PowerPoint® 4 for Windows™
QuickStart

Craig Bobchin

Bernice Glenn

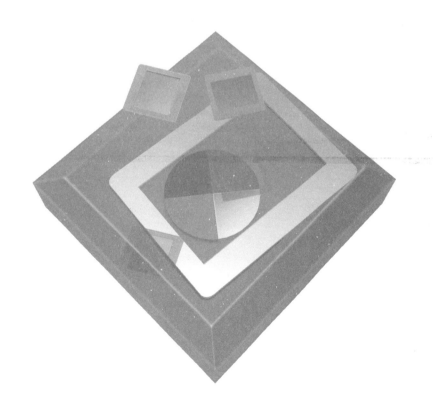

PowerPoint 4 for Windows QuickStart

Copyright © 1994 by Que® Corporation.

Library of Congress Catalog No.: 94-65148

ISBN: 1-56529-682-6

97 96 95   4 3 2

Interpretation of the printing code: the rightmost double-digit number is the year of the book's printing; the rightmost single-digit number, the number of the book's printing. For example, a printing code of 94-1 shows that the first printing of the book occurred in 1994.

Screen reproductions in this book were created using Collage Plus from Inner Media, Inc., Hollis, NH.

PowerPoint 4 for Windows QuickStart covers version 4 of PowerPoint for Windows.

Publisher: David P. Ewing

Associate Publisher: Corinne Walls

Publishing Director: Lisa A. Bucki

Managing Editor: Anne Owen

Marketing Manager: Ray Robinson

About the Authors

Craig Bobchin is a freelance writer with more than 100 published articles. Bobchin is also president and founder of CMB Systems Design, a microcomputer consulting firm specializing in applications development and training. Craig lives in Orange County, California, where when he is not spending time in front of his PC, he spends time with his twin boys, Michael and Steven.

Bernice Glenn, principal, Glenn and Associates, combines experience in technology and communications for print, electronic, and video media. As an author, Glenn develops content for books, training manuals, and documentation. She also develops content for multimedia and presentation graphics projects.

Publishing Manager
Lisa A. Bucki

Acquisitions Editors
Thomas F. Godfrey III
Nancy Stevenson

Product Director
Kathie-Jo Arnoff

Production Editor
Anne Owen

Editors
Jo Anna Arnott
Elsa Bell
Heather Kaufman
Jeanne Lemen

Technical Editors
Tamara Bryant
Matthew Lafata

Book Designer
Amy Peppler-Adams

Cover Designer
Dan Armstrong

Illustrator
Kathy Hanley

Production Team
Angela Bannan
Karen Dodson
Teresa Forrester
Joelynn Gifford
Brook Farling
Carla Hall
Joy Dean Lee
Tim Montgomery
Aren Munk
Linda Quigley
Dennis Sheehan
Tina Trettin
Sue VandeWalle
Mary Beth Wakefield

Indexer
Johnna VanHoose

Composed in *Stone Serif* and *MCPdigital by* Que Corporation.

Trademark Acknowledgments

Contents at a Glance

Table of Contents

7 Adding Clip Art to Slides   149

Introduction

In today's world of information overload, it's important to be able to present data in a quick, concise, and effective format. To that end, presentation of information has become one of the paramount concerns in business. PowerPoint has always been at the forefront of Windows presentation packages. PowerPoint allows people to present information easily and quickly via a variety of methods, such as on-screen slide shows, 35mm slides, and handouts.

In this new version of PowerPoint, Microsoft has even further enhanced a great product. They have added many new features and have improved most of the old ones. PowerPoint now shares the same look and many of the features of Microsoft Excel and Word for Windows. You can also edit objects from one application to another, subject to certain limitations, of course.

This book, *PowerPoint 4 for Windows QuickStart,* takes you into PowerPoint and teaches you how to get started with this program. It teaches you the basics and gives you a few pointers along the way. New and improved features for this version are one of the main focuses of this book. There are many illustrations included to help clarify both the text and the program.

What Is in This Book?

Each of the lessons in this book relates to a particular PowerPoint procedure or procedures. The basic composition of *PowerPoint 4 for Windows QuickStart* reflects the normal operations of someone creating presentations. It starts with the basics of becoming familiar with the look and use of the components of PowerPoint and progresses through creating text slides, using the drawing tools, and adding clip art and other objects. It also looks at creating full multi-slide presentations and getting the final output.

This book also contains a Visual Index. The Visual Index will let you locate a particular subject easily. It shows various aspects of PowerPoint and where you can find information about using them.

Part I, "Getting Started," examines the basics you need to use PowerPoint, and covers some of the basics about using Windows and PowerPoint. Part I looks at the PowerPoint screens and features and discusses how to create a slide. Part I is where you also put together your first slide presentation.

Part II, "Working with Text," explores adding text to slides. You learn how to both manipulate and enhance text. Part II also shows you how to check spelling and perform search and replace operations on text.

Part III, "Enhancing Your Presentation," shows you how to add features such as color and images to your slide. It explains how to use Powerpoint's tools to draw your own pictures. Also discussed is working with color, charts, and tables, and creating printed material for your audience's use.

Part IV, "Putting It All Together," shows you how to pull together all the pieces that you've created and show them as a presentation. It also delves into the procedures needed to create printouts and photographic slides.

Lesson 1, "Getting to Know PowerPoint 4 for Windows," introduces you to the world of PowerPoint. It explains what the program is about and gives a brief overview of its features. It teaches you how to start the program, understand the various parts of the program, and how to get help if needed. The lesson ends by explaining how to save your work and exit the program.

Lesson 2, "Working with Slides," examines what is involved with creating a basic slide. It gives a brief look at adding text and other objects into a slide. It then introduces you to the concept of adding an additional slide. Finally, it teaches you how to navigate within your presentation and how to start and view your multi-slide presentations.

Lesson 3, "Creating Your First Presentation," focuses on what a presentation is and how to create one. It explains about defaults for a presentation and how to use Wizards and templates. The lesson then introduces Slide Masters and tells how to use them to speed up the development of your presentation. The lesson then goes into detail to discuss working with presentations; it covers topics such as viewing slides in various formats, moving, copying, hiding, and deleting slides, as well as creating notes for slides.

Lesson 4, "Adding Text to Slides," explores in detail the processes involved with adding text to slides and how to manipulate it afterwards. The lesson looks at bulleted lists and how to use them, and searching for and replacing text is also covered. Checking the spelling of text is another topic examined.

Lesson 5, "Enhancing Text on Slides," shows you how to modify and improve the look of your text. It tells you how to add lines, fills, and shadows. It discusses how to change fonts, styles, and colors, and how to justify text.

Lesson 6, "Working with Color on Slides," explains how to increase the effectiveness of your presentations through the use of colors and backgrounds. Topics covered include using shading and patterns, managing existing color schemes, and creating new ones.

Lesson 7, "Adding Clip Art to Slides," examines how to use clip art to make your presentations more effective. It includes such topics as using the ClipArt Gallery, choosing clip art, resizing and positioning clip art, editing clip art, and converting clip art between various formats. Adding other types of images as well as cropping and recoloring clip art are also looked at here.

Lesson 8, "Adding Drawings to Slides," covers using PowerPoint's drawing tools to create your own artwork for inclusion into slides. It examines how to create lines, arcs, and shapes. It then goes into detail about using patterns and colors. The lesson also explains how to change an object's style and shadows. Working with multiple items and guidelines are other topics that are covered.

Lesson 9, "Adding Charts to Slides," discusses how to create and modify charts in PowerPoint and how to add them to your presentation slides. This lesson also looks at the different types of charts. Creating organizational charts in slides is briefly discussed at the end of the lesson.

Lesson 10, "Organizing Data and Datasheets," looks at what it takes to add tables to PowerPoint slides. It starts with how to work with data sheets and then looks at how to format and change the way the data looks in the table.

Lesson 11, "Creating Handouts, Outlines, and Notes" concentrates on how to create supplementary materials for your presentations. These tools will help you stay organized and allow your audience to follow your presentation. Creating speaker's notes is another topic that is covered.

Lesson 12, "Viewing and Organizing Your Presentation," covers what you have to do in order to preview your presentation and rehearse it, so that it flows smoothly. It discusses what you have to consider in terms of timing and pacing yourself during a presentation.

Lesson 13, "Printing Your Presentation," shows how to set up the printer to print your materials. It also discusses how to send output to Genigraphics to create slides.

Lesson 14, "Displaying Your Presentation," explains how to set up a slideshow by using transitions between slides and building slides in a particular order. Rehearsing a slideshow and using hidden slides are also discussed. Running a slideshow and using the PowerPoint 4 Viewer Disk are the other topics covered in this lesson.

Lesson 15, "Working with Other Windows Applications," explores how you can use PowerPoint with other Windows applications, such as Microsoft Excel and Word from Windows. It also explains what Dynamic Data Exchange (DDE) and Object Linking and Embedding (OLE) are and how to use them.

Appendix A, "Installing PowerPoint 4 for Windows," details the installation of PowerPoint 4. The appendix also lists the minimum and recommended requirements for running PowerPoint.

Who Should Use This Book?

This book is written for the novice PowerPoint user as well as for the user upgrading from an earlier version. It is not intended as a replacement for the normal set of user documentation that comes with PowerPoint. It is also not a full reference book for the program. Rather, its purpose is as a "how to" tutorial on putting together effective presentations, using the tools Microsoft provides in PowerPoint.

PowerPoint is an easy program to learn, and you may find yourself exploring in a hopscotch fashion rather than progressing from start to finish. If that is how you work, this book will be of great use to you. While each lesson builds on previous concepts, it does not rehash them endlessly. So, feel free to skip about and explore piecemeal, or take the tutorial one step at a time in order. *PowerPoint 4 for Windows QuickStart* works both ways.

These lessons and book assume that you have some knowledge of DOS and Windows operations, and that you know how to use a mouse to select items from menus and press on-screen buttons. Since this is a tutorial style book, some of the more advanced features of the program are not included in this book.

Conventions Used in This Book

There are certain conventions used throughout *PowerPoint 4 for Windows QuickStart*. They are intended to make it easier for you to follow along. They also clearly define the various actions and displays you will see. Following are the general conventions this book follows:

- The first term, and one that you will see most frequently, is *clicking*. Clicking refers to pressing and releasing a mouse button. In this book, it is assumed that the left mouse button is the button being pressed unless otherwise noted.

- *Double-clicking* means quickly pressing and releasing the mouse button twice.

- *Selecting* means highlighting or otherwise choosing an object. To select text, press and hold the left mouse button while dragging it across the text you want to work with. To select any other object, click on it with the mouse pointer.

- **Boldface type** denotes any text you type.

- Any key combinations are shown as Shift+F1. This means press and hold the Shift key while you next press the F1 key.

- To select a menu choice with the keyboard, press the Alt key, then press the underlined letter on the menu. (In this book, the underlined letter is shown in boldface.) For example, to choose the **F**ile menu, press the Alt key, then press the F key.

- Important words will appear in *italics*; this will usually be the first time they are mentioned.

- Screen elements and any messages will be in a `special typeface`.

Where To Go for More Information

There are many sources you can use to find out more information about PowerPoint. The first one is the PowerPoint manuals that come with the program. You can also call Microsoft's technical support at (206) 635-7145. In Canada, call (905) 568-3503. Que has a complete line of books on PowerPoint 4 for Windows. For a comprehensive guide to PowerPoint, refer to Que's *Using PowerPoint 4 for Windows*. For a very simple and more visual beginning level book on PowerPoint, see *Easy PowerPoint for Windows*.

You may want to find out if there are any user groups in your area. User groups are a wonderful way to find out about the ins and outs of a program from people who use it on a daily basis.

New Features of PowerPoint 4

PowerPoint 4 is chock full of new and improved features. Below is a brief list of what has been added and improved.

- There are now seven predefined toolbars for specific tasks. Microsoft has made the toolbars similar to those in Excel and Word for Windows, in that they can be resized, moved around, or anchored to any edge.

- All the toolbars are user definable. You can drag and drop buttons on and off a toolbar, and even between toolbars.

- PowerPoint now sports improved dialog boxes that have a sculptured three-dimensional look.

- The new scroll bars allow you to scroll from slide to slide and inform you as to what slide you're currently viewing.

- There are optional ToolTips that pop up when the mouse pointer passes over the toolbar buttons.

- PowerPoint now allows you to specify the zoom level in any view. You can choose any percentage from 25 percent to 400 percent, no matter where you are in the program.

- PowerPoint supports "Windows" standard Multiple Document Interface (MDI). This allows you to work with multiple presentations and keep one or more presentation windows minimized on the PowerPoint screen.

- PowerPoint makes it easier than ever for new users to get started creating presentations. New in version 4 are Cue Cards that provide step-by-step instructions for common multistep tasks, such as adding a logo to every slide.

- Microsoft has added two Wizards to assist users. Wizards prompt you for information about your presentation and slides, and then put together a full presentation for you with the exception of text. Of course, you can override the result whenever you want.

- You can drag and drop slides between presentations.

- The Files Open dialog box allows you to select several documents to open at once.

- You can search for all slides that contain a specific text string. You then can copy or move those slides to a new presentation.

- Microsoft has added a Format Painter tool. This allows you to select objects and text on a slide and copy just the format or style of it to another object or objects.

These are just a few of the many improvements made to this program. In the pages that follow, you will explore most of these and other features too numerous to list here. PowerPoint now offers even more tools to make it easier to create professional presentations.

Visual Index

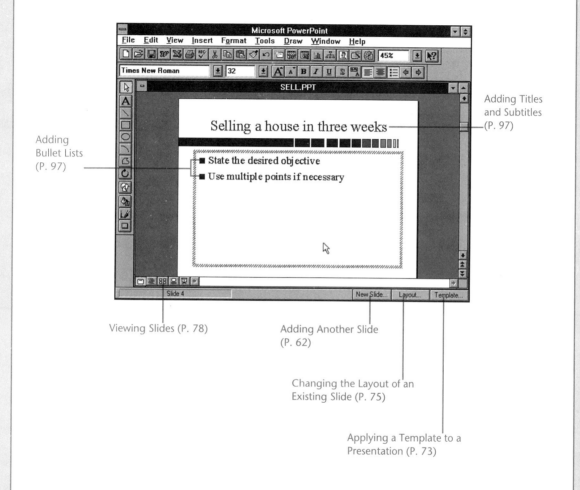

Adding Titles and Subtitles (P. 97)

Adding Bullet Lists (P. 97)

Viewing Slides (P. 78)

Adding Another Slide (P. 62)

Changing the Layout of an Existing Slide (P. 75)

Applying a Template to a Presentation (P. 73)

Using Grids, Guides, and Rulers (P. 197)

Coloring and Shading Objects (P. 139)

Changing the Color of Text (P. 145)

Using AutoShapes Tool (P. 183)

Working with Color Schemes (P. 128)

Drawing Arcs (P. 176)

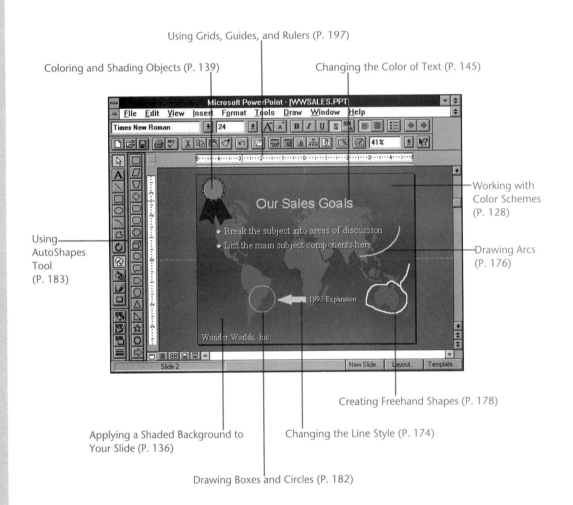

Creating Freehand Shapes (P. 178)

Applying a Shaded Background to Your Slide (P. 136)

Changing the Line Style (P. 174)

Drawing Boxes and Circles (P. 182)

Using the Drawing Tools (P. 171)

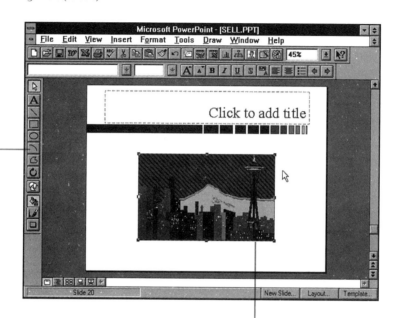

Adding Clip Art Images to a Slide (P. 157)

Adding Text to Charts (P. 233)

Adding Arrows to a Chart (P. 235)

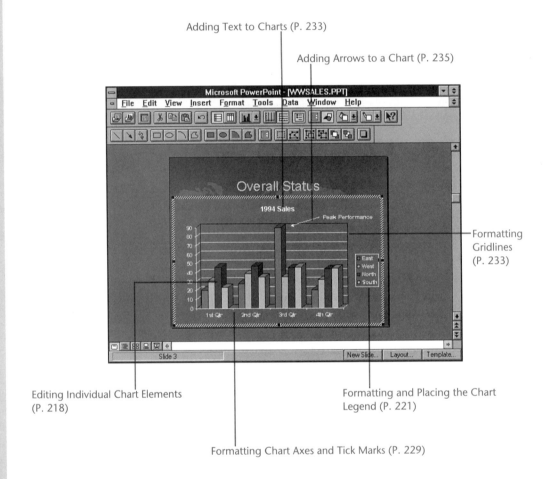

Formatting Gridlines (P. 233)

Editing Individual Chart Elements (P. 218)

Formatting and Placing the Chart Legend (P. 221)

Formatting Chart Axes and Tick Marks (P. 229)

Selecting Cells, Columns,
and Rows (P. 247)

Adjusting Column
Widths (P. 249)

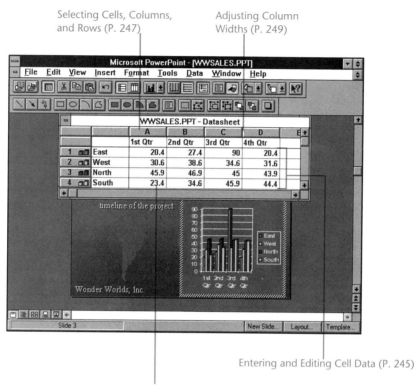

Entering and Editing Cell Data (P. 245)

Formatting a Datasheet (P. 257)

Using the Pick a Look Wizard to
Prepare Materials (P. 263)

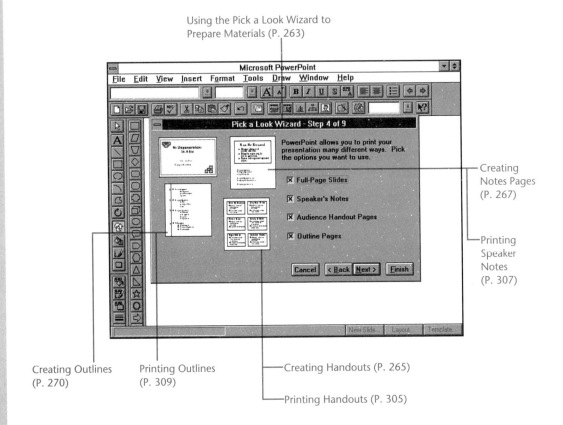

Creating
Notes Pages
(P. 267)

Printing
Speaker
Notes
(P. 307)

Creating Outlines
(P. 270)

Printing Outlines
(P. 309)

Creating Handouts (P. 265)

Printing Handouts (P. 305)

Formatting Text in Outline View (P. 289)

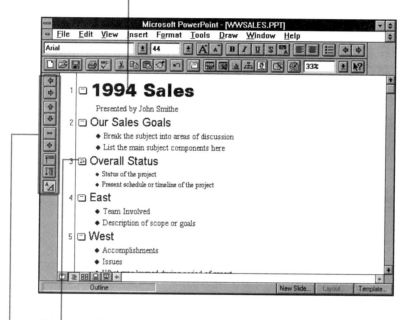

Using the Outline Tools (P. 284)

Selecting a Slide or Slide Text in Outline View (P. 286)

Using Transitions
(P. 317)

Building Slides (P. 320)

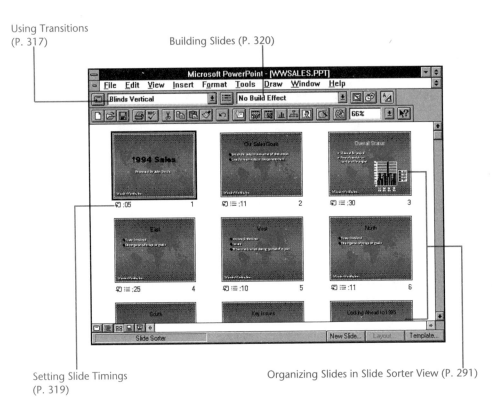

Setting Slide Timings
(P. 319)

Organizing Slides in Slide Sorter View (P. 291)

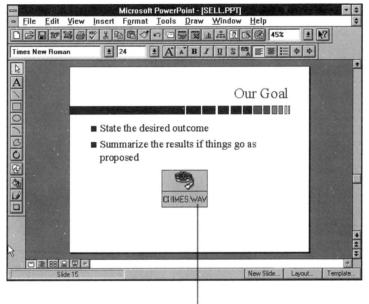

Adding an Embedded Object to PowerPoint (P. 340)

Part I
Getting Started

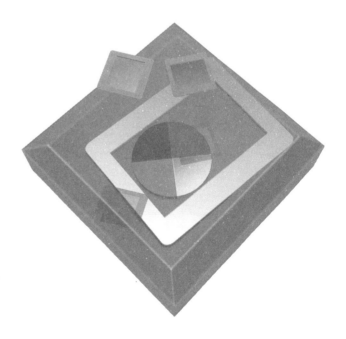

Getting To Know PowerPoint 4 for Windows

This lesson covers the basics of PowerPoint 4. It looks at why you should use it and what hardware and software you need to run PowerPoint 4. Among the other topics discussed are: starting PowerPoint, becoming familiar with the PowerPoint screens and components, and using the PowerPoint help system and cue cards. The lesson ends with instructions on how to save your work and exit PowerPoint. In this lesson you learn to:

- Define PowerPoint 4

- Start PowerPoint

- Decide how to create your presentation

- Get to know the PowerPoint screens

- Use the toolbars

- Navigate in PowerPoint

- Get Help

- Close and save your work

What Is PowerPoint 4?

Microsoft PowerPoint 4 for Windows is a highly sophisticated, powerful, and flexible graphics presentations software program. It provides you with the means to create, view, and present slide shows on your PC. It also allows you to print a variety of handouts and notes to give to your audience.

Why Should You Use PowerPoint 4?

PowerPoint 4 allows the user to disseminate information quickly, easily, and efficiently. It provides you with the means to create effective presentations that will captivate your audience and retain their interest. It allows you to create color slide shows and print materials; it also gives you the flexibility to include in your presentation sounds, video clips, and documents from other applications—and even slides from other presentations. The slides you create can graph data from spreadsheet tables and can even be linked in such a way that if the data changes, the graph changes along with it. PowerPoint also lets you draw your own pictures, create overhead transparencies, and output to 35mm slides. PowerPoint also links up to Genigraphics, a company that creates high quality slides from your presentations. When linked with Excel or other Microsoft programs, PowerPoint's power is limited only by what you want to do with it and your creativity.

What Is Required To Run PowerPoint 4?

PowerPoint is a Windows product, and as such, it has the same minimum requirements as Windows; it requires an 80386SX or better computer, DOS 3.3 or higher, two megabytes of Random Access Memory (RAM), and Windows 3.0 or higher. A hard disk and VGA card in addition to a display are also required. A mouse is optional, but pretty much a necessity.

However, to really tap the power of Windows and have PowerPoint work at a reasonable rate of speed, we recommend the following configuration: an 80386DX 25 MHz or better computer; DOS 5.0 or higher; four megabytes or more of RAM; a memory management software package such as QEMM or Memmaker; Windows 3.1; an 80 megabyte or larger hard drive; and a Super VGA card, with one megabyte or more, together with a monitor capable of 800x600 or greater resolution. A disk cache, such as Smartdrive, will also help speed performance. You can use the keyboard for most tasks in PowerPoint, but a mouse or other pointing device is really necessary because there are a couple of things you can't do without one.

1

The system just described will enable you to run PowerPoint very comfortably; however, like any other Windows program, your performance will vary based on how you work and what programs you regularly use.

Task: Starting PowerPoint 4

Before starting PowerPoint, you must be sure Windows is running. Then, you can start PowerPoint 4 in one of two ways:

- From the PowerPoint 4 Program Group

- From the File Manager

Even though the first method may require fewer steps, it is a matter of preference on the part of the user as to which method to use. Following is an in-depth, step-by-step description of each method.

Starting PowerPoint from the PowerPoint Program Group

Since PowerPoint is a Windows application, during installation it creates a Windows program group to store its icons. In this case, the group is named Microsoft Office, a name the user can change at installation time (see Appendix A, "Installing Powerpoint 4 for Windows," for details on installation). This Program Group contains five items: Microsoft PowerPoint, PowerPoint Setup, Media Player, Graphics Link, and PowerPoint Viewer.

Note: *If you haven't installed PowerPoint yet, see Appendix A for installation instructions.*

To start PowerPoint from the Program Group, follow these steps:

1. With the Program Manager active, double-click on the Program Group icon if the group isn't already open.

The Program
Manager shows
the PowerPoint
Program Group
icon.

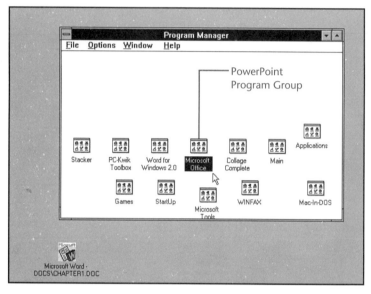

2. After the Program Group is opened, double-click on the PowerPoint icon. The PowerPoint program will then open.

The PowerPoint
Program Group
includes the five
PowerPoint icons.

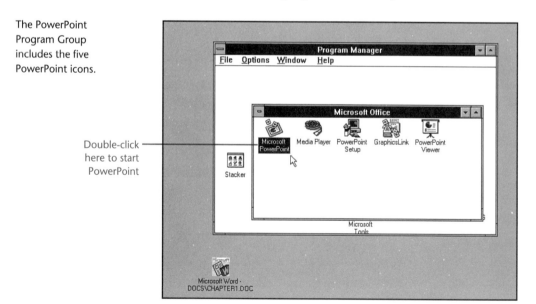

Starting PowerPoint from Windows File Manager

If Windows is anything, it's flexible! So, you can start PowerPoint by using another method. Follow these steps to start PowerPoint from the Windows File Manager:

1. Start the File Manager by opening the Main Program Group, or if you have moved the File Manager to a different group, open that group. Double-click on the File Manager icon.

2. Scroll down the list of directories until you come to the \POWERPNT subdirectory. In the list of files, you see a POWERPNT.EXE file. This is the program for PowerPoint.

3. Double-click on POWERPNT.EXE to launch PowerPoint.

PowerPoint starts from the File Manager.

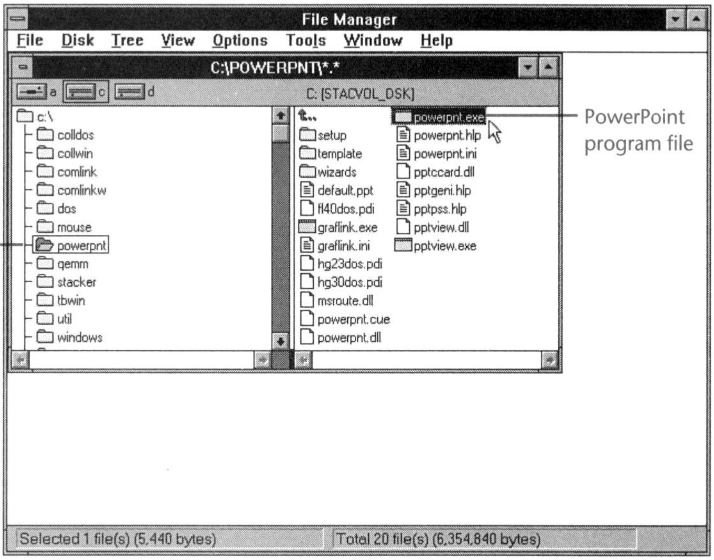

PowerPoint directory

PowerPoint program file

Note: *You can start PowerPoint with a presentation already opened if you double-click on a file with an extension of PPT. PPT files are PowerPoint presentations. When PowerPoint is installed, it creates an association that tells Windows to launch PowerPoint with the selected file.*

The PowerPoint opening screen is displayed.

Tip of the Day Screen

When you start PowerPoint, the first thing that you see is the Tip of the Day screen; it provides the user with an optional series of hints and tips that Microsoft has put together. These tips can help you understand what PowerPoint can do for you and how you can use it to your best advantage. This screen also offers hints on how to make your presentations more effective. For example, one tip is: "If you give a slide show, most people can't see text smaller than 18 points in size."

Tips of the day offer many useful suggestions.

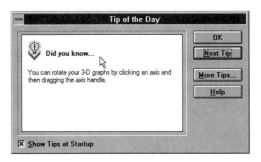

When you're in the Tip of the Day dialog box, you have several options available to you:

■ You can close the dialog box and continue using PowerPoint by clicking on the OK button.

■ You can look at the next tip in the series by choosing the **N**ext Tip button.

■ You can get more tips by choosing the **M**ore Tips button. The **M**ore Tips button brings up the PowerPoint 4 Help system. More information on the Help system is presented later in the lesson.

■ You can specify that you don't want the tips to display during startup by unmarking the **S**how Tips at Startup check box.

Tips of the day can be viewed at any time by choosing the Tip of the Day choice from the **H**elp menu.

Note: *The Tip of the Day dialog box is specific for PowerPoint version 4. Users of earlier versions should ignore this section.*

Deciding How To Create Your Presentation

There are several manners in which you can create a presentation. They range from having Powerpoint do all of the work to you doing it all. How you finally decide to create a presentation is dependent on your experience with Powerpoint and your level of comfort with creating presentations in general. The following steps examine each of your alternatives.

After the tips of the day are displayed, you're presented with the PowerPoint dialog box which allows you to start creating your presen-tation.

The PowerPoint dialog box allows many options for creating presentations.

Wizard
A feature of PowerPoint that asks you questions and uses your answers to automatically format your presentation.

Template
A presentation that you apply to other presentations to use the same format and color schemes.

You have several choices:

- You can use one of the two *Wizards*: AutoContent Wizard or Pick a Look Wizard.

- You can create your own look from choosing a *template* style.

- You can go with a blank presentation which gives you full control from the start.

All of the options are explained in the text that follows.

Note: *All of the options under this dialog box are specific for version 4 of PowerPoint. They do not appear in earlier versions.*

The AutoContent Wizard

Choosing the **A**utoContent Wizard option from the PowerPoint dialog box brings you to the first of the Wizards in PowerPoint 4. It leads you down a very straight path and creates a whole presentation for you. All that you're required to do is answer a couple of questions to help the Wizard pick a layout.

After you answer the questions, PowerPoint creates a full presentation for you. Once the presentation is created, you, of course, will have to fill in the text on the slides since there's no way for the Wizard to know what you want to put on them.

The AutoContent Wizard can do most of the work for you.

The Pick a Look Wizard

Choosing the **P**ick a Look Wizard option brings you to the second Wizard that comes with PowerPoint. This Wizard is a little more complex than the AutoContent Wizard. It creates the slide presentation, but it gives you much more control over the look of the presentation each step of the way. After the Wizard creates your slides, you go to the **V**iew **S**lides so you can immediately start working on your presentation.

The Pick a Look Wizard makes it easy for you to keep control of your presentation.

Template

Choosing the **T**emplate option allows you to choose one of PowerPoint's many predefined template styles for the look of your presentation. The Presentation Template dialog box shows in the lower right corner a preview of what the style looks like. After you choose the style you want, you go to the New Slide dialog box. The New Slide dialog box is discussed later in the lesson.

Blank Presentation

By choosing the **B**lank Presentation option, you give yourself full control over the look of your presentation. You have to select the background and the type of presentation you're giving. This option gives you the most flexibility from the start.

AutoLayout
An AutoLayout is a slide that contains specific object placeholders already on them. The placeholders are locations for different objects such as images or charts. These layouts appear on the AutoLayout screen.

Open an Existing Presentation

The **O**pen an Existing Presentation option allows you to create and save a new presentation with the same style as an already open presentation.

The New Slide Dialog Box

After you decide to use a new presentation based on a blank presentation, you go to the New Slide dialog box. This is also called the AutoLayout screen. This is where you select the type of slide that you want to add.

There are several other methods you can use to display the AutoLayout screen. They are outlined below and each will be discussed at the appropriate time later in this book.

■ Press the New Slide button on the bottom of the screen.

■ Press the Ctrl+N key combination.

■ Choose the New **S**lide command from the **I**nsert menu.

The New Slide dialog box allows you to select the type of slide you want to work on. The dialog box presents thumbnail samples of what a slide's layout looks like. You have a choice of 20 predefined layouts and one blank layout that you can customize.

The New Slide
dialog box allows
you to choose from
predefined slide
layouts.

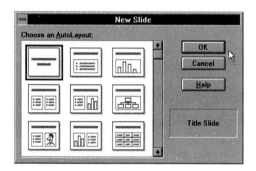

Task: Becoming Familiar with the PowerPoint Screens

PowerPoint 4 has a slightly different screen look from previous versions. Also, while Windows products adhere to a certain look and feel, there is a lot of leeway for a company to create its own look for a line of products. If you're not familiar with Microsoft's look of their latest version or you've never worked with PowerPoint before, you should take some time to review this section.

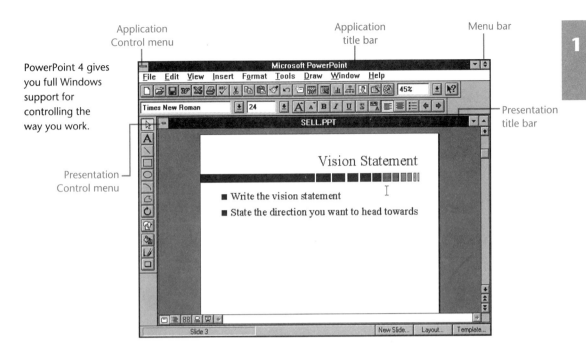

PowerPoint 4 gives you full Windows support for controlling the way you work.

The Title Bar and Control Menu

When you look at a PowerPoint screen, you'll notice along the top of the screen the *title bar* and a gray dash on the left corner. The title bar is used to show what application you're working on. You also can click on the title bar with the mouse and drag the window to another location. Also, along the top of the screen you find the first of two Control menus. This is the gray dash located to the left of the title bar.

This Control menu is used to modify various aspects of the application window. If you single click on the Control menu, you find choices that allow you to Move, Restore, Size, or Close the application.

There are also two other choices on the Control menu. One of these allows you to switch to any other application that is running at the same time. The second choice brings up a dialog box with two choices: the Windows Clipboard and the Windows Control panel.

Note: *You can also access the Application Control menu by pressing the Alt+space bar key combination.*

You'll also notice that there is another title bar and Control menu on the screen. These are to control the current document you're working on. Like the Application Control menu, you can move the window, resize it, and close it. It doesn't have the run option nor does it have the capability to switch between tasks. If, however, you have more than one presentation open, you can switch between them.

Note: *You can switch between the open presentations by pressing Ctrl+F6. You can also access the document Control menu by using the Alt+ – key combination.*

The Menu Bar

Under the title bar you find the *menu bar*, your main method to control the power of PowerPoint. From it, you can choose commands that tell PowerPoint what you want to do. The menu can be accessed with the mouse or via the keyboard.

The PowerPoint main menu has the following choices: **F**ile, **E**dit, **V**iew, **I**nsert, **F**ormat, **T**ools, **D**raw, **W**indow, and **H**elp. Each menu item has a submenu with commands that support that function.

As with all Windows programs, the menus are very easy to use. You choose menu items by clicking on the choice with the mouse pointer. You can also activate a menu choice with the keyboard by pressing the Alt key and the highlighted letter from that menu selection. For example, if you want to select the **P**icture command from the **I**nsert menu, follow these steps:

1. Click on the **I**nsert menu with the mouse, or press the Alt+I key combination.

This action displays the **I**nsert menu.

2. Choose the **P**icture command. You can do this three different ways:

   ■ Press P.

   ■ Click on the Picture option with the mouse.

   ■ Scroll through the menu with the cursor keys and press Enter when Picture is highlighted.

PowerPoint's Rulers

Rulers are used in PowerPoint to align text and graphics on a slide. You can use rulers to set tab stops, hanging indents, and word wraps for text objects. In PowerPoint 4, you now have both vertical and horizontal rulers. You display the rulers by choosing **R**uler from the PowerPoint **V**iew menu.

PowerPoint now has one integrated set of rulers for all objects.

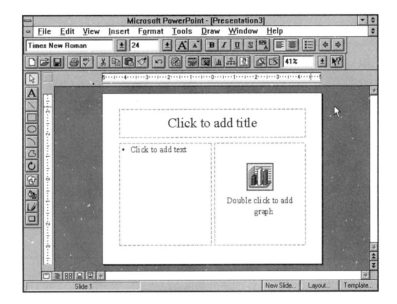

Note: *In earlier versions of PowerPoint there were some differences in the rulers. First, there used to be a ruler for each text object. In version 4, there is only one ruler and it affects whichever object you have selected. You now can use the same ruler to align text and graphics. Second, you now have a vertical ruler to assist you in lining up objects vertically and horizontally.*

The Scroll Bars in PowerPoint

One of the advantages of Windows is the capability to work with an object larger than the current screen or monitor is capable of displaying at one time. Of course, you need a method to move around the image to view and modify various parts. You can move around the image with *scroll bars*, which are at the right and bottom edges of the image. The use of these scroll bars changes depending on what view mode you're in and what your zoom level is.

If you are zoomed in on an image at 100 percent or more, the scroll bars can move you around the image. If you can see the whole slide on-screen, the scroll bars may not be active or they may move you to the next slide.

The scroll bars can move you around the screen or between slides.

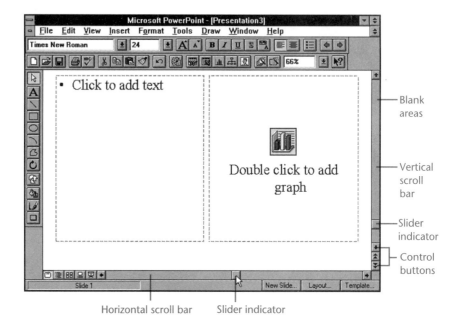

To use the scroll bars, follow these steps:

1. Position the mouse pointer over one of the control buttons.

2. Press the directional control button. These buttons are dimmed if you're unable to use them for the current operation.

3. You can also click on the slider indicator and drag it to the location you want.

Note: *You can also maneuver through the scroll bars by clicking on a blank area before or after the slider indicator. This action moves the slider in the same manner as pressing the arrow buttons.*

The *vertical scroll bar* provides different functionality based on what you're doing at the time. During normal operations, it moves you from slide to slide. If you're in Outline view, the vertical scroll bar moves you within the outline. If you switch to Slide view, the vertical scroll bar moves you to another slide in the presentation. Whether you move to a previous slide or a later slide depends on which direction you move. If you enlarge a slide, you move within the slide rather than moving from slide to slide.

To move from slide to slide each time, use the control button with two arrows on it. This will always move you between slides.

The *horizontal scroll bar* is only functional when the image of the slide is larger than the screen can display. Any other time, the horizontal scroll bar is inactive.

Dialog Boxes

Dialog boxes are small screens that allow you to perform a task—they are one of the methods that PowerPoint uses to make life easier. Dialog boxes frequently have buttons and drop-down lists for you to choose from. An example of a dialog box is the Open dialog box. It has a scrolling list of both files and directories, several command buttons, and a check box.

The Open dialog box has many common dialog box features.

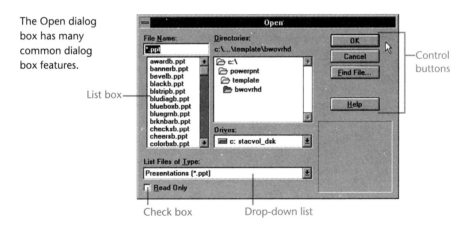

You move around a dialog box by using the mouse or the Tab key. An item is selected when it changes appearance. The boxes with arrows next to them are called *combo boxes*. You can either type into the combo box, or press the arrow button to see a drop-down list of selections to choose from.

Using the Toolbars

Toolbar
A group of on-screen buttons that can provide shortcuts to menu options.

PowerPoint has a set of highly customizable *toolbars* in its arsenal. A toolbar is a set of buttons that performs various functions. Toolbars are generally customizable by the user and frequently appear under a menu bar. They may or may not have graphic images on them. They perform a function of allowing you to execute sometimes complex tasks with a single mouse click rather than navigating through many menus. These toolbars are easy to use, can be utilized in a variety of places, and can even be used to start or link to other Microsoft applications.

Some of the toolbars are the same as in other Microsoft applications. This way, once you know one toolbar, you know them all. The toolbars can be docked or anchored to any edge of the screen. They can also be free-floating icon palettes that can be moved and resized on-screen. You can find out more about specific toolbars by reading about them later in the book. They will be discussed throughout where applicable. For example, the Drawing and Drawing+ toolbars will be discussed in the lessons on drawing pictures.

PowerPoint's toolbars are easily customized and displayed by the user.

Formatting toolbar

Standard toolbar

Drawing toolbar

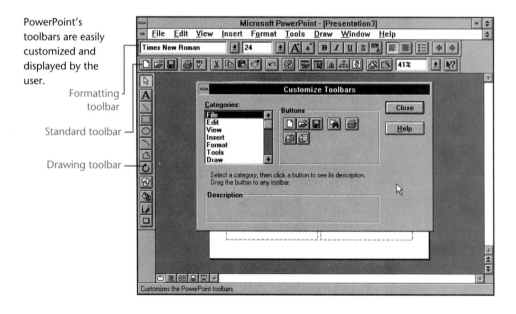

Opening and Closing Toolbars

By default, when you start PowerPoint, certain toolbars are open and closed. The open toolbars are Standard, Formatting, and Drawing. To open other toolbars or close any that are open, follow these steps:

1. From the **V**iew menu, choose **T**oolbars. The ellipsis following the menu choice tells you that a dialog box will be displayed next.

The Toolbars dialog box makes it easy to set which toolbars you want to see.

2. From the Toolbars dialog box, select the toolbar whose display you want to change. An X in the box next to the choice means that it is currently displayed.

3. To change a toolbar from visible to closed, click once in the box next to the toolbar to modify it. This will either display or close the toolbar, depending on the previous state.

4. Choose the OK button to save your changes. Or choose Cancel to ignore any changes that you have made.

Any changes you save here will be saved as the new defaults and will be in effect the next time you use PowerPoint.

Deciding Which Toolbars To Display

This decision is often one of the hardest tasks in using toolbars. On the one hand, it's nice to have access to all of your menu choices and tools at the click of a mouse. On the other hand, if you open up all or too many of the toolbars, the screen gets cluttered and you can have overkill. My suggestion is to keep only the default toolbars open and then open any extra ones when needed.

There is a special toolbar called a Custom toolbar. The Custom toolbar is blank when you first open it. You must add buttons to it yourself with the Customize Toolbar function. Customizing toolbars is covered briefly in the next section.

Customizing Toolbars

Customizing toolbars falls into two categories:

- Adding or modifying tools on the toolbar

- Changing the position of toolbars

While this text does not go into details about all of the options available to you, this lesson does look at how you can add and delete items from a toolbar. This example uses the Custom toolbar.

Adding Items to a Toolbar

The first order of business is to open up a toolbar for customization. Follow these steps to select the Custom toolbar for modification and to add tools to it:

1. From the **V**iew menu, choose **T**oolbars.

2. Click on the Custom check box and make sure that the X is visible in it.

   Note: *The Custom toolbar will be empty and show up as a small square. You may have to drag the Customize window out of the way to see it.*

3. Choose the **C**ustomize button in the Toolbars dialog box to display the Customize Toolbars dialog box.

   Note: *You can also access the customize option by using two other methods:*

   - Select the Customize command from the Tools menu.

   - Click the right mouse button on a toolbar and select the Customize command from there.

You can customize
any toolbar by
dragging tools
to and from it.

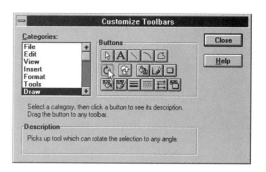

4. Select one of the tool categories on the left to see the tools associated with it.

5. Click on one of the tool icons on the right and drag it to the Custom toolbar.

6. Release the mouse button to drop the tool onto the toolbar.

7. Continue this process until you have built the toolbar you want to see. Choose the Close button when you're done.

Note: *You can also drag and drop tools in different positions on the toolbar. Simply open the Customize window and drag a tool to a new location on the toolbar.*

Deleting Items from a Toolbar

To remove tools from a toolbar, use a similar method:

1. Start to customize the toolbar.

2. Instead of dragging tools on to the toolbar, drag them off and release them anywhere on-screen.

3. Choose Close when you finish.

Resizing and Relocating Toolbars

Any toolbar can be converted into a free-floating icon palette. This allows you to free up screen space and place the toolbar wherever you want it.

To convert a toolbar that is docked to the screen, follow these instructions:

1. Click on an empty space on the toolbar.

2. Drag the toolbar to the slide screen. You'll notice that the toolbar outline changes shape when it's on the slide screen.

3. Position the toolbar and release the mouse button.

To dock a free-floating toolbar, reverse the preceding steps:

1. Click on the toolbar title bar.

2. Drag the toolbar to the edge where you want it docked.

3. When the toolbar outline changes shape, release the mouse button to set the toolbar.

   Note: *There is a shortcut to converting toolbars to and from docked and free-floating positions. Simply double-click on a blank area of the toolbar to change it.*

Resizing a free-floating toolbar is done in the same manner as any other window in Windows:

1. Move the mouse pointer to the border of the toolbar.

2. When the pointer changes to a double-headed arrow, press and hold the left mouse button.

3. Drag the border to the size and shape you want the toolbar to be.

4. Release the mouse button.

Displaying Tools in Color

In PowerPoint 4, the toolbars now have colored icons. No longer do you have to see drab, black-and-gray icons as you did in version 3. To ensure that your toolbar icons are in color, select the Color Buttons check box in the Toolbar dialog box.

Looking for Tooltips

A second new feature in PowerPoint 4 is Tooltips. *Tooltips* are little flags that pop up when you place your mouse pointer on the tool. These tips tell a little about what the tool is used for. You can shut off these tooltips by clearing the X in the **S**how Tooltips check box on the Toolbar dialog box.

Note: *Powerpoint 4 has two new features for its toolbars. One is Color Buttons and the other is Tooltips.*

Navigating in PowerPoint

There are two primary modes of moving around the PowerPoint screen: with the mouse and via the keyboard. While it's possible to run PowerPoint via the keyboard, the use of a mouse makes it easier and faster than just keyboard.

Using a mouse is undoubtedly the preferred mode of running PowerPoint. Using the mouse also presents some unique shortcuts that are otherwise unavailable to strict keyboard users.

Using the Left Mouse Button

You'll use the left mouse button the most. It's used for selecting and clicking on objects. By clicking and holding down the left button, you can drag objects around the screen. The left button is also used to switch between slides when you're in Slide Show view.

Using the Right Mouse Button

The right mouse button is rarely used in Windows, in general, but PowerPoint 4 makes significant use of it. By pressing the right mouse button, you're able to bring up a menu that gives you shortcuts to modify objects and the screen.

The right mouse button brings up a shortcut menu for many tasks.

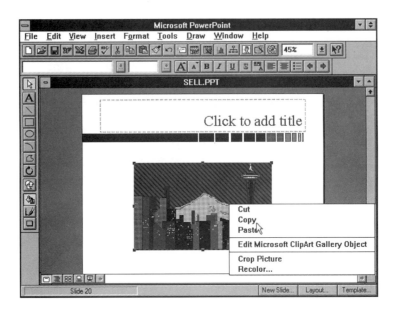

The shortcut menu that appears when you click the right button changes based on where the mouse pointer is at the time and what mode you're in. For example, if you point at a toolbar with the mouse and press the right mouse button, you see a menu that allows you to access and modify toolbars. The menu changes if you're in Outline mode and you point at a text object.

Using the Keyboard

The keyboard is used in PowerPoint primarily to type in text. It can be used for other things like controlling all aspects of PowerPoint. You normally do this via the menu system. (Refer to the section on menus to see how to use the keyboard for menu choices.) But there are a few shortcuts that make your keyboarding easier. For example:

- To move between different objects on a slide, use the Tab key. The selector box will move from object to object. When you land on an object, it's automatically selected.

- If you have multiple presentations open at the same time, pressing Ctrl+F6 switches you between presentations.

- The F7 key starts the spell checker.

- Ctrl+N creates a new slide into a presentation.

These are just a few of the keyboard shortcuts that are available to you. Many menu choices also show the keyboard shortcut keys for that choice.

Getting Help in PowerPoint

With such a powerful program as PowerPoint, you need a really good Help system. Naturally, PowerPoint has just that. There are several methods to get help in PowerPoint. You're already familiar with a couple of them: the Tooltips that appear when you select a tool from a toolbar, and the Tip of the Day. In addition to showing up when you start PowerPoint, Tip of the Day is also available from the Help menu. The text that follows looks at the other Help actions available to you.

The Help Options

Normally, you choose **H**elp by pressing the F1 key or selecting an option from the Help menu.

The PowerPoint Help system is very powerful and allows you to search for specific topics.

Contents

Search

History

Back

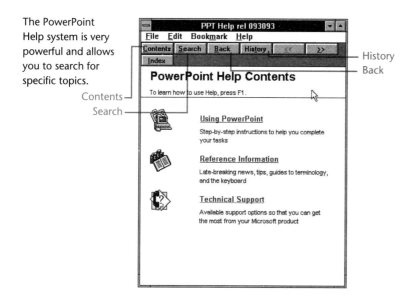

Note: *You can also get help by clicking the Help button on the toolbar. The Help button looks like an arrow with a question mark next to it. It will change the pointer to the shape of an arrow and a question mark. Clicking on anything in the PowerPoint screen will bring up Help on whatever was clicked on.*

If you have problems...   If your toolbar doesn't have the Help button visible, you can switch your pointer to a help pointer by pressing Shift+F1.

Cue Cards

Cue cards are step-by-step instructions that help you through multistep tasks. Cue cards are similar to Wizards, but they don't do any work. All they do is lay out the steps for you to take. You can navigate the cue cards by pressing the buttons that appear on them. One button brings up a menu of different cue cards, and the others are used to navigate forward and backward in that cue card. You access the cue cards by selecting **Cu**e Cards from the **H**elp menu.

Quick Preview

PowerPoint also has an overview of program features, what the program can do, and how you can use it. This is called the *Quick Preview*. The Quick Preview is displayed when you start PowerPoint for the first time after installation. After that, you can run it at any time by choosing **Q**uick Preview from the **H**elp menu.

The Help Table of Contents

In PowerPoint, you have two different Help screens. One is the *table of contents*, which allows you to keep track of where in the Help system you are. Simply click on an underlined topic to see Help for it. The Help will appear in the Help window. This feature allows you to keep the table of contents visible and helps minimize confusion.

To use the table of contents:

1. From the **H**elp menu choose **C**ontents.

2. You will see the PowerPoint Help table of contents.

3. Click on one of the hot points. Hot points are underlined and are a different color than the rest of the text.

4. In some cases, another window with the table of contents for that topic is displayed. In other cases, it is not.

5. Select a topic from the Topic Contents. The help for that topic is shown in the usual Help screen.

The Help table of contents is now visible whenever you need it.

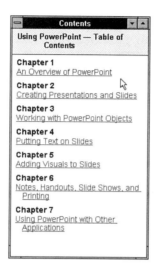

Searching for Help

One of the advantages to the Windows Help system is the capability to search for a topic anywhere in Help.

To search for a Help topic, follow these steps:

1. Press the F1 key to bring up the Help system.

2. Click on the **S**earch button at the top of the Help screen.

3. In the dialog box that appears, type your search criteria in the top text box. You'll notice the scrolling list moves as you type in the letters.

4. When you've entered the topic, you can either click on the Show Topics button or press Enter.

A list of available topics appears in the bottom half of the screen.

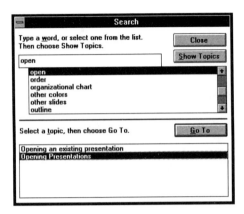

5. Double-click on the subtopic to view information about it.

The Help Index

In addition to the table of contents, PowerPoint also contains an index to the Help system. This can also be used to quickly find a topic or to get an alphabetic listing of topics.

To use the help index:

1. From the **H**elp menu choose **I**ndex.

2. The Help Index screen is displayed.

3. Press the first letter of the topic you want to get help on. You can also press the Tab key to get to the letter you want, then press
   Enter.

4. The Index will move to the first topic that starts with that letter.

5. Click on the topic you want to get help for. If you don't see the topic you want, use the scroll bars to find it.

The Help index can be used to find all the topics covered in the Help system.

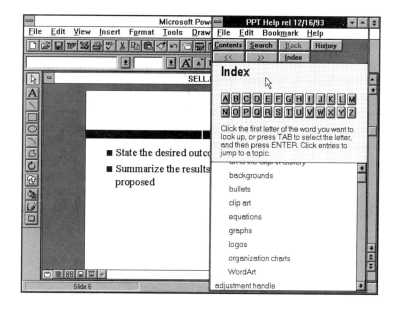

Using the Keyboard in Help

In the Help system, as with all open windows, the keyboard can be used just as readily as a mouse. To move between topics on the Help screen, use the Tab key and press Enter. The Help system jumps to your selection.

While in Help, you can access the Help menus by pressing Alt+letter of the menu selection combination. The buttons at the top of the Help window are also accessed this way.

Getting Help on Dialog Boxes

When you're in a dialog box and you're not sure how to proceed, you have the Help system at your disposal. You can either press the F1 key to bring up the Help window or, if there is one present, press the Help button in the dialog box. You then proceed as outlined earlier to make Help work for you.

Closing PowerPoint and Saving Your Work

After you create something in PowerPoint, you need to know how to save it. There are several ways to save your work:

- Close PowerPoint entirely.

- Close the current presentation.

- Save and keep working.

- Save in another format.

Each method has its advantages and disadvantages which are discussed at greater length in subsequent lessons.

Save and Keep Working

Caution

If you do not save your changes, all of the work you have done is lost. If you press the No button on the dialog box, you don't save your changes.

PowerPoint gives you complete control over where you save your presentations.

It's easy to save a new presentation and not close your presentation or PowerPoint:

1. From the File menu, choose **Save** or press Ctrl+S. You receive a dialog box asking you to type in a name for your presentation.

2. Scroll through the drives and directories until you find the path where you want to save the presentation.

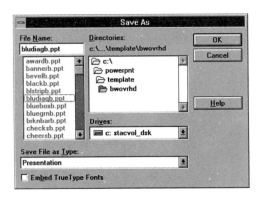

3. Give the presentation a valid DOS name of no more than eight characters. PowerPoint automatically adds the PPT extension.

4. Press OK to save your presentation.

   You then return to your presentation to continue working on it.

If you have problems...	If you save a presentation with a name of an existing presentation, PowerPoint prompts you to overwrite the old file. Choose Yes to overwrite or No to enter a new file name.

Save and Quit the Presentation

Another method of saving involves closing the presentation and leaving PowerPoint running. Follow these steps to perform this task:

1. From the **F**ile menu, choose **C**lose.

   If you haven't previously saved this presentation, you get the same Save As dialog box as in the preceding section.

2. Follow the instructions on saving and keep working.

3. PowerPoint saves your file and closes the presentation.

4. If you've already saved the file and have made any changes since the last save, PowerPoint asks whether you want to save changes to the presentation. Press the appropriate button on the dialog box to save or erase your changes.

   Note: *You can also press the Ctrl+F4 to close a presentation. Double-clicking on the presentation Control menu also closes it.*

Printing Your Presentation

If you want to print your presentation before you quit PowerPoint, choose **P**rint from the **F**ile menu. This action puts you into the standard Windows printing system. Press the OK button to print. Printing is thoroughly examined in Lesson 13.

Closing PowerPoint

There are three ways to close PowerPoint; all three will ask whether you want to save your work (see the preceding section on how to save your work):

- You can close PowerPoint by choosing E**x**it from the **F**ile menu.

- You can press the Alt+F4 key combination.

- You can double-click on the application Control menu.

After saving your work or discarding it, you return to the Windows Program Manager.

Summary

To	Do This
Start PowerPoint 4	While the Program Manager is active, double-click on the Microsoft Office icon and then double-click on the Powerpoint icon.
Use the menu bar	Select the menu with the mouse or by pressing Alt+ the highlighted letter of the choice.
Use the scroll bars	Press the arrow keys on the scroll bar. Click and drag the indicator. Click on a blank area of the scroll bar.
Select toolbars to view	Choose **T**oolbars from the **V**iew menu. Select the toolbars you want to see from the dialog box.
Customize toolbars	Open the Customize Toolbars dialog box. Drag tools to and from the toolbars.
Use a mouse	Press the left mouse button to click and select. Press the right button for a pop-up menu of options for your current object.
Use the keyboard	Press Alt+letter to select from menus. Use the PgUp/PgDn keys to move between slides. Use Tab to select objects on a slide.
Get help	Press F1 or Shift+F1. Choose **H**elp from the menu. Press the Help button in dialog boxes. Press the Help button on the toolbar.
Print your work	Choose Print from the File menu or click on the Print button on the toolbar.
Save your work and close PowerPoint	Press the Save button on the toolbar or choose **S**ave from the File menu. Press Alt+F4 to close PowerPoint or choose E**x**it from the File menu.

On Your Own

Estimated time: 10 minutes

1. Start PowerPoint.

2. Use the AutoContent Wizard to create the base presentation.

3. Minimize the presentation.

4. Minimize the PowerPoint application.

5. Restore the application and the presentation.

6. Display the rulers.

7. Close all of the toolbars.

8. Open the Standard, Formatting, and Drawing toolbars.

9. Change the Standard toolbar from docked to free-floating.

10. Anchor the Standard toolbar at the bottom edge of the screen.

11. Return the Standard toolbar to the normal position.

12. Bring up the Help table of contents.

13. Search for the topic "Moving Slide by Slide."

14. Display the cue cards.

15. Close PowerPoint. Answer No when asked whether you want to save your changes.

Working with Slides

Lesson 1, "Getting To Know PowerPoint 4 for Windows," looks at the PowerPoint interface and how to use some its features. In this lesson, you learn how to create slides and add different objects to them. You learn how to add text and modify various text attributes. You also learn how to add images and graphs and how to draw your own objects. You learn how to do the following:

- Add the first slide
- Add text to a slide
- Add objects to a slide
- Add another slide
- Move between slides
- View a slideshow

Understanding Key Presentation Terms

Before you begin working on a presentation, you must first learn some of the terms PowerPoint uses. Below are three terms you use throughout this book. Understanding them will help you comprehend how PowerPoint works.

Presentation
A file that contains a series of related slides that are used to create some form of output; also known as a *slideshow*.

- *Presentation.* A presentation is a file that contains a related series of slides. These slides are then output on-screen, one at a time, used to create overhead transparencies in color or black and white, or used to create 35mm photographic slides.

Slide
The basic element of a presentation.

■ *Slide.* A slide is the basic building block of a presentation. It's made up of several elements; these elements can be text, images, sound, or other slides. You can add many more things to a slide; these will be discussed later.

Objects
The various elements that make up slides, usually containing text or images.

■ *Object.* Objects are the basic building blocks of a slide. They are individual items that are placed on a slide template. In most cases, you'll be working with text objects and image objects; there are other objects as well that you look at in more depth in later lessons.

Task: Adding the First Slide

The first step in developing a presentation is to create a slide. When you first create a presentation, you're greeted by a sometimes bewildering array of options. To simplify this first task, you will create a very generic slide. The following steps detail what it takes to create a slide:

1. Start PowerPoint. If you're not sure how to do this, see Lesson 1, "Getting To Know PowerPoint 4 for Windows," for instructions.

2. Click the OK button in the Tip of the Day dialog box.

3. In the New Presentation dialog box, choose **T**emplate and choose OK.

Choosing **T**emplate gives you more control of what appears on a slide.

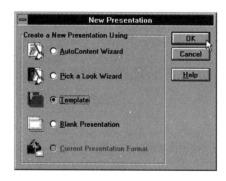

4. From the Presentation Template dialog box, select a template background to use. For this example, use the EMBOSSDB.PPT template from the Template\BWOVRHD subdirectory.

   Note: *The Presentation Template dialog box has a location to see a thumbnail view of a template style. The view box is located in the lower right corner of the dialog box. Click on a few styles to see what they look like.*

The Presentation Template dialog box allows you to see a style before you apply it.

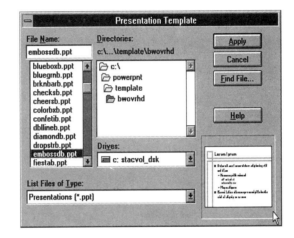

5. Press the **A**pply button to create a slide with the selected style.

6. The AutoLayout dialog box displays. Scroll through the layouts provided and highlight the one you want to use. For this example, select the first layout, the Title Slide.

7. Press the OK button.

Title Slide
The first slide in a presentation. It contains a title (usually the title of your presentation) and a subtitle.

You have just created a blank slide with a style but no text. Notice that two boxes are on the slide. One box is to add a title and the other is for a subtitle. This type of slide is known as a *Title Slide* and is usually the first slide in a presentation.

The Title Slide contains two text objects: title and subtitle.

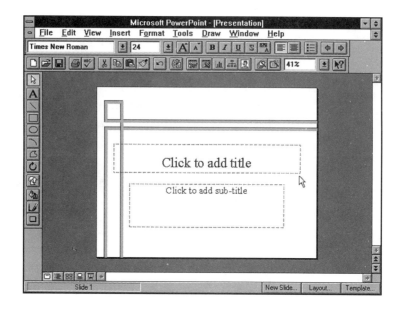

These two sections are *text objects*. These are also called *placeholders*. A text object is an object that contains any sort of text, be it letters or numbers. In the next section, you will look at how to use these text objects.

Placeholder
A location on the slide that holds text or other objects.

Text object
Any placeholder that you can type alphanumeric text into.

Task: Adding Text to a Slide

The first step in using a text object is to add text to it. There are three types of text objects in PowerPoint. The first is a *title*. The title is the line or lines of text at the top of a slide. The next type of text object is a *subtitle*. This usually appears on the first slide under the title. The last type of text object is the *bullet list*. The majority of text in a presentation is bullet lists.

The placeholder automatically wraps any text that is longer than it is. Adding text to the text object is as simple as clicking on the object and typing in what you want to say. These steps show how it's done:

1. Click once in the text object that says `Click to add title`.

Adding text is as simple as clicking and typing what you want to appear.

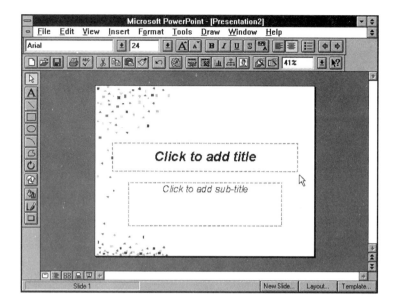

2. Start typing the text you want. Don't worry about formatting the text yet; that is discussed later in this lesson.

3. When you have typed the title for the slide, click the mouse outside of the placeholder. This action tells PowerPoint that you have finished with the title. The text you typed will replace the placeholder.

Formatting Text

Formatting text comprises many different issues: anything from changing justification to entirely changing the font and color of the text. This section discusses just a few items regarding how to format text. Lesson 5, "Enhancing Text on Slides," covers this topic in more detail.

Changing Text Justification

The first thing you learn is how to change the *justification* of the text. Justification of text is the manner in which text aligns along the edges of a paragraph. There are four types of justification: Left, Right, Full, and Center. Following is a brief look at each type of justification.

Left justification is the most common form of justification. The text aligns along the left edge, leaving the right side looking a little ragged. This paragraph shows an example of left justification.

Right justification is when the text aligns along the right edge. Right justification is mainly for numeric text and in numeric columns. This paragraph is an example of right justification.

Full justification is when both edges are flush and aligned. This is commonly used for letters and correspondence. This paragraph is an example of fully justified text. You can see how both edges of the text are fairly aligned. In order for full justification to work, you must use a proportional font.

The last form of justification is **Center** justified. This type of justification centers the text in between the margins set for the document. This paragraph is center justified.

You can vary the justification to make an emphasis. Titles are usually centered, while bulleted lists are left justified. The following steps show how to change the text justification in PowerPoint:

1. Start PowerPoint if you haven't done so already. Add some text to a slide as outlined in the previous section.

2. Highlight the text; then, from the **F**ormat menu, choose **A**lignment. The little arrowhead indicates that there is a submenu.

   On the submenu, notice that there are four choices: Left, Center, Right, and Justify. These are the same choices discussed in the preceding section. Notice a little bullet next to the current justification; in many cases, the current justification is Center.

You can also set the alignment before you start to type.

The Format Alignment menu allows you to change the justification of the text you type.

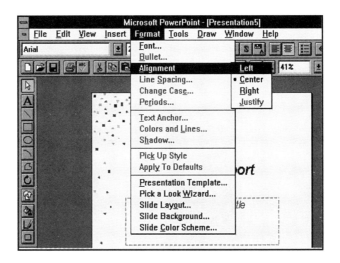

3. Choose **R**ight and watch how the text moves over to one side. Choose **L**eft and see what happens now. You will see the text moves back to the left.

4. Return the text to its original alignment. You do this by selecting the text and then selecting the correct alignment from the **F**ormat menu.

Task: Adding Objects to a Slide

You can have more than text in your slides; clip art, drawings, organizational charts, graphs, sound, and even video clips can all be added as objects to your slides. The easiest objects to add are drawings you make yourself.

Drawing Objects on Slides

To draw an object on a slide requires no special skills. You can place your objects anywhere you want on a slide. To draw an object on the title slide, follow these simple steps:

1. Start PowerPoint and create a title slide as discussed in the previous section. (If that slide is still active, use that one.)

2. Select the Rectangle tool from the Drawing toolbar. (This tool is along the left side of the screen.)

The Drawing toolbar allows you to draw directly on your slides.

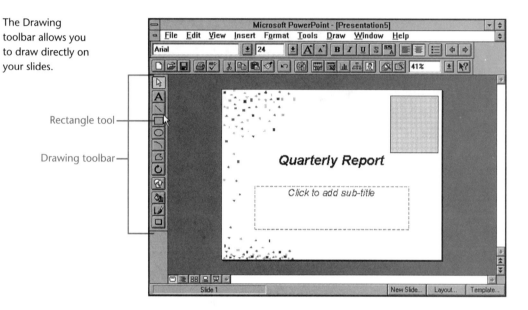

Rectangle tool

Drawing toolbar

3. With the mouse positioned on the Rectangle tool, click and drag the pointer until you see the outline of a rectangle.

4. When you're satisfied with the size of the rectangle, release the mouse button.

The rectangle will appear with a color filled in. In Lesson 8, "Adding Drawings to Slides," you learn how to enhance your drawings.

Adding Text Labels to an Object

After you have drawn one or more objects, you may want to add labels to them for emphasis, or to add supporting text. Again, PowerPoint makes this an easy task.

To create a text label for any object, one you have drawn or one you have added to a slide, follow these steps:

1. Click the Text tool on the Drawing toolbar. (The text tool looks like a button with the letter A on it.)

The Drawing
toolbar allows
you to add text
anywhere on
your slides.

Text tool

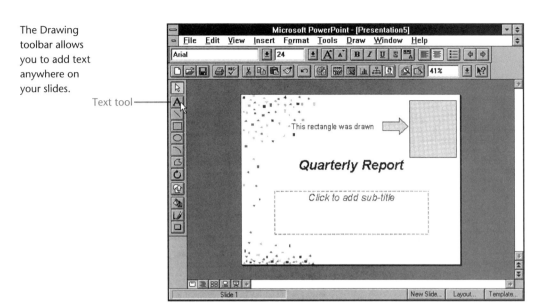

2

2. The pointer changes to a text insertion point. Position the text
insertion point where you want to start typing and press the left
mouse button.

3. Type whatever text you want.

4. When you're finished typing, click the mouse pointer outside the
text area.

Lessons 4 and 5 discuss in detail how to modify and enhance your text
with different fonts, shadows, colors, and more.

Adding Additional Objects to Slides

Suppose that you want to add something other than boring text or some
crude, handmade drawings to your presentation. How would you like to
be able to add some clip art, or even a full motion video clip with sound?
With PowerPoint, it's simply a matter of choosing the correct menu
option.

To add any other object to a slide, follow these steps:

1. Choose the **I**nsert menu.

From the **I**nsert menu, you see a variety of objects you can insert
into a slide. (If none of these objects fits your needs, choose **I**nsert
Object.)

2. Choose **O**bject to open up a dialog box listing all the possible objects you can add to a PowerPoint slide.

The Insert Object dialog box gives you access to many different objects you can add to a presentation.

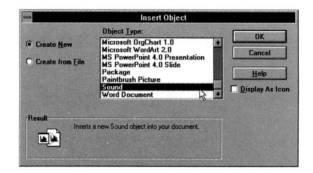

Note: *These objects can be pictures or charts from a variety of other programs such as CorelDRAW! or AmiPro, or they can be MIDI files or video clips.*

3. Select the type of object you want to insert into the slide.

4. If you're creating a new object to add, PowerPoint launches the application and lets you create the object in that application. When you're finished and you exit the application, you are prompted as to whether you want to update the slide. Respond with either Yes, No, or Cancel.

5. If you want to link to an already existing file, click the Create from **F**ile option button. You then can browse for the file you want to link to.

   If you choose **D**isplay as Icon, PowerPoint places an icon on-screen. Double-clicking the icon launches the application with the selected file.

Lesson 15, "Working with Other Windows Applications," examines this topic in more detail.

Task: Adding Another Slide

If you're not creating your presentation with one of the Wizards but are using the Template or Blank presentation instead, you may need to refer to this section. Even if you have created your presentation by using the

Wizards, you still may find it necessary to add a slide now and then. Adding one or a dozen slides is a simple procedure:

1. Move to the location in the slideshow where you want to add the slide. (The new slide is added *after* the current slide.)

2. From the **I**nsert menu, choose **N**ew **S**lide; or press Ctrl+M.

   Note: *You can also press the New Slide button along the status bar. The status bar is located at the bottom of the slide worksheet. Then, follow the rest of the directions.*

3. Choose a layout for the slide from the AutoLayout dialog box. Press OK when you have selected a layout.

The new slide is created with the layout you specify.

Note: *You can tell what slide you're currently on by looking at the status bar. On the left side of the status bar is the slide you're currently viewing.*

Task: Moving between Slides

Once your presentation contains more than one slide, you need to be able to maneuver between the slides. If you're still creating your presentation, you can go from slide to slide in PowerPoint by using the mouse or the keyboard. If you want to view your presentation as a slideshow, see "Viewing a Slideshow" later in this lesson.

Moving between Slides with the Mouse

There are different ways you can use the mouse to maneuver between slides, depending on what you're doing at the time and how you're viewing the current slide:

- If you're viewing the entire slide, you can press the up or down arrows on the Vertical scroll bar to move between slides.

- If you're zoomed in on a slide, you can use the Next Slide or Previous Slide buttons on the Vertical scroll bar. These buttons are the ones with two arrowheads.

- You can grab the indicator button on the Vertical scroll bar. As you move it along the length of the scroll bar, you see the slide number displayed to the left of the indicator. Stop when you're on the slide you want.

PowerPoint allows you to use the mouse in a variety of ways to move between multiple slides.

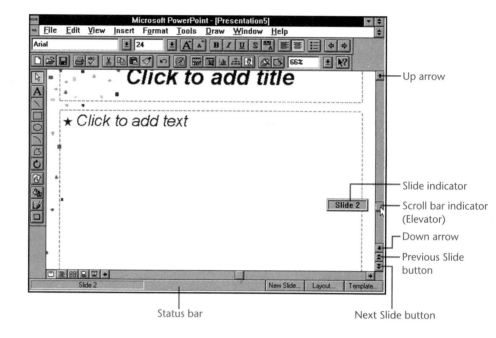

Moving between Slides with the Keyboard

For those users who don't want to use the mouse, or otherwise are not using a mouse, you can move between slides by using the keyboard. The only method available is to use the page up (PgUp) or page down (PgDn) keys. This method works no matter how closely you're zoomed in on a slide.

Note: *You can also move between slides by going into Slide Sorter view and double-clicking on the slides you want to see.*

Task: Viewing a Slideshow

There are two methods you can use to view a slideshow; neither of them requires the presentation to be finished. While Lesson 14, "Displaying Your Presentation," goes into greater detail concerning creating the final output, the basics are outlined here.

The first method allows you to view the presentation—to see how it flows or to rehearse. You're still in PowerPoint when using this method:

■ From whatever view you're in, click the Slide Show button at the bottom of the slide; this button is denoted by a picture of a screen.

■ You can also choose Slidesho**w** from the **V**iew menu. By doing so, you have a few options available to you that you won't see if you press the Slide Show button. These options concern how the slideshow runs. For the details on this option, see Lesson 14, "Displaying Your Presentation."

The second method is useful if you want to take your slideshow to another PC that does not have PowerPoint installed. However, for this to work, you need to first install the PowerPoint Viewer Program on the host PC. The PowerPoint Viewer Program is a stand-alone program you can use to distribute your presentation.

Using the PowerPoint Viewer is simple. Follow these steps:

1. Start the PowerPoint Viewer Program from the PowerPoint Program Group.

You see a File Open dialog box.

The PowerPoint Viewer allows you to take your presentations with you without having PowerPoint loaded on a PC.

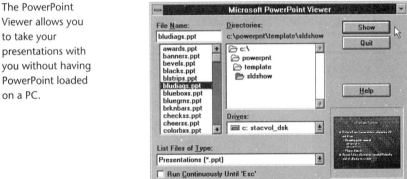

2. Select your saved presentation from the list. (You may first have to change to the directory in which it is stored.)

3. Choose the Show button from the dialog box. You can also double-click on the file name to start the slideshow. If you have checked the box that is marked Run **C**ontinuously until 'Esc', the slideshow will repeat until the Esc key is pressed.

Note: *If you have not set up any timings for the transition between slides, single-click the left mouse button to advance to the next slide. If you have transition timings set up, the viewer uses those timings to advance the slides.*

Summary

To	Do This
Add text to a slide	Click on the text placeholder and type your text.
Change text alignment	Select Alignment from the Format menu and choose the justification you want.
Draw objects	Use the Drawing toolbar to create shapes and lines.
Add a text label to an object	Use the text tool from the Drawing toolbar.
Add more objects to a slide	Use the Insert menu choices to select an object.
Add an additional slide	Press Ctrl+M or press the New Slide button.
Move between slides	Use the Vertical scroll bar or press the PgDn/PgUp keys.
View a slideshow	Use the Slide Show Viewer Program or view the slideshow from within PowerPoint. (Press the Slide Show button or select from the menu.)

On Your Own

Estimated time: 10 minutes

1. Create a new presentation.

2. Make a title slide.

3. Add the title `Starting a Home-Based Business`.

4. Change the alignment to left.

5. Draw a circle on the slide.

6. Create a label on the slide for the circle. It should read `This is a drawn circle.`

7. Create a second slide.

8. Move between the slides with both the mouse and the keyboard.

9. View your slideshow.

10. Close PowerPoint but don't save your presentation.

Creating Your First Presentation

Creating a single slide is easy; however, the real power of PowerPoint becomes apparent when you produce multiple slides and put them together in a presentation for an audience.

Creating presentations ranges from easy to difficult, depending on what you want to do. You can have PowerPoint do all, some, or none of the work for you. It is your choice.

This lesson helps you do the following:

- Understand what a presentation is
- Use Wizards and templates
- Use Slide Masters
- Create and view slides
- Copy, delete, and move slides

Task: Understanding What a Presentation Is

A *presentation* is a group of slides that you use to present an idea or subject to an audience. This can take any of the following forms:

- A slideshow that runs on your computer in either color or black and white
- Overhead transparencies
- 35mm slides

Your presentation may also have audience notes, speaker notes, an outline, or another form of handout. PowerPoint helps you create and combine all these items effectively.

PowerPoint also makes it easy for you to gain and retain the interest of your audience; it enables you to enhance your presentations through the use of a variety of mediums, such as:

- Sound

- Full motion video

- Branching to other parts of a presentation and then returning

- Adding documents and files from other Windows applications

Task: Using PowerPoint's Wizards

Wizard
A Wizard is an interactive method to create a presentation. Wizards ask you some questions and then create the presentation for you.

PowerPoint's *Wizards* enable you to create presentations with a professional look quickly and easily. You can create presentations even if you have very little knowledge about PowerPoint. PowerPoint's Wizards can help you develop your ideas for a presentation and then assist you in designing your presentation's look.

A Wizard is a guided method to create a presentation. All you do is answer a few questions that appear on-screen.

Wizards are a new feature in PowerPoint 4; PowerPoint has two Wizards. The AutoContent Wizard helps you decide on the best kind of presentation and then creates the presentation for you. You do not have to worry about what slide background or text styles to use. Of course, you are free to modify any aspect of the presentation after it is created.

The Pick a Look Wizard helps you pick a look for your presentation by selecting from a variety of templates. You also can use the Pick a Look Wizard after you develop a presentation to help fine-tune or entirely change a presentation's style for you.

Remember that even if you use Wizards, you can override any options they may set up.

In most cases, you use Wizards to cut down your development time when creating a new presentation. As mentioned earlier, you can use the Pick a Look Wizard at any time.

Starting a Wizard

You can start the Wizards in the following ways:

- Choose one of the Wizards when you create a new presentation.

- Choose the appropriate button from the toolbar.

  Note: *The AutoContent Wizard creates a new presentation, whereas the Pick a Look Wizard modifies the open presentation or creates a single slide with a particular look.*

- Choose Pick a Look **W**izard from the F**o**rmat menu. This can be done only after a presentation is active.

Creating a Presentation with the AutoContent Wizard

The following steps illustrate how to use the AutoContent Wizard to create a slide show:

1. Start PowerPoint. If PP4 is already running from the **F**ile menu, choose **N**ew Presentation. This brings up either the tips of the day or the New Presentation dialog box.

   Note: *The Tip of the Day dialog box will only be displayed if the Show Tips at Startup box on the Tip of the Day dialog box is checked. If it has not been checked, the New Presentation dialog box will be the first displayed.*

2. Select the AutoContent Wizard and press OK.

3. Respond to the questions in the Wizard's first dialog box and choose **N**ext. The Wizard asks what you want to talk about, your name, and any other information you want to appear on the slides. This information appears on your title slide. Choose **N**ext.

4. Respond to the question in the Wizard's second dialog box. Here, you determine what type of presentation you want to give. You have a choice of six types: Recommending a Strategy, Selling a Product, Service, or Idea, Training, Reporting Progress, Communicating Bad News, or General Presentation. Choose **F**inish.

Along the left side of the dialog box is a brief outline of the various types of slides that can be created.

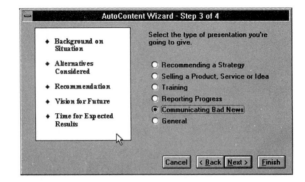

After creating your presentation, the AutoContent Wizard displays an Outline view of the slides it created.

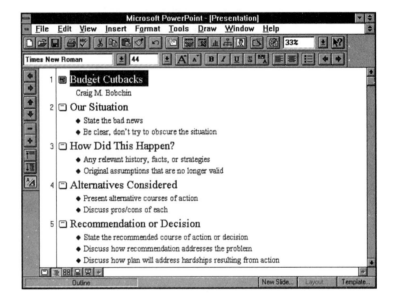

You then can edit the text in Outline view, or switch to Slide view and work on the slides there.

Note: *You can switch to Slide view in several ways. The quickest way is to double-click on the slide icon next to the slide to which you want to go. Other methods to switch views are discussed later.*

Modifying a Presentation with the Pick a Look Wizard

To pick your own look for a presentation by using the Pick a Look Wizard, follow these steps:

1. From the New Presentation dialog box that appears when you start PowerPoint, choose the Pick a Look Wizard. Or, from the **Fo**rmat menu, choose Pick a Look. Or, press the Pick a Look Wizard button on the toolbar.

   The first dialog box tells you about the Wizard you have chosen.

2. Choose **N**ext to proceed to the next step.

   Note: *You can have PowerPoint do the rest of the work for you at any time by choosing **F**inish. PowerPoint then uses whatever defaults are set for that type of slide presentation. This gives you the freedom to request a couple of items and let PowerPoint handle everything else.*

3. Answer the prompts. Through the prompts, you select the type of output you want, the template to use for these slides, and any handouts you want to produce. The prompts also ask you for the information to appear on both the slides and the handouts, such as Date, Page Number, and Company Name.

The Pick a Look Wizard helps you create handouts and other items.

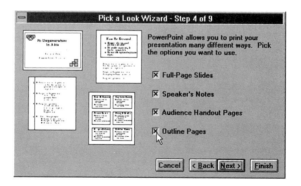

   Note: *Along the left side of each dialog box is a miniature image (thumbnail) or preview so that you can get an idea as to what the final products will look like. If you want to change an option you selected, simply choose **B**ack until you reach the point where you want to make the change.*

4. After you make all your choices, choose **F**inish to have PowerPoint create the title slide for you.

While the AutoContent Wizard creates the entire presentation for you, the Pick a Look Wizard only creates a title slide. After you have the style that you want, you then have to add additional slides. Adding more slides is covered later in this lesson.

If you have problems...

If you have any problems using the Wizards and want to reverse your steps to correct an error or change a choice you made, simply choose **B**ack. You can then backtrack as many steps as you need—all the way back to the new presentation dialog box if you so desire.

Task: Using Templates

Template
A template is a presentation that has been designed to fit a particular look, style, or color scheme.

A *template* is a presentation in which the text and the colors have been especially designed for a particular style. Templates define what your slide looks like. They also offer a complete color scheme for your presentation. PowerPoint provides you with more than 100 predefined professionally designed templates, but you also can create your own.

When you save a presentation, it can then be used as a template for other presentations. When this occurs, the text and color scheme of the template replace the text and color scheme of the open presentation.

The best way to understand what templates can do for a presentation is to browse through the templates themselves. You can do this by choosing **F**ormat **P**resentation Template and single-clicking on a presentation in the dialog box. You then see a thumbnail image of what the template looks like in the lower right corner of the dialog box.

An example of the template is displayed in the lower right corner of the dialog box.

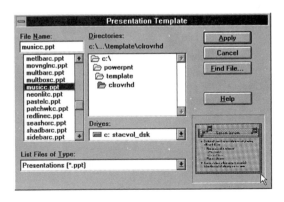

You apply a template to start creating a presentation or after you have created all or part of a presentation. In either case, follow the steps in the next section. Remember, if you do not like the look of a template you have applied, you can readily apply a different one.

Applying a Template to a Presentation

Applying templates is easy no matter where you are in the process of creating your presentation. Follow these steps:

1. If you are starting a new presentation, select the **T**emplate option from the New Presentation dialog box. Or, from an existing presentation, choose **P**resentation Template from the F**o**rmat menu.

3

In either case, the Presentation Template dialog box is displayed. There are several directories of templates for your particular needs.

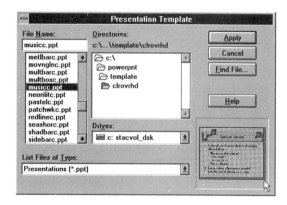

2. Select what type of presentation you want to create from the Directories list.

   Note: *PowerPoint creates a directory structure under TEMPLATE with several subdirectories. They are BWOVRHD (Black and White Overhead transparencies), CLROVRHD (Color Overhead transparencies), and SLDSHOW (on-screen or 35mm photographic slides).*

3. When you know the type of presentation you want to create, scroll through the various templates in that directory and select the one that suits your needs.

4. Choose **A**pply, and PowerPoint creates the title slide with the chosen style.

Note: *A quick way to change the template of an existing presentation is to open a presentation, and then click the Template button at the bottom right corner of the work area. Then follow steps two and three preceding, and choose **A**pply when you have the template you want.*

Understanding Layouts

When you create a presentation in PowerPoint, PowerPoint generates one slide for you (unless you use the AutoContent Wizard). As you continue to develop your presentation, you may need to add one or more slides, which is easy to do at any time with PowerPoint. Some of these slides may have text, some may contain artwork, and others may include graphs. You decide the layout of a new slide by picking the layout you want to use in the New Slide dialog box.

Layout

A basic organization of objects on a slide. Several predesigned layouts, called *AutoLayouts,* are shipped with PowerPoint.

A *layout* is simply an arrangement of objects on a slide. These objects can be text, graphs, images, or anything that can be added to a slide. PowerPoint comes with about two dozen predefined layouts. These are called *AutoLayouts* and are available from the AutoLayout dialog box.

You use layouts to create new slides or to change the layout of an existing slide. The steps for both processes are very similar and differ only in where the layout is applied. All new slides are added *after* the current or active slide.

Using Layouts To Create a New Slide

You can add a new slide to a presentation in the following three methods; all are of equal ease:

- From the **I**nsert menu, choose New **S**lide.

- Press Ctrl+M.

- Click on the New Slide button on the status bar.

All these methods bring up the AutoLayout dialog box. Select your layout, and you can immediately proceed with the design process.

To create a new slide to be placed *after* the current slide, follow these steps:

1. From the **I**nsert menu, choose New **S**lid, or click on the New Slide button on the bottom right corner of the screen. Another option is to press Ctrl+M.

The New Slide
dialog box,
showing the
AutoLayout
options, is
displayed.

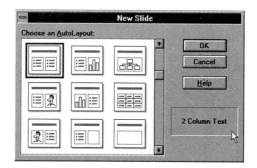

Note: *It makes no difference which PowerPoint view you are in.
PowerPoint adds the slide following your current, or active, slide.*

2. In the AutoLayout dialog box, scroll through the layouts to get a
   feel for the ones provided.

   On the layouts, you see placeholders for various objects. Some are for
   titles and text; others are for clip art, graphs, or organizational charts.
   In the lower right corner, you see a description of the layout.

3. Click on an AutoLayout to select it.

4. Choose OK to create a new slide with that layout.

Changing the Layout of an Existing Slide

To change the layout of an existing slide, choose the Layout button on
the status bar, or choose Slide Layout from the Format menu. Follow all
the preceding steps, and after choosing ReApply, the current slide's layout is changed to the new one.

Task: Setting Common Elements with Slide Masters

If you create many similar slideshows, you can make your life easier by
setting certain defaults for PowerPoint to use, such as the same background or font. Setting defaults is done via *Slide Masters*.

Slide master

A Slide Master is a slide that controls the defaults such as background or text format and color for a presentation.

A *Slide Master* is a slide that contains the format and controls the characteristics of the slide's title and text. PowerPoint sets up the format of the text so that you do not have to create it each time. If you make a change to a Slide Master (for example, choose a special font for the text or underline the slide title), the change affects all the slides in your presentation that follow the Slide Master's format.

Note: *Each of the different views has its own master style; you can have a Slide Master, Outline Master, Handout Master, or Note Master. Using them is the same as using the Slide Master.*

Date stamp

PowerPoint can automatically add the current date and time to a printout or a slide. This date is called the date stamp.

The Slide Master also is where you add any background items that you want to appear on every slide in the presentation, such as your company logo or a *date stamp*.

Note: *If you want certain objects to appear on each slide in your presentation, place them on a Slide Master. That way, you only have to create common items once. PowerPoint automatically includes them on every slide.*

Caution

Although you do not lose any text or objects added to a slide if you change the layout, you do have to make some changes, including moving and resizing objects. You might also have to delete one or more objects, depending on what you are changing.

You can change a Slide Master's format any time: before, during, or after you create a presentation. For example, you may decide at the last minute to add your company name to every slide. Just use the Text tool to type it outside the placeholders on the Slide Master. PowerPoint applies it to all the slides in the presentation in a single step.

Deciding What To Include on a Slide Master

Not every slide must follow the Slide Master. Slides use the color scheme of the Slide Master, but individual slides can have their own color schemes. As you build a slide, you have the option of using or not using any elements from the Slide Master.

No hard or fast rules exist for when to create or edit a Slide Master. It is all up to you. A few suggestions of when you might want to modify a Slide Master are as follows:

- *If you want to add a border to your slides.* Borders serve as frames for your graphics and text. You can use a border on slides to emphasize the content of the slide. A border is generally a shape such as a rounded rectangle.

- *If you want the date, time, or page number symbols on all your slides.* PowerPoint handles the printing/displaying of the correct information on each slide or page.

■ *If you want to add background items to appear on all your slides, such as clip art that forms the basic look of your slides.* If you do this, the title and text always appear on top of the background items on your slides.

As mentioned earlier, you use Slide Masters to change the look of your entire presentation. PowerPoint changes all your slides accordingly. If you make any changes to the format of the title and text on individual slides, PowerPoint remembers them as exceptions to the Slide Master. If you later change the Slide Master or apply another template, PowerPoint applies the new format and "remembers" all your exceptions.

Changing the Slide Master

Changing the Slide Master is very similar to changing any other slide in a presentation.

Follow these steps to modify the Slide Master:

1. From the **V**iew menu, select **M**aster. Then choose Slide Master.

The Slide Master appears.

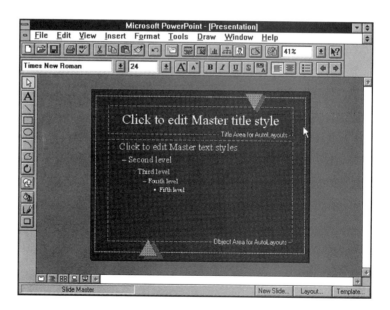

2. Make any changes you want. You can work on the master just as you work on a slide. You can add a logo, change text attributes, or add a picture to act as background for the slides.

*Note: To access the ClipArt Gallery, press the Insert ClipArt button from the toolbar or choose **C**lipArt from the **I**nsert menu. For more details on using PowerPoint's clip art, see Lesson 7, "Adding Clip Art to Slides."*

Caution

If you accidentally delete the title or any text placeholder on the Slide Master, you can restore it while you have the Slide Master on your screen. Choose Master Layout from the F**o**rmat menu. This gives you a dialog box with the choices of **A**dd Title or Add **T**ext.

3. When you are finished making changes, choose **S**lides from the **V**iew menu. When you look at the slides in your presentation, you can see the changes you made on every slide.

Removing Elements from a Slide Master

Sometimes you may want to delete certain items, such as text, graphs, or drawings from a Slide Master. This may especially come in handy when you set defaults for common elements and use the Slide Master for numerous presentations.

The steps to delete elements from a Slide Master are as follows:

1. With the Slide Master displayed, click on the object you want to delete.

2. Press Del to delete the object.

If you have problems...

If you accidentally delete something from the Slide Master, or from any slide for that matter, you can reverse your actions by choosing **U**ndo from the **E**dit menu, or by choosing the Undo button on the toolbar. Just make sure that you make no other changes in between.

Task: Viewing Slides

When you have more than one slide in your presentation, you may want to view your slides in various formats. For example, you may want to run a test of what the final slide show will look like, or see a thumbnail view of all your slides. To accommodate you, PowerPoint provides you with multiple options to view your presentation. The following sections look at each of the different views.

Using Slide View

Slide view is the most commonly used view mode in PowerPoint. This is where you do most of your work, and also see the slide in full view. By using the Zoom control, you can zoom to greater detail on the slide. You can use any of the following methods to switch into Slide view if you are not there already:

■ From the **V**iew menu, choose **S**lides.

■ Click on the Slide View button on the bottom left of the status bar.

The Slide View button is represented by an icon that looks like a single slide.

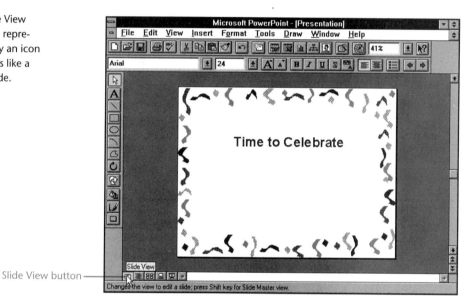

Slide View button ——

■ From Outline view, double-click on the screen icon next to the slide you want to go to.

In Outline view, double-click to switch to Slide view.

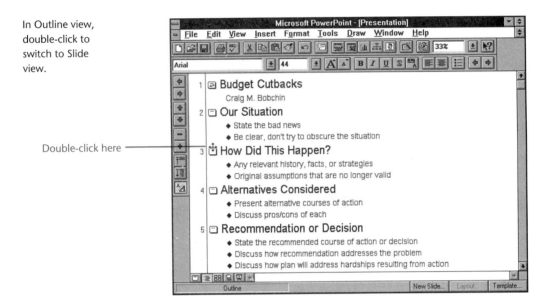

Double-click here

■ From Notes view, double-click on a slide.

■ From Slide Sorter view, double-click on a slide.

In Slide Sorter view, double-click to move to Slide view.

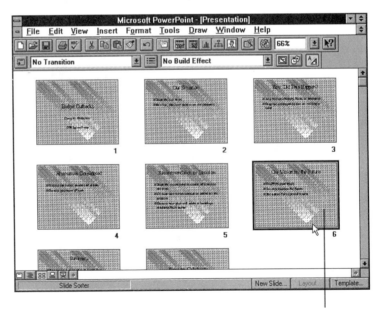

Double-click here

Using Outline View

Outline view enables you to see your slides as a written outline. In this view, you work only with the titles and main text of your slides. You do not see a graphical representation of the slides on-screen.

Outline view enables you to quickly get a handle on the message of your presentation.

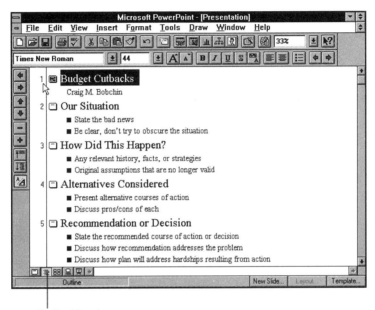

Outline View button

As you start to create a presentation, Outline view is useful for quickly organizing your thoughts and message. After you create a number of slides, you can use Outline view to move slides around and get a good overview of what you will be saying with your presentation.

You can access Outline view in either of the following ways:

■ From the **V**iew menu, choose **O**utline view.

■ Click on the Outline View button on the lower left side of the PowerPoint window. The Outline View button icon looks like a series of lines in an outline format on the button.

Lesson 11, "Creating Handouts, Outlines, and Notes," and Lesson 12, "Viewing and Organizing Your Presentation," show you how to use the outline feature in detail.

Using Slide Sorter View

Slide Sorter view enables you to see all your slides in a miniature format. You see all the text and graphics on the slides. Slide Sorter view is equivalent to working on a physical light table.

Slide Sorter view is useful when you want to move slides around, as well as to set up transitions and timings for electronic presentations. Use either of the following two methods to get to Slide Sorter view:

■ From the **V**iew menu, choose Sli**d**e Sorter View.

■ Click on the Slide Sorter View button on the lower left side of the PowerPoint window. The Slide Sorter View button is represented by an icon that looks like a group of four squares on the button.

If you have a large number of slides in a presentation, it may take a few moments to display all the text and graphics of your slides in Slide Sorter view mode. You can minimize this time by clicking on the Show Formatting button on the Slide Sorter View toolbar.

Click on the Show Formatting button to toggle on and off the display of graphics.

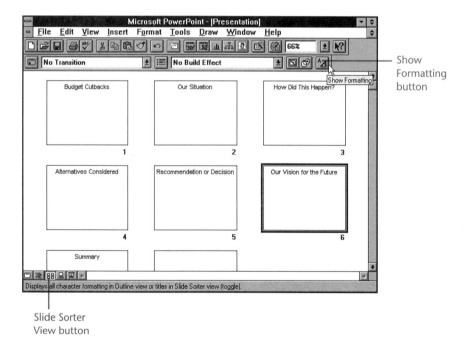

Show Formatting button

Slide Sorter View button

Later in this lesson, you examine how to use Slide Sorter view to move your slides around in a presentation.

Using Notes Pages View

Notes Pages view enables you to create a set of speaker's notes for your presentation. You use the notes as a guide while you are giving your speech. You can add text or drawings to the notes.

The notes pages have an area for a thumbnail view of the slide and an area to add text. You can add text or images to either section, and they are not reflected on the actual slide. You can get to Notes Pages view in two ways as follows:

- From the **V**iew menu, choose Notes Pages.

- Click on the Notes Pages View button on the lower left side of the PowerPoint window. The Notes Pages View button is represented by an icon that looks like a box above a couple of lines.

Notes Pages view allows you to create speaker's notes for your presentation.

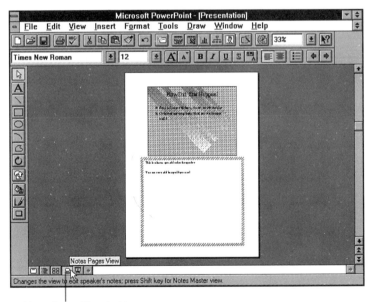

Notes Pages View button

Note: *You can switch to Slide view at any time while in Notes Pages view by double-clicking on the image of the slide.*

Lesson 11, "Creating Handouts, Outlines, and Notes," shows you how to use the Notes Pages feature.

Task: **Managing Your Slides**

Working with presentations in PowerPoint can be fun. PowerPoint has many features and much flexibility built in. In addition to creating slides, you also can copy, move, and delete slides. All these features are discussed in detail on the following pages.

Copying Slides

Occasionally, you may need to create a slide more than once in a presentation. For example, you might want to make a point, show some comparisons, and then show the main point again. You could re-create the slide manually, but that might be a great deal of work, and there is no guarantee that the slide will be an exact duplicate. PowerPoint makes it easy to copy or duplicate a single slide or a whole set of slides.

You have two methods of copying slides. The first method enables you to copy the desired slide *to another position* in the presentation; the second method creates a *duplicate immediately after the current slide.*

To copy slides anywhere in your presentation, follow these steps:

1. Switch to Slide Sorter view by clicking on the Slide Sorter View button on the PowerPoint status bar or by choosing Slide Sorter from the **V**iew menu.

   Note: *You also can copy slides from Outline view. Simply change to Outline view and proceed with the following steps.*

2. Tag a slide by clicking on it. If you want to tag more than one slide, hold down Shift while you click on the slides.

3. From the **E**dit menu, choose **C**opy; or press Ctrl+C.

4. Move the slide indicator to the slide after which you want the copied slide(s) to appear.

5. From the **E**dit menu, choose Paste, or press Ctrl+V to paste a copy of the slide(s).

   Note: *You also can copy slides by selecting them in the preceding manner and then pressing and holding down Ctrl while dragging them with the mouse to the location you want. A vertical insert line appears between slides. When the line is where you want it, release the mouse button, and the slides are copied.*

Here a slide is being copied by clicking and dragging with the mouse.

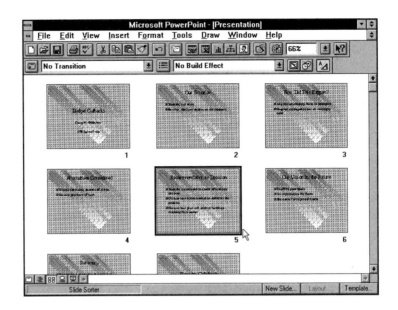

Follow these steps to duplicate slides:

1. Switch to Slide Sorter view by clicking on the Slide Sorter View button on the PowerPoint status bar or by choosing Sli**d**e Sorter from the **V**iew menu.

   Note: *You also can duplicate slides from Outline view. Simply change to Outline view and proceed with the following steps.*

2. Tag a slide by clicking on it. If you want to tag more than one slide, hold down Shift while you click on the slides.

3. From the **E**dit menu, choose **D**uplicate; or press Ctrl+D.

The slide(s) are inserted immediately after the last tagged slide. You then can move the slides wherever you want. Later sections in this lesson explain how to move slides in a presentation.

Deleting Slides

Just as it is important to copy and duplicate slides, it is important to be able to delete slides. Once again, follow a few simple steps to delete slides:

1. Select the slide(s) you want to delete. See the section on copying slides for directions on selecting slides.

   2. Press Del; or from the **E**dit menu, choose Delete Slide.

The slide(s) you selected are deleted.

Moving Slides within a Presentation

During the design phase of your presentation, you may want to move slides around or otherwise change the order of your presentation. You can always do things the hard way by manually re-creating all the slides in the new area and then deleting the old ones, or you can simply move slides from one location to another. You can do so from either Outline view or Slide Sorter view.

To move a slide from one location to another in Outline view, follow these steps:

   1. Select the slide.

   2. Drag the title icon from its present spot to its new spot.

   Note: *While you are dragging the icon, a horizontal insert line appears. This makes it easier for you to place the slide just where you want it.*

Rearrange slides in Outline view by dragging the title.

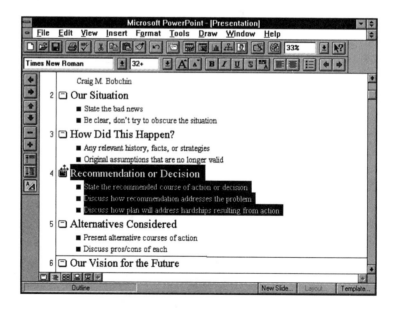

Follow these steps to change the order of your slides in Slide Sorter view:

1. Select the slide or slides you want to move.

2. Drag the selected slide(s) from the present location to the new location. When you reach a spot between two slides where you can place the slide(s), an indicator shows you where the slide(s) will appear in the presentation.

   Note: *As you drag the slide(s), a slide icon appears above the pointer. The slide icon shows the number of slides you are moving. While you are dragging them with the mouse to the new location, a vertical insert line appears. When the line is where you want it, release the mouse button. The slides are moved to that location.*

Rearrange slides by dragging them in Slide Sorter view.

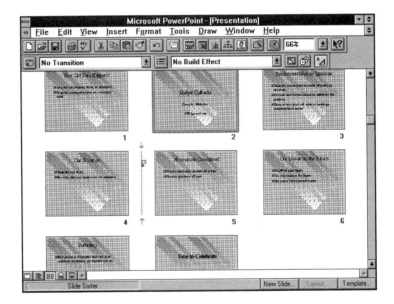

Moving Slides between Presentations

As you create more and more presentations, you may want to pull slides from one presentation into another. This is true especially if your presentations are simply variations on a theme. With PowerPoint, you easily can add slides from one presentation to another. You must have one presentation active and another one saved on disk.

PowerPoint enables you to either copy or move slides from one presentation to another. The steps you follow for each procedure are very similar, and thus discussed together at this point.

To copy slides from a presentation saved on disk to an active presentation, follow these instructions:

1. In the active presentation, choose the slide that you want to insert after.

2. From the **I**nsert menu, choose Slides From **F**ile.

You see a dialog box asking you to select a presentation from which to copy slides.

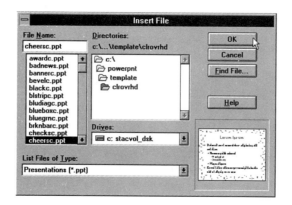

3. Select the presentation from which you want to copy the slides. Then choose OK.

   The entire slideshow will be inserted *after* the active slide in the first presentation. You then must edit, move, and/or delete slides to get the exact presentation you want.

Caution
Any slides moved or copied between presentations take on the attributes of the receiving presentation.

You can use the following alternative method to copy slides between presentations:

1. Open both presentations and then arrange the windows so that they are both visible. Place both presentations in Slide Sorter view.

2. Select the slide(s) from the first presentation—the one from which you want to move/copy.

3. Press Ctrl and the mouse button simultaneously while you drag the highlighted slides to the different window—the one you want to copy to.

If you want to move slides between presentations, follow the first two steps in the preceding list; then press the left mouse button only and drag the highlighted slides from one presentation window to the next— the one you want to move to. You can only copy or move slides in this manner from Slide Sorter view.

Here slides are being inserted from another presentation by dragging them between the two presentations.

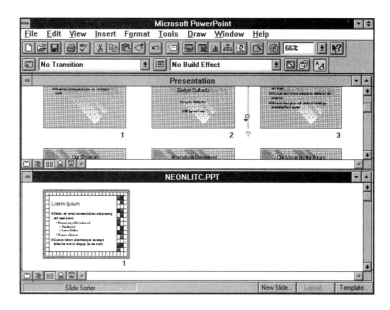

Caution
If you move slides from one presentation to another, you remove them from the first presentation.

Note: *The slides are copied or moved depending on whether you press Ctrl at the same time you press the mouse.*

Summary

To	Do This
Automatically create a presentation	Use the AutoContent Wizard to create a presentation.
Create a style for the slideshow	Use the Pick a Look Wizard.
Use AutoLayouts to create a slide	Press the New Slide button or select New Slide from the Insert menu. Then select the proper layout for your slide. Press the Ctrl+M keys.
Change defaults for a slide presentation	Modify the Slide Master. From the menus choose **V**iew **M**aster **S**lide Master.

(continues)

To	Do This
Change views	Press the correct view button from the group on the bottom of the screen. Select the proper view from the **V**iew menu.
Copy slides	Use **C**opy and **P**aste from the **E**dit menu, or press and hold down Ctrl while dragging the slide. (Only works in Slide Sorter view or Outline view.) Press the Ctrl+V keys.
Duplicate slides	Select the slide(s) to duplicate. Then press Ctrl+D or choose **D**uplicate from the **E**dit menu.
Delete slides	Select slide(s) to delete. Then press Del or select Delete Slide from the **E**dit menu.
Move slides	Go into either Slide Sorter view or Outline view. Click and drag a slide(s) to move it where you want.
Move or copy slides	Open both presentations and drag slides between them to move

On Your Own

Estimated time: 15 minutes

1. Create a presentation using the AutoContent Wizard.

2. Change the look of the presentation using the Pick a Look Wizard.

3. Change the look using a template.

4. Add an object to all the slides in one step.

5. Create four additional slides.

6. View your presentation as an outline.

7. Copy the title slide to the end of the presentation.

8. Duplicate your slide with the clip art on it.

9. Delete the second copy of the title slide.

10. Move the last slide to the second position.

11. Open or create a second presentation and move slides from one to the other.

12. View the slideshow.

13. Close PowerPoint but do not save your work.

Part II
Working with Text

Lesson 4

Adding Text to Slides

As you saw in Lesson 2, "Working with Slides," it is very easy to add text to slides. This lesson goes into more detail about text in slides:

- Create text

- Create bulleted lists

- Control text objects

- Search and replace text

- Check text spelling

Text is the most common aspect of slides. You will use the text tools of PowerPoint more than any other tools. Creating text in PowerPoint is similar to using a word processor. You have most of the features that you expect in a Windows word processor. Alignment, font control, and special effects are all available and easy to use. In fact, you can write your text in Word for Windows and simply drag and drop the text to add it to a slide. This is covered in Lesson 15, "Working with Other Applications."

Task: Creating Text Objects

To create a text object, use the Text tool.

The Text tool is located on the Drawing toolbar on the left side of the screen; it is the button denoted by an uppercase A.

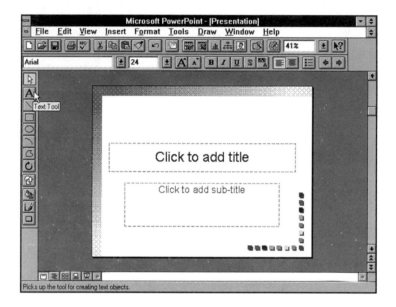

When you want to add text—other than a slide title or main text—to a slide, use the Text tool. When you use the Text tool, you can choose whether to have text word wrap. If you create a text box, word-wrap is on automatically.

Follow these steps to add a text object with the Text tool:

1. Click on the Text tool.

2. Position the pointer where you want to insert text and click.

3. Start typing the text.

4. When you are finished typing, click the mouse pointer outside the text area.

Text objects have a shape. By default, this shape is a rectangle, and the border is not visible. You can make the border visible by selecting the text object and clicking on the Line On/Off button. This button is located on the Drawing toolbar on the left-hand side of the screen and is denoted by a square with a paintbrush drawing a line.

You can change the rectangle to any AutoShape using menus as follows:

1. Select the text object that you want to modify.

2. Make the text object border visible, if it is not already, by clicking on the Line On/Off button on the Drawing toolbar.

3. From the **D**raw menu, select **C**hange AutoShape to display a cascading menu of different shapes.

Changing the shape of a text box is easy.

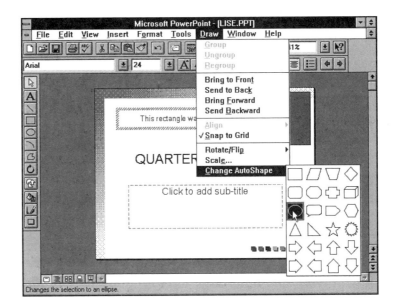

4. Select the shape you want to change to.

5. Release the mouse button.

> **Note:** *When you change the shape of a text object, the size of the text does not change. The object is sized for the current text size. If you want to make the text larger or smaller, select the text to change, and then change the font size. To make the shape and the text resize as one, use the Scale command on the Draw menu.*

Caution
Text created with the Text tool does not appear on the slide in Outline view.

You can change the word wrap for a text object by selecting the Word-Wrap Text In Object check box in the Text Anchor dialog box. See the next section on how to use this dialog box.

Changing the Anchor Point for a Text Object

Text Anchor
The point on the text placeholder from which the text grows or to which it shrinks when edited. This is also known as the *anchor point*.

Text fits into a shape depending on the setting in the Text Anchor dialog box. The *text anchor*, also known as the *anchor point*, is the location in a text object where the text starts. For example, setting the text anchor in the center keeps the text's insertion point centered in the shape's text area.

You can set the text anchor by following these simple steps:

1. Select an Object to anchor.

2. From the F**o**rmat menu, choose **T**ext Anchor.

The Text Anchor dialog box appears in which you control the text anchor point and other text settings.

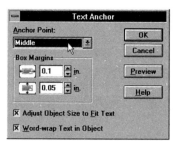

3. From the **A**nchor Point drop-down list, select the position from which you want the text to start to appear. You have six choices: Top, Middle, Bottom, Top Centered, Middle Centered, and Bottom Centered.

4. If you want to see the effect of your selection, choose **P**review on the dialog box. If the dialog box covers the text to be modified, simply drag the dialog box out of the way.

5. Select the Word-wrap Text in Object box, if desired.

6. Choose OK when you are finished.

If you have problems...

Unless the text box is larger than the text in it, you probably will not notice any changes. If this is the case, resize the text box by clicking on one of the handles and dragging it to the proper size.

Adding Titles and Subtitles

By default, titles are found on all slides. To add a title to a slide, simply click in the title text placeholder and start typing. The title normally is centered, but the alignment can be modified (see Lesson 2, "Working with Slides," in the "Changing Text Justification" section, for details on how to do this).

Subtitles appear only on the title slide and can be treated just like a normal title.

Note: *When you add a new slide, you can add a title without clicking on the title object. Simply start typing. Your text automatically is added to the title.*

You can create a slide *without* a title; either use the blank AutoLayout or select and then delete the title and/or subtitle.

Adding Bullet Lists

The next major form of text that you will work with on a regular basis is the bullet list.

The text placeholders on some AutoLayouts are set up to create bullet lists for you automatically; just select one of these layouts and then follow these steps:

1. Click on the bullet list placeholder and start typing.

Caution
You should also check the Adjust Object Size To Fit Text check box in the Text Anchor dialog box. This ensures that PowerPoint resizes the object to fit around the text. If the check box is not selected and you make the object smaller, text may run over the edges.

Bullet lists are easily created and controlled.

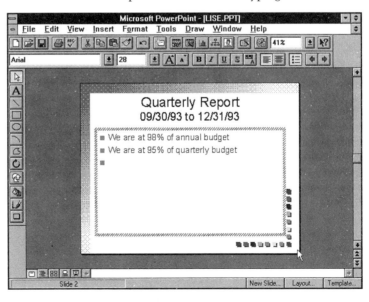

2. When you press Enter, a new bullet is added so that you can type the next item on the list.

You have full control over the look of the bullets' style, color, and placement. These can be changed by using menu commands and toolbar buttons. You also can turn off a bullet for an item on a list.

Bullets can be moved around and can act as a mini outline on a slide.

To move a bullet on a bullet list, follow these steps:

1. Make the bullet list the active object by clicking on it.

2. Place the mouse pointer over a bullet.

Notice that the pointer changes into a directional pointer with arrowheads on each arm.

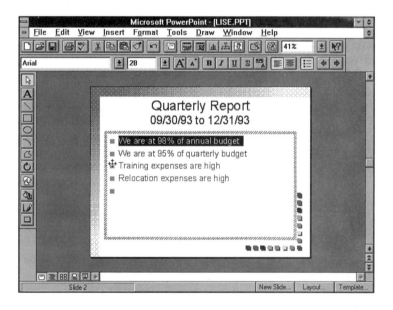

3. Click and drag the bullet to the location that you want. While you are dragging the icon, a horizontal insert line appears. This makes it easier for you to place the bullet just where you want it.

Note: *Notice that the text changes each time you move the bullet item in or out a level. The style and fonts for this are controlled by the Slide Master. You can change them, if you want, by changing the Slide Master. See Lesson 3 "Creating Your First Presentation," for details on how to change the Slide Master.*

While you can change all the properties of a bullet list via the Slide Master, occasionally you might want to modify only one or two bullet items or a part of them. For example, you may only want to change the look of a particular bullet. The steps are as follows:

1. Make the bullet list the active object by clicking on it with the mouse.

2. Position the pointer anywhere on the line with the bullet that you want to change.

3. From the F**o**rmat menu, choose **B**ullet.

The Bullet dialog box is displayed, from which you can change a bullet's style.

Special color drop-down box

Size spinner

Use a Bullet checkbox

Bullets From drop-down box

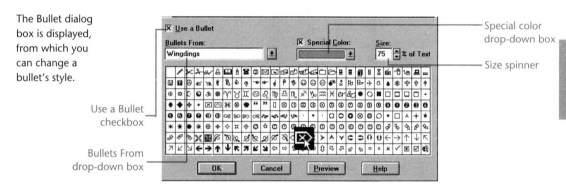

4

4. Select the character for the bullet style from the available choices.

5. If you want to change the font, size, or color of the bullet, use the options in this dialog box.

6. When you have the bullet looking the way you want it, choose OK.

You can turn off a bullet by unmarking the **U**se a Bullet check box in the upper left side of the Bullet dialog box.

You can add a bullet to any text that you want; simply click on the Bullet button on the Formatting toolbar. The Bullet button is represented by an icon that looks like a button with a bullet list on its face.

Note: *You can see what the selected bullet looks like by choosing **P**review from the Bullet dialog box. This updates the slide box while keeping the dialog box active. You may have to drag the Bullet dialog box out of the way to see the slide. Changes are made to the slide only when you choose OK.*

Task: Manipulating Text Objects

After you create text objects, you need to be able to manipulate them, including moving and deleting the text, or changing size and justification.

One of the most basic facets of text manipulation is the alignment of text—ensuring that the text lines up the way you want it. Another aspect of aligning text is setting indents and tabs if you want the text to word wrap. PowerPoint makes it easy for you to handle all these issues.

The next few sections show you how to manipulate and manage your text. Lesson 5, "Enhancing Text on Slides," goes into more detail about how to modify your text by changing fonts, colors, lines, and shadows.

Changing Margins for Text

The margins assigned to text determine how close the text comes to the borders of the text object. You can adjust both the vertical (top and bottom) and horizontal (left and right) margins.

To change the margins around text that is in a shape, follow these steps:

1. Select the object.

2. From the Format menu, choose Text Anchor. The Text Anchor dialog box appears.

3. To modify the horizontal margins, click on the top set of up or down (spinner) arrows, next to the image of text with a horizontal arrow in the Box Margins area of the dialog box.

4. To change the vertical margins, click on the bottom set of up or down (spinner) arrows in the Box Margins area of the dialog box. This is next to the image of text with a vertical arrow.

   Note: *Each up or down increment changes the margin in steps of 0.05 inches. You also can highlight the numbers and type new ones to get an exact setting, such as 0.13 inches.*

5. Choose Preview if you want to see the effect before applying the changes. If the dialog box covers the text, drag it out of the way.

6. Choose OK when you are finished.

Changing the Indentation

You can have up to five indentation levels. Each indentation level has a default setting. You can use these, or you can reset the default settings.

Follow these steps to set text indents:

1. From the **V**iew menu, choose **R**uler to display the ruler.

Upper Indent Indicator   Lower Indent Indicator

The Ruler appears with the indent markers for each level along the lower edge. You can set the paragraph indentation by dragging the indicators.

Move both indicators control

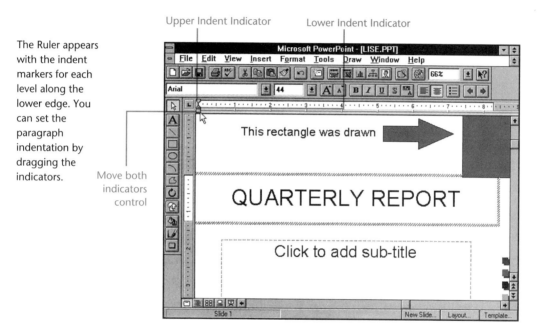

The top indicator shows the indentation amount of the first line of a paragraph. The lower indicator shows the indentation amount of the remaining lines in the paragraph. The default indent setting is zero for all lines. You can have a separate indent for each level in a text object.

Note: *You must be adding or editing text for the markers to display and be functional.*

2. Click and drag the indicators to the new indent positions you desire.

For example, if you want the first line of a paragraph to be indented by one inch, set the top marker at one inch and leave the lower marker at zero.

You can adjust one indicator at a time, or you can drag both of them at the same time. To move both indicators, click and drag the little square located at the bottom of the lower indicator. Dragging both indicators indents the entire paragraph.

You can watch the text change indentation as you drag the indicators.

Moving Text

As you saw in Lesson 2, "Working with Slides," you can select an object and then drag and move it to a new place on a slide or anywhere in your outline. Moving text around a slide or text box works in exactly the same way.

Follow these steps to move text using the mouse:

1. Highlight the text you want to move.

2. Click the left mouse button and drag the text to its new location, as you hold the mouse button down.

As you move, a box appears at the bottom of the pointer, and a small dotted line precedes your pointer to show you where the text will be placed when you release the mouse button.

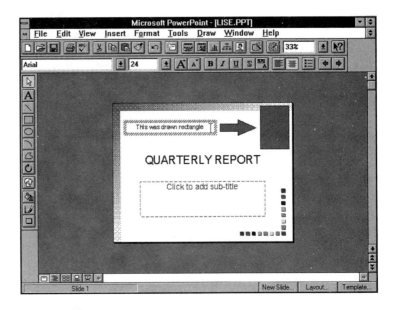

3. Release the mouse button when you have the text positioned where you want it. The selected text moves to its new location.

You also can move text with the keyboard using the cut and paste method as follows:

1. Highlight the text to be moved.

2. From the **E**dit menu, choose Cu**t**, or press Ctrl+X.

3. Move the pointer to the new location where you want to move the text and choose **P**aste from the **E**dit menu. Alternatively, you can press Ctrl+V.

   The text appears in its new location.

Copying Text

PowerPoint also enables you to copy text. Copying text is very similar to moving text.

Follow these steps to copy text via the keyboard:

1. Select the text to be copied.

2. From the **E**dit menu, choose **C**opy. This command places a copy of the text in the Clipboard so that you can paste the text in the new location (see the next step).

3. Move the pointer to the new location and press Ctrl+V; or you can choose **P**aste from the **E**dit menu. Your text then is copied to the new location.

To create a copy of text by dragging with the mouse, use these steps:

1. Select the text to be copied.

2. Press Ctrl while pressing the left mouse button. When you press Ctrl, the pointer changes into an arrow with a + sign next to it.

3. Drag the copy of the text to its new location and release the mouse button.

Deleting Text

When you delete text, you can either delete it entirely or place it on the Clipboard so that you can paste it elsewhere. Cutting and pasting is covered in the preceding section on moving text.

To delete a character, position the pointer after the character you want to delete and press Backspace.

To delete a block of text, highlight the text to select it and then press Backspace or type the replacement text.

Using Shortcuts for Deleting and Copying Text

A few keystrokes make it easier for you to edit and manipulate text. They are as follows:

Delete character left	Backspace
Delete word left	Ctrl+Backspace
Delete character right	Del
Delete word right	Ctrl+Del
Cut	Ctrl+X
Copy	Ctrl+C, Ctrl+Insert
Paste	Ctrl+V, Shift+Insert
Undo	Ctrl+Z

Task: Searching for and Replacing Text

Frequently, you may need to change some of the text in a presentation. PowerPoint enables you to find a word and replace it with a new word or phrase.

For example, you can use the Find and Replace commands to find every instance of *First Quarter* and change it to *1st Quarter*, or you can Find and Replace a phrase such as *3rd Quarter 1994* with *First Quarter 1995*. This comes in handy when you must update slides from an earlier presentation.

To find and replace text, use these steps:

1. From the **E**dit menu, choose R**e**place.

The Replace dialog
box is displayed.

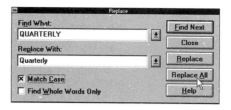

2. In the Find What text box, type the text you want to locate.

3. In the Replace With text box, type the text you want to replace it with. For example, to replace all occurrences of *Bryan* with *Brian*, type **Bryan** in the Find What box and **Brian** in the Replace With box.

4. Click on the option check boxes if you want them activated:

   ■ Match **C**ase: locates and replaces only those words that match the case of the Find word or words.

   ■ Find **W**hole Word Only: locates and replaces only whole words. For example, if you want to replace *Jones* with *Johnson*, PowerPoint does not locate *Jonesburg* if this box is checked.

5. Choose the button appropriate for the action you want to take:

   ■ The Find Next button continues to search the presentation to find the next occurrence of the text. The text is selected, but *not* replaced. Use this option if you are not sure that you want to replace the text.

   ■ The Replace button changes the first occurrence of the selected text and then finds the next occurrence of that text, but does *not* replace it. Use this option when you know you want to change the selected text, but are not positive that you want to change the next occurrence of it.

   ■ Replace All changes every occurrence of the located text. To stop the replacement of all text, press Esc.

6. When you finish searching and replacing, choose Close.

4

Task: Checking Text Spelling

If you were a perfect typist and speller, you would have no need for dictionaries and spelling tools. But because you are bound to make spelling mistakes, PowerPoint includes a spelling tool.

The spelling tool checks the spelling of all text in the entire presentation, including all slides, outlines, notes pages, and handout pages. If PowerPoint cannot find a word in its main dictionary, it then checks a custom dictionary that you can customize by adding words to it.

To check the spelling in a presentation, follow these steps:

1. From the Tools menu, choose Spelling; or press F7.

    Note: PowerPoint checks the spelling starting at the current selection in the presentation.

When PowerPoint finds a word it does not recognize, that word appears in the Not In Dictionary box of the Spelling dialog box.

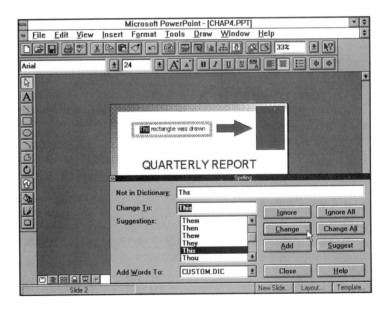

2. Choose from the following options:

    ■ You can manually correct the word. Simply retype the word in the Change To box and then choose Change. If you want to change any other occurrences of the same misspelling, choose Change All.

■ Pick one of the suggested alternatives. PowerPoint lists possible spellings for the misspelled word in the Suggestio**n**s box. You can scroll through the list, locate the word you want, select it, and then choose either **C**hange or Change A**ll**.

■ Ignore the misspelling. Choose the **I**gnore button when the word is spelled correctly but is not in the dictionary. Selecting **I**gnore does not add the word to a custom dictionary, and PowerPoint tells you it does not recognize the word each time you check the presentation's spelling. If you choose I**g**nore All, PowerPoint then ignores that word any time it encounters it in the presentation.

■ Add. When you choose **A**dd, PowerPoint adds the word to a custom dictionary. Your choices of custom dictionaries are listed in the Add **W**ords To box. If you have multiple custom dictionaries, you can select one from the drop-down menu. Click on the arrow next to the Add **W**ords To box to see the list.

4

3. When PowerPoint reaches the end of your presentation, it either tells you that it checked the entire presentation, or asks whether you want to continue checking at the beginning of the presentation, (in case you started the spell check in the middle of the presentation). In the first situation, press OK to quit the spell check. In the second situation, choose either Yes to check from the beginning of the presentation, or No to stop.

Summary

To	Do This
Create text	Use the Text tool and type.
Change the anchor point for text	Use the **T**ext Anchor dialog box located on the F**o**rmat menu.
Create bullet lists	Click on a bullet list placeholder, or choose the Bullet list button.
Change the bullet	Choose Format **B**ullet and then choose the desired format from the dialog box.

To	Do This
Change margins on a text box	Use the **T**ext Anchor dialog box and adjust using the margin controls.
Change the size of a text object	Grab the handle and drag to resize.
Change paragraph indentation	Use the rulers to move the indentation indicators.
Move text	Click and drag the text.
Copy text	Press Ctrl while dragging the highlighted text.
Delete text	Highlight text and press Del.
Search for and replace text	Use the **F**ind or **R**eplace options on the **E**dit menu.
Check the spelling of a presentation	Press F7 or use the **S**pelling checker from the **T**ools menu.

On Your Own

Estimated time: 10 minutes

1. Type two paragraphs of text on an otherwise blank slide.

2. Change the anchor point to the left.

3. Make the text a bullet list.

4. Set the margins to .75 inch all around.

5. Make the text box larger.

6. Change the paragraph indentations to make it 3/4 inch for the first line and 1/4 inch for the rest of the paragraph.

7. Replace the word *AND* with the word *OR*.

8. Spell check the text.

Enhancing Text on Slides

One of the things you can do to enhance your presentation and make it more effective is to enhance your text. Probably 85 percent of your presentation is based on text. By adding items such as boldface, larger fonts, or changing the justification, you can make an impact on your audience. This lesson shows you how to enhance your text and covers the following topics:

- Change fonts

- Add boldfacing, italics, and other text effects

- Justify text

- Change case

- Modify text styles and colors

The Formatting toolbar and the Format menu give you access to many text styles. You can change the color, size, or typeface of your text, or add shadows, boldfacing, italics, and so on.

Task: Changing Fonts

Font
A complete collection of characters in a particular typeface.

During the development phase, you may want to change a font in your presentation. Changing fonts falls into two categories: changing fonts before you start typing, and replacing all instances of one font with another.

You can use either the menus or the toolbar to change fonts before you start typing. To use the menus, perform the following steps:

1. From the F**o**rmat menu, choose **F**ont.

The Font dialog box appears.

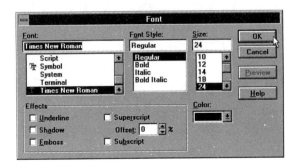

2. Scroll through the Font list to select a new font; highlight the one you want to use.

3. Choose OK to close the dialog box and continue typing with the new font.

Follow these steps to use the toolbar:

1. On the Formatting toolbar, click on the down arrow next to the Font list to display a list of available fonts.

2. Select the one you want from the list.

Note: *PowerPoint also enables you to modify some text that you already typed. First, highlight the text with the mouse or keyboard. Then select the appropriate font using the techniques just described.*

If you have problems...   If a font you want to use does not appear in the Font list, you may have to install it into Windows. See your Windows documentation for instructions.

Replacing Fonts

The procedures outlined in the preceding section are fine if you have a small amount of text to change or are just beginning to develop a presentation. But, what if you want to change all of a particular font in a presentation? You could go in and change the font slide by slide, but that could be time-consuming and tiring, depending on how many slides you must go through.

Instead, use the Replace **F**onts menu command. When you replace a font with the Replace **F**onts menu command, all the text using that font in your presentation changes.

To replace fonts, follow these steps:

1. From the **T**ools menu, choose Replace **F**onts.

The Replace Fonts dialog box appears, where you can choose to swap one font for another throughout your presentation.

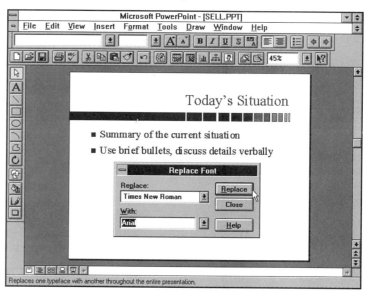

If you highlight text before choosing Replace **F**onts, the font of the selected text is listed in the Re**p**lace box. If no text is selected, the font previously listed on the Formatting toolbar appears in the Re**p**lace box.

Note: *You can scroll through the list in the Re**p**lace box to see all the fonts used in your presentation.*

Caution
Other text attributes such as italics and size are not affected during the replace.

2. Scroll through the **W**ith drop-down menu to see all the fonts installed on your system. Highlight the one that you like.

3. Choose **R**eplace. The new font you just selected in the preceding step replaces the old font on the slide and now appears in the Re**p**lace box.

4. Choose Close to accept the new font.

Changing Font Size

You may discover that some of your text is just too small to be seen by people at the back of the room. Remember that your presentation should be designed so that the message has impact. To this end, you may need to resize your fonts to make them larger.

Caution

When you select text to change, make sure that you select *all* of it, and not just part of it; otherwise, you may end up with half a line in one font size and half a line in another—unless, of course, that is the effect you want.

You have two methods to change the size of a font: the menus or the toolbar. Regardless of which method you use, to change the font size of *previously existing* text, you must first highlight the text and then proceed with the following steps. If you do not select any text before you change the point size, only new text that you create appears in the new size.

To use the menus to change font size of selected text, follow these steps:

1. From the F**o**rmat menu, choose **F**onts. The Font dialog box appears.

2. On the right side of the dialog box, either type a number between 1 and 999 in the **S**ize text box, or select a point size from the scroll list.

3. To see the effect of your selection, choose **P**review on the dialog box. Drag the dialog box out of the way if it covers the text to be modified.

4. Choose OK to close the Font dialog box and apply the new point size to your fonts.

You also can use the toolbar to change the font size by performing the following steps:

1. On the Formatting toolbar, click on the down arrow next to the Font Size to display a list of available font sizes.

2. Select the one you want from the list.

Note: *Alternatively, click in the Font Size box and type the size you want. Use a font size between 1 and 999.*

As an alternative method, you can use the Increase Font and Decrease Font buttons on the toolbar, next to the Font Size box. The Increase Font button is an icon containing a big, capital letter A and an arrow pointing up in the upper right corner of the button. The Decrease Font button icon looks like a button with a small, capital letter A and an arrow pointing down in the upper right corner of the button.

Using the Increase and Decrease Font buttons, however, only increases or decreases your font size by four points. For example, if your current font size is 40 and you click on the Decrease Font button, the new font size is 36. If you want to increase or decrease your font size by more than four points, you can continue clicking on the Increase or Decrease Font buttons, or you can use either the Font Size box or the menus.

Adding Bolds, Italics, and Other Text Effects

PowerPoint enables you to easily add some special effects to your text for emphasis or style; you can add **boldfacing**, *italics*, underlining, and shadow. Once again, you can use either the menus or the toolbar to accomplish these tasks. Regardless of the method you choose, to make any changes to *previously existing* text, you must first select the text and then proceed with the following steps. If no text is selected before you make your changes, only the new text you create has the changed attributes.

To add effects to selected text with the menus, follow these steps:

1. From the Format menu, choose **F**ont.

   The Font dialog box appears.

2. In the Font dialog box, select the styles you want from the available font styles in the Font Style box. If you want to bold the font, select Bold, and so on.

   - To underline your text, mark the **U**nderline check box in the Effects section.

   - To shadow your text, mark the Sh**a**dow check box in the Effects section.

   - To emboss your text, mark the **E**mboss check box in the Effects section.

   Note: *You can emboss your text only from the Font dialog box. There is not a button on the Formatting toolbar.*

5

3. If you want to see the effect of your selections prior to applying them, choose **P**review on the dialog box. Drag the dialog box out of the way if it covers the text to be modified.

4. Choose OK when you are happy with your changes.

If you use the toolbar to change these attributes, the procedure is the same for all of them; the only difference is in which buttons you use. Clicking on the text editing buttons on a toolbar toggles an attribute on and off.

To change the text attributes via the toolbar, select one of the tools on the Formatting toolbar and make the changes you want to the text. The text attributes buttons are represented as follows on the Formatting toolbar: the Bold button has a **B** on it, the Italics button has an italic *I* on it, the Underline button shows a <u>U</u> with a line under it, and the Text Shadow button has an S in shadow type.

The toolbar can be used to add enhancements to your text.

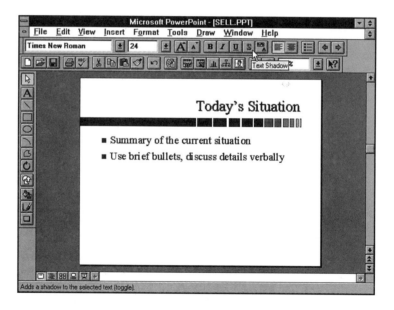

To add either superscripts or subscripts to your text, you must use the menus. Unlike the other text attributes, you cannot use the toolbar to create superscripts and subscripts unless you customize it. As with the other attributes discussed earlier, to make any changes to *previously*

existing text, you must select the text first and then proceed with the rest of the steps. If you do not select text before you make changes, only the new text that you create has the changed attributes.

To add superscripts or subscripts, follow these steps:

1. From the F**o**rmat menu, choose **F**ont to display the Font dialog box.

2. In the Effects section, check either Supe**r**script or Su**b**script, depending on what you want to do.

3. If you want to see the effect of your selections prior to applying them, choose **P**review on the dialog box. Drag the dialog box out of the way, if it covers the text to be modified.

4. Choose OK when you are finished.

    Note: *The offset is to help you determine the placement of the super and subscript text. Click on the arrows to change the value or type it in after highlighting the existing offset value.*

Task: Justifying Text

Justification
The justification is the margin along which the text has a flush edge. You have four types of justification, Right, Left, Center, and Full.

In many instances, you may want to change paragraph alignment. You can align paragraphs on the right, left, or center, or they can be fully justified. You can set alignment in two ways. You can set alignment in the Slide Master, or you can set alignment for each individual paragraph in the slide. To change alignment, once again, you can use the menus or the toolbar. However, the toolbar only allows you to align the paragraph on the left or the center unless you customize the toolbar to add right alignment and full justification tools.

Regardless of the method you choose, you first must select the paragraph or paragraphs you want to change. To change the alignment of paragraphs in a text object, select all the text. To change the alignment of more than one paragraph, select some text in each of the paragraphs to be changed. To change the alignment of a single paragraph, place the insertion point any place in the paragraph.

If you want to change your text alignment using the menus, follow these steps:

1. From the Format menu, select Alignment.

2. From the cascading Alignment menu, choose the alignment you want.

The Alignment menu allows you to change the justification of your text.

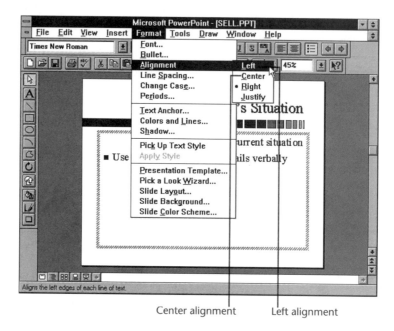

Center alignment   Left alignment

To change a paragraph's alignment via the toolbar, click on either the left or center alignment buttons on the toolbar. These buttons are in the upper right-hand side of the screen, to the right of the Bold, Italic, and Underline buttons. The Left Alignment button is represented by an icon that looks like a number of text lines all lining up on the left. The Center Alignment button icon looks like a number of text lines lining up in the center.

If you have problems...   You can add the right and fully justified alignment to the toolbar by customizing the toolbar. See Lesson 1, "Getting to Know PowerPoint 4 for Windows," for instruction on how to customize the toolbar.

Task: Adjusting Line Spacing

If you want to adjust the space between the lines of your text and/or between paragraphs, the Line **S**pacing menu choice is what you need. The Line **S**pacing menu choice enables you to increase or decrease the spacing between lines and paragraphs to make text fit better in a slide or to make text more readable.

Follow these steps to change line or paragraph spacing:

1. Select the paragraph or paragraphs in which you want to change either the line or paragraph spacing.

2. From the F**o**rmat menu, choose Line **S**pacing.

The Line Spacing dialog box appears in which you change line and paragraph spacing.

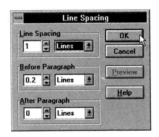

3. Change the spacing by either typing the value you want or clicking the up or down arrows to change the value.

   ■ To adjust the line spacing, enter a new value in the Line Spacing box.

   ■ To adjust the spacing before or after a paragraph, use the **B**efore Paragraph or **A**fter Paragraph box.

   You can modify the spacing in either lines or points by using the drop-down menu to the right of each adjustment box. Choose **P**review to see what effect the new line or paragraph spacing has on the text. Move the dialog box out of the way, if it covers the text to be modified.

4. Choose OK to save your changes.

5

Task: Changing Case

If you want to change the case of any text in your presentation, the For-mat menu contains a command that enables you to alter lowercase and uppercase text after you have typed it on a slide. Several case choices are available; they include, but are not limited to, ALL UPPER, all lower, and Title Case.

To change case, perform the following steps:

1. Select the text you want to change.

2. From the Format menu, choose Change Case.

The Change Case
dialog box appears.

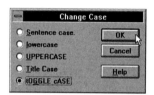

3. Select the case you want to change to and choose OK. The text changes to the case selected.

Task: Adding or Deleting Periods

You have the option to add or delete periods at the end of selected para-graphs. You can perform this while in Slide, Outline, and Notes Pages views. The change only adds or deletes periods in the main text. It does not affect slide titles or text added using the Text tool.

Follow these steps to add or delete periods:

1. Select the text to which you want to add or delete periods.

2. From the Format menu, choose Periods.

The Periods dialog
box appears.

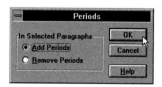

3. Choose either **A**dd Periods or **R**emove Periods.

4. Choose OK to save your changes.

Task: Modifying Text Styles and Colors

Although the default color schemes that come with PowerPoint are nice and the text and background complement each other, you probably will want to experiment with your own colors. PowerPoint makes it easy for you to do this.

You also can add lines and fills to text objects. When you have a style you like, you can then apply it to other text objects in your presentation.

Changing the Color of Text

Perhaps the most common change you will make to text is to change the color. You may want to make all the text the color of your company logo, or make certain labels a bright color for emphasis. You can change color by using the menus or the toolbar.

To change the font color from the menus, use these steps:

1. From the F**o**rmat menu, choose **F**ont to display the Font dialog box.

2. From the **C**olor drop-down palette, select the color you want.

3. If you do not see the color you want, choose Other Color; then pick a new color in the Other Color dialog box. If you still do not see a color that fits your needs, go to the More Colors dialog box.

In the More Colors dialog box, you can create your own colors if you cannot find any existing ones that you like.

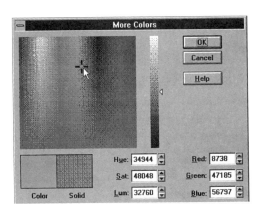

5

Follow these steps to use the toolbar to change text color:

1. Select the text you want to change. If you are starting a new text object and want to specify the color, go to step 2.

2. On the Formatting toolbar, click on the Text Color button.

Clicking on the Text Color button displays a palette of colors.

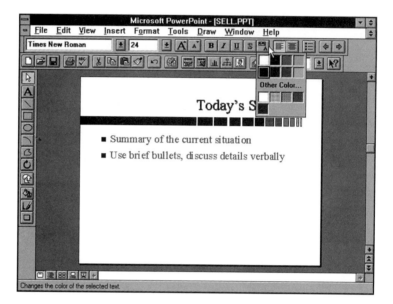

3. Select a color from the choices available. If you want to see more colors, double-click on the Other Color option.

4. If you do not want to use one of the colors in the Other Color dialog box, you can create your own by choosing More Colors.

The More Colors dialog box enables you to drag the pointer to create virtually any color imaginable, or any color your system is capable of displaying.

Adding Lines and Fills

PowerPoint text can have attributes that define how the objects appear on a slide. The attributes are as follows:

■ The border around a text object

■ The background color of a text object—called the Fill

A line can exist on its own, without acting as a border for an object. Both lines and borders have similar attributes, although there are a few differences. For example, lines, arcs, and freeform shapes can have arrowheads; borders cannot.

PowerPoint objects come with a predefined set of attributes. These default settings are taken from the presentation's Slide Master. The default settings are automatically available when you use one of the toolbar buttons to assign an attribute. For example, use the Apply Fill Defaults button on the Drawing toolbar to apply the default fill color. To select a different fill color, use the Colors And Lines command from the Format menu, or the Fill Color button on the Drawing+ toolbar. It is easy to change the defaults for whatever you want.

Border
A line added to an object that defines its shape.

A *border* is a line around an object that defines its shape. PowerPoint, by default, adds a thin border to any object you draw; also by default, this border is not visible. You can add borders to text boxes, pictures, and artwork that you imported into your presentation. You also can delete a border, and change its style, color, and border weight.

To add a border to a text object, follow these steps:

1. Select a text object to change.

2. From the Format menu, choose Colors and Lines.

The Colors and Lines dialog box appears. You can easily add any style of border to a text object.

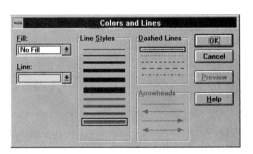

3. In the Color and Lines dialog box, click on the Line Style you want to apply. If you want to make the border a dashed line, click the dashed line that you want to apply. Click on the color combo box to see the options that you have for the line color.

4. To view your changes before accepting the border style, choose **P**review.

5. Choose OK to save your changes.

Fill

A color and/or pattern that acts as background for an object.

You also can select fills from this same dialog box. A *fill* is the color that acts as background for a text object. For example, say you want to have white text on a red background. Set the text color to White as outlined in the earlier section on choosing text color, and then set the fill to red.

Note: *When you select a color for the fill, you see several other options. You have the chance to add shading and a background pattern to the fill. Select the appropriate item from the menu and follow the dialog box.*

You can add and change fills as easily as you can borders.

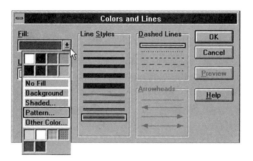

It might be useful to use the buttons on both the Drawing and Drawing+ toolbars to make quick changes to borders and fills.

Applying New Text Styles

After you create a text object with just the right border, fill color, and so on, it is possible to "pick up" all the attributes of that object and apply them to another object, by using the Format Painter button on the standard toolbar.

With this button, you can quickly change the appearance of a text object by copying the attributes (color, shadow, font, and so on) of another text object whose appearance you like. The Format Painter button works only with objects and their attributes, *not* with graphs and pictures.

To pick up and apply style using the Format Painter button, follow these steps:

1. Select the text object whose attributes you want to copy.

2. Click on the Format Painter button on the standard toolbar. This is represented by an icon with a paintbrush on it. The pointer changes to a paintbrush.

3. Click inside the object to which you want to apply the attributes. The selected object takes on its new attributes.

Summary

To	Do this
Change fonts	Select the new font from the toolbar or the Font dialog box.
Replace fonts	Use the Replace Font option from the Tools menu.
Change font size	Use the Font dialog box or the toolbar to select a font size.
Add bolds, italics and other text effects	Select the text; then choose the attributes from the toolbar or the Font dialog box.
Justify text	Select the paragraph to align and then select the alignment from the toolbar or the Format Alignment menus.
Change line spacing	Use the Line Spacing dialog box.
Change case	Use the Change Case command from the Format menu.
Change Periods	Use the Periods command from the Format menu.
Change the color of text	Use the Color and Lines dialog box or the toolbar.
Add lines and fills	Use the Color and Lines dialog box.
Apply new text styles	Use the Format Painter button to drag and drop text formats.

5

On Your Own

Estimated time: 12 minutes

1. On the title of a new slide, change the font to Arial.

2. In an existing presentation, replace all the Times Roman fonts with Arial.

3. Change the subtitle to 33 points.

4. Create a text object and make it bold with shadows.

5. Make the text object right justified.

6. Change the line spacing to two lines.

7. Change the text case to all lowercase.

8. Add periods to all the bullet lists. If periods are already used in the bullet lists, remove them.

9. Change the text color to Bright Green.

10. Add a yellow border to the text object.

11. Make the fill Light Blue.

12. Apply this style to the slide title.

Part III
Enhancing Your Presentation

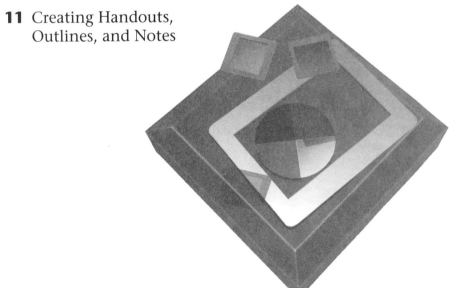

Working with Color on Slides

PowerPoint enables you to choose from more than 16 million colors for a presentation, depending on the configuration of your computer. With so much to choose from, you have the power to enrich or ruin your presentation, depending on how wisely you pick a color scheme. Fortunately, PowerPoint has made it easy for even nonartists to choose colors that ensure a professional look to any slide show. You learn how to do the following in this chapter:

- Use color schemes

- Change colors or create new colors

- Use a color scheme from another application

- Rearrange colors on a slide

- Change colors of pictures, text, and other objects

Understanding Color in a Presentation

Color provides cohesiveness to a slide presentation. If the main points on a slide stand out and you use the same colors consistently from slide to slide, your show has more impact. It's the same for all the other elements you are using—the bullets and other text, art, graphs, and other graphic elements communicate your ideas more vividly when a consistent use of color is applied to them.

Color also separates the background from the text and the illustrations you are using on a slide. Some colors appear to come forward; these are the ones you want to use for text and art. Cool or grayed-off colors recede and are best used for backgrounds. If colors you use for the text don't contrast strongly from the background, your audience will not be able to read what you have put on your slides—especially if they are seated in the back of the room.

Color Schemes
These are sets of coordinated color palettes. Each color scheme is made up of eight harmonizing colors.

I'm not an artist, you say! How do I know what the right colors are? Well, PowerPoint has made it easy for you with its new Color Schemes color palette sets.

If you are just starting out as a slide presenter, you also might want to use the Pick a Look Wizard to get you started. It helps you define the *look* of your presentation. You can also review the many templates that PowerPoint provides and choose one that appeals to you.

Note: *To get started with the Pick a Look wizard, click its button on the Standard toolbar.*

Task: Working with Color Schemes

If you are one of those people who has always had problems working with color, the color schemes PowerPoint provides will help to ensure pleasing results. In a color scheme palette, each of the eight colors blends with others in the set. Color harmonies exist whether your color scheme is shown on a computer screen as slides or as printed output. Colors have been specifically chosen for each one of the elements that makes up a slide—the text, background, object fills, and the graphics you may include.

When you need to change colors to match a new scheme, the entire presentation can be changed in a single step. If you only want to change colors for one or two slides within the set, that is done just as easily.

If you add pictures from an outside source to a presentation, these, too, can be recolored to match your scheme.

Using Existing Color Schemes

When you develop a presentation using one of the many templates provided by PowerPoint, you are already using a color scheme. It includes the following object elements:

- *Background.* Just what it says. It is the color that appears behind all the other elements on the slide.

- *Text and Lines.* The color applied to text that is created with the Text tool, the lines drawn with one of the draw tools, and the frames created with the Line command in the Object menu.

- *Text Title.* The color used for the title of a slide.

- *Shadows.* The color applied to text or objects when the Shadow command is used.

- *Fills.* The color inside an object.

- *Accents.* The colors used for emphasis or for coloring a chart. Three accent colors are provided in a color scheme.

Changing or Creating Color Schemes

Color is one of the features or attributes connected to an object in PowerPoint. If you recall from earlier chapters, attributes connected to an object can be changed at any time.

What if you like the design of a particular template, but prefer the colors used in another one? Or, you need to change one of the colors to match a company logo. Not to worry. Color schemes can be modified or changed entirely.

It is important to keep in mind that the color scheme is your main palette for a specific presentation. It is the one that PowerPoint keeps track of as you continue to add slides. If you change your color scheme at any time while putting together your presentation, PowerPoint will automatically update all the slides. *However, if you add other colors that are not part of a color scheme, these will not be updated.* You have to recolor these additions manually.

Applying a Color Scheme from Another Template

You can copy a color scheme from a template whose colors you like to one whose layout you prefer. Begin by selecting an individual slide from the template whose color you like.

Note: *You can't apply a template to an individual slide. Whenever you apply a template, you affect the entire presentation.*

6

To apply a color scheme from another template, follow these steps:

1. In the Slide Sorter view, select the slide whose colors you want to apply to the presentation. The selected slide is surrounded by a thick border.

2. Use **Edit Copy** or Ctrl+C to copy the slide to the Clipboard.

In the Slide Sorter view, select the slide whose colors you want to apply in order to copy to other slides in the presentation.

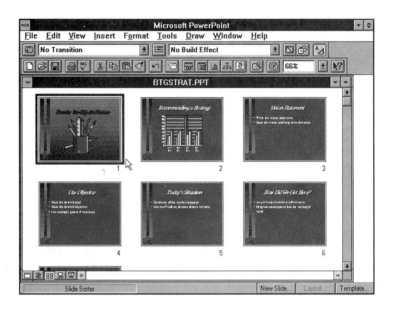

3. Click the Format Painter button on the toolbar. It picks up the color scheme of the selected slide and the arrow pointer changes to the icon of the Format Painter.

Format Painter button

Format Painter is a toolbar button that enables you either to copy or apply formatting.

When you use the *Format Painter button* with a graphic, a single click picks up line, fill, shades, and shadows. (With a double-click, formatting is applied to text.) When Format Painter is used in the Slide Sorter view, it picks up the color of the selected slide. You can then apply the colors to any or all slides in the presentation.

4. Select the slide whose colors you want to change; the color scheme you selected previously is applied to these slides and the pointer returns to its arrow shape.

5. Repeat steps 1 through 4 to copy slide color schemes to additional slides.

A slide selected for a color change in the Slide Sorter view.

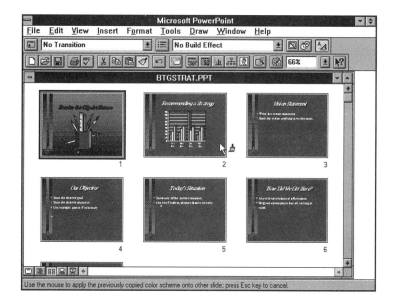

Choosing a New Color Scheme

If you want to experiment with new color schemes or rearrange the colors on your present scheme, PowerPoint acts as a guide. The new color scheme will be based on the background and text colors that you choose.

To choose a new color scheme, follow these steps:

1. From the Format menu, choose Slide Color Scheme to display the Slide Colors dialog box.

At the top of the Slide Color Scheme dialog box, you see the current palette for your presentation.

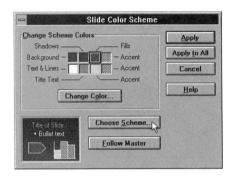

2. Click the Choose **S**cheme button.

The Choose Scheme dialog box appears.

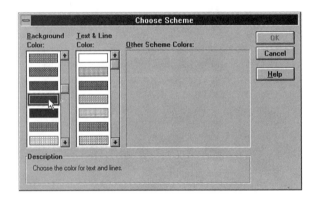

3. Select a background color from the **B**ackground Color box on the left. Use the scroll bar to view all the color choices.

   After you have chosen the background color, colors that harmonize with the background color you have chosen appear in the **T**ext & Line Color box.

4. Choose a **T**ext and Line Color.

After you have
chosen a text and
line color, four full
color schemes
appear in the **O**ther
Scheme Colors
dialog box.

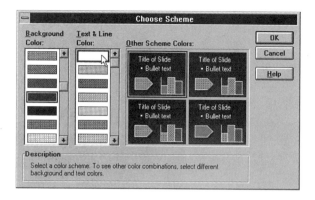

5. Review the color schemes, select the one you like, and click OK.
    Or, start a new background and text selection process until you
    find a color scheme that pleases you.

Changing a Color

Occasionally you may want to change only one or two colors to match
a logo or to provide particular emphasis. Individual colors in a color
scheme palette are also changed by choosing Slide **C**olor Scheme from
the F**o**rmat menu.

Note: *If you are working with the Master Slide, all the slides in your presentation change colors to match the changes you make.*

To change a color, follow these steps:

1. From the F**o**rmat menu, choose Slide **C**olor Scheme. The Slide
    Color Scheme dialog box appears displaying the colors of the
    Master Slide.

    At the top of the dialog box you see the color palette for the
    scheme that your slide presentation is based on. Eight boxes are
    shown for shadows, background, text and lines, title text, fills, and
    accent colors.

2. Select the element whose color you wish to change.

6

The Slide Color
Scheme dialog box
with a color
selected in the
color palette.

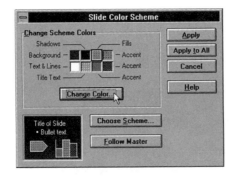

3. Click the Change Color button.

The Fill Color dialog
box appears with a
color palette for the
element you want
to change. The
colors in the palette
have been chosen
by PowerPoint to
harmonize with the
other colors in the
color scheme.

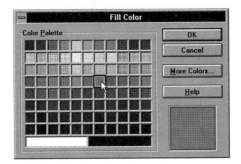

4. Select the color you want to use.

5. Click OK and you return to the Slide Color Scheme dialog box.
Notice that the original color you selected has changed to the
new color you just selected.

**Change Color
button**

The Change Color
button below the
palette enables you
to change colors
for each of the
elements on a
presentation
master or slide.

Look at the preview box on the left below the *Change Color
button*; that shows you the colors as they appear when applied
to the elements on your slide.

6. If you are not satisfied with your choice, click the **F**ollow Master
button to restore the template's original colors, or select the color
again and repeat the preceding steps.

Creating New Colors

If you are not satisfied with the colors that you saw in the palette for
Change Color, you still have more choices from a color picker containing
all the colors your system is capable of showing.

To create a new color, follow these steps:

1. In the Color **P**alette of the Fill Color dialog box, click on the color you want to change.

2. Click the **M**ore Colors button.

The More Colors dialog box appears with the crosshair in the color picker and the slider box.

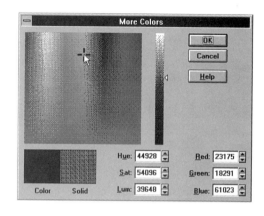

Notice that when you place your pointer in the color picker, it changes from an arrow to a crosshair to enable you to select a color with precision.

Note: *The color directly in the center of the crosshair is the color that will be selected when you click the mouse button.*

3. Click on the color of your choice with the crosshair pointer. It appears in the sample box below the color picker box.

To the right of the color picker is a narrow rectangle with a slider triangle. It enables you to darken or lighten the color you have chosen.

Caution

When you choose colors from the color picker, you are on your own. These colors have not been reviewed by PowerPoint to harmonize with a color scheme.

4. Use an upward movement to brighten the selected color, or move the slider down to make the color darker and blacker.

Notice that the numbers in the boxes for RGB and HSL change as you move the color picker cursor or the slider. RGB represents the basic colors the computer blends to make all other viewable screen colors. HSL represents an alternative method for describing colors

6

that some people find more descriptive. Hue stands for the *actual color*, such as blue. Saturation represents the *amount of color* that is used, changing it from gray to full color. Luminosity is the *intensity of the color* from black to white.

Note: *If you know the numbers for the color you want, you can type them directly into the RGB or HSL boxes.*

RGB
Red, Green, and Blue.

HSL
Hue, Saturation, and Luminosity, another way of describing computer color specifications.

5. Click OK and you return to the Color Palette. The color you selected originally has changed to the new color you just selected in the color picker.

6. Select the new color to apply to the element you chose in the Slide Color Scheme dialog box. Choose OK to continue.

7. Click the **A**pply button for color changes on the slide you are working with. Apply **t**o All automatically applies your color changes to all the slides in your presentation.

   Click **F**ollow Master to restore the master slide color scheme if you are unhappy with the changes that you made.

Note: *If you need some reminders to help you change colors in a slide, choose* C**u***e Cards from the* **H***elp menu. Then click on Change Colors in the Color Scheme step-by-step guidance.*

Note: *If you decide you don't like a color scheme when you return to the Slide view, you can undo it immediately by using the* **U***ndo command in the* **E***dit menu.*

Applying a Shaded Background to Your Slide

A shaded background can add interest and drama to your presentation, and it is easy to create one. If you want this background to appear on all the slides, work with the Slide Master. Otherwise, just select the slide you want to change.

To apply a shaded background to your slide:

1. From the F**o**rmat menu, choose Slide Back**g**round.

When the Slide Background dialog box appears, you find that there are several choices available to you.

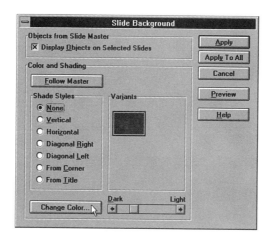

2. To change the background color, click the Change Color button at the bottom left.

The Background Color dialog box is displayed.

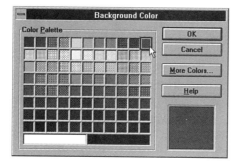

Select an alternative color and click OK.

3. To change the shaded appearance of the background, select one of the Shade Styles from the area on the left.

6

The style you select appears with up to four variations in the Variants box to the right. Try several styles before you make a final decision.

4. The scroll bar at the bottom of the Slide Background dialog box controls effects from light to dark. Move the scroll box and view the changes in the Variants box.

5. When you are satisfied with the choices you have made, select the variant you like best.

6. Click **A**pply.

Note: *If you forgot to select the Slide Master when you started, click Apply to All if you want the background to be added to all the slides in the presentation.*

Using Color Schemes from Other Applications

There are occasions when you need to match colors that were used in another application or graphic.

If the color scheme you want to copy was created in another PowerPoint application, you can embed the original into your current application and use it as a reference for coloring a new master.

Color schemes can also be copied as a graphic from another application. To do so, follow these steps:

1. Copy the item containing the colors you like as a screen shot and paste it into a PowerPoint slide as a bitmapped object.

2. Manually copy its colors to a slide color scheme following the directions in the "Changing a Color" section earlier in this chapter.

Task: **Coloring and Shading Objects**

All objects in PowerPoint have attributes whose colors can be changed from their default settings. These include lines, fills, colors, patterns, and shadows. Pictures, text, or other objects copied or embedded from other applications or presentations can be recolored to match the presentation you are currently working on.

Changing the Color of an Object

Recolor
The **R**ecolor command enables you to change *any* color in any scanned or bitmapped image when the Colors option is chosen.

The Recolor dialog box appears with the object you want to recolor visible in the center.

Several simple steps enable you to *recolor* a picture or graph for aesthetic reasons, or to match other objects on a slide.

To change the color of an object on a slide, follow these steps:

1. On the slide, select the object that you want to recolor.

2. From the **T**ools menu, choose **R**ecolor.

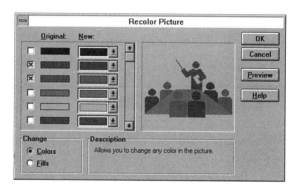

3. Make sure that the **C**olors option is selected in the Change box on the lower left. This enables you to change any color in the picture.

   If the **F**ills option is chosen, only background and fill colors are affected; line colors are not affected. The color choices default to color scheme selections.

   At the top left, you find two columns of color samples, one labeled **O**riginal and the other labeled **N**ew.

4. Select the **O**riginal colors you want to change by clicking in the check box to the left of the color sample. To view all the colors, scroll through them. An x appears next to the colors you have selected.

6

5. To select a replacement color in the **N**ew column, go to the color to the right of the one selected in the Original column. Click on the drop-down button to the right of the color to display a list. Select an appropriate replacement.

Your changes appear in the view window as you make them.

6. When you have completed making changes, click the **P**review button to preview them in full size.

7. If you are satisfied, click OK to accept your changes.

Note: *If you click the **F**ills option button in the Recolor dialog box, only the background or fill colors change.*

Using the Toolbar Drop-Down Lists to Change Colors

Another way to add or change colors in PowerPoint is through the toolbar drop-down lists for text, fill, line, and shadow.

This is the Fill Color drop-down list on the Drawing+ toolbar.

This is the Text
Color drop-down
list on the Standard
toolbar.

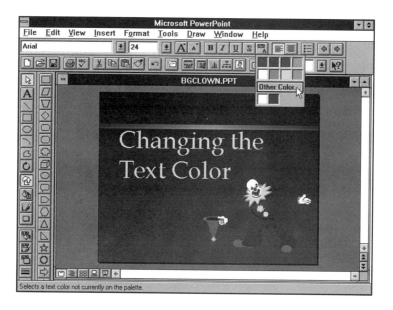

To add the color of an existing object to a color drop-down list, follow
these steps:

1. On a slide, select the object whose color you want to add to the
   drop-down list.

2. From a toolbar drop-down list (text, fill, line, or shadow), choose
   Other Color.

Adding Colors to the Toolbar Drop-Down Lists

You can also add a new color to a toolbar color drop-down list. The new
color replaces one of the eight colors in the palette.

To add a color to a toolbar drop-down list, follow these steps:

1. Choose Other Color from a toolbar color drop-down list.

2. When the Other Color dialog box appears, choose a color to add to
   the drop-down list.

3. Click OK. The newly selected color is added to *all* the color drop-
   down lists (text, line, fill, and shadow), replacing a previously
   added color.

6

Changing the Color of a Fill or a Line

PowerPoint assigns a default color to all created shapes based on user preference. However, you are not bound by the default settings. You can change fill or line colors and line thicknesses for any picture or shape.

To change the color of a fill or a line, follow these steps:

1. Select the picture you want to recolor on the slide you are working with.

2. From the Format menu, choose Colors and Lines.

The Colors and Lines dialog box appears if you choose from the Format menu.

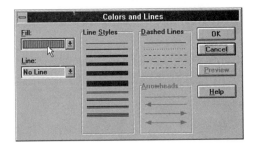

3. In the Fill drop-down box, scroll through and select the color you want to change to.

Here is the Colors and Lines dialog box with a color selected.

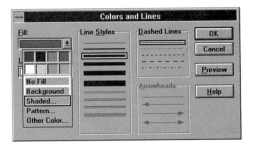

4. In the Line drop-down box, scroll through and select the line color you want to change to.

5. Select a line style if you want to make a change to the style or thickness of a line.

6. Click Preview to view your results.

7. When you are satisfied with the results, click OK.

Changing the Pattern of a Fill

Patterns can also be selected using the Colors and **L**ines command from the F**o**rmat menu.

To change the pattern of a fill, follow these steps:

1. Select the object you want to apply a pattern to.

2. From the F**o**rmat menu, choose Colors and **L**ines.

3. From the **F**ill drop-down box, choose Pattern to display the Pattern Fill dialog box.

These are examples of patterns that can be applied to an object.

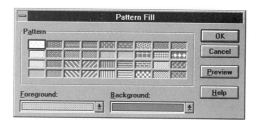

4. Select the pattern you want to apply and click OK.

Shading the Fill Color

When a fill color is shaded, the graphic can assume a more interesting three-dimensional form.

To shade the fill color, follow these steps:

1. Select the object you want to shade.

2. Display the Fill Color drop-down list from the Drawing+ toolbar and choose Shaded.

The Shaded Fill dialog box appears.

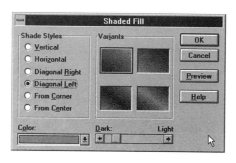

6

3. To change the color for your shaded object, make a selection from the Color drop-down list.

4. Select the shading style you want. As you make your selections, notice the appearance of each choice and the variations that are available in the Variants box to the right.

    Note: *Selecting a shading style for an object is similar to selecting one for a slide background.*

5. To make the shading lighter or darker, move the scroll bar box at the bottom.

6. When you see a shading in the Variant box that you want, select it.

7. Click OK in the Shaded Fill dialog box.

8. Click OK in the Color and Lines dialog box.

Changing the Color of Shadows

You can add a default color shadow quickly to any object, or you can opt to select a nondefault shadow color.

To change the color of a shadow, follow these steps:

1. For a quick shadow treatment, select the object you want to shadow.

2. Click the Shadow On/Off button on the Drawing toolbar and view the results.

If you are not satisfied with PowerPoint's default selection, you can go farther:

1. Make sure that your object is selected.

2. From the Format menu, choose Shadow.

The Shadow dialog
box appears.

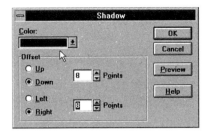

3. Select the color of the shadow you want to see on the selected object.

The color selections
are displayed in the
Color drop-down
list.

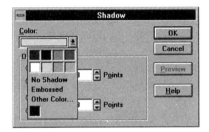

If you want to make the shadow color heavier or thinner than the default selection, you can also adjust the amount of the shadow offset in the Shadow dialog box. Adjust the thickness with the options available to you until you find a pleasing result.

Choose Other Color button for more color options.

4. Click OK when you are pleased with the resulting shadow color.

Changing the Color of Text

You have several options when changing the text color in a presentation. To apply a color change to all the text, change its color in your color scheme as described earlier in this chapter. You can also change the text color in an individual slide.

To change the color of text, follow these steps:

1. Highlight the text whose color you want to change.

2. From the F**o**rmat menu, choose **F**ont.

The Font dialog box is displayed. Here you see the Color option displayed in a drop-down list.

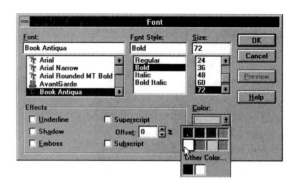

This dialog box not only enables you to make color changes, but also gives you the opportunity to add effects such as Shadow or Emboss.

3. Review the colors in the **C**olor drop-down list on the lower right and select an appropriate color.

   You can also choose other options such as Shadow or Emboss at this time.

Text can also be recolored through the text color drop-down list by following these steps:

1. Highlight the text whose color you want to change.

2. Choose the text color drop-down list from the Standard toolbar. Select the color you want to change the text to.

3. Click the color to apply it to the text.

4. Click OK.

   Note: *If the color you want is not there, add it by choosing Other Color from the drop-down list.*

Summary

To	Do This
Select a color scheme	Choose a template whose color scheme you like. In the Slide Sorter view, replace the colors of your presentation with the template colors by using the Format Painter tool in the toolbar.
Modify a color scheme	Choose Slide **C**olor Scheme from the Format menu and select the color you want to change from the color scheme palette. Select a new color from the color scheme palette that appears.
Create a new color scheme	Choose Slide **C**olor Scheme from the F**o**rmat menu and click the Choose **S**cheme button.
Change one or two colors in a color scheme	Choose Slide **C**olor Scheme from the F**o**rmat menu and select the color you want to change from the color scheme palette. Select a new color from the color scheme palette that appears.
Add a new color to your color scheme	Choose Slide C**o**lor Scheme from the F**o**rmat menu and select the color you want to change from the color scheme palette. Click the **M**ore Colors button and make a selection.
Add a shaded background to a slide presentation	Choose Slide Back**g**round from the Format menu.
Recolor a picture	Select the picture and choose **R**ecolor from the **T**ools menu.
Add a shaded fill to an Autoshape or other object	Click on the Fill Color drop-down box in the Drawing+ toolbar and select Shaded.
Change text color for a single slide	Select the text for color change. Choose Font from the Format menu. Make the change using the Color box.
To apply a color change	Make your change on the master slide.
Change text color for an entire slide	Choose Slide **C**olor Scheme from the F**o**rmat menu and select the color for the text. Choose an alternative color from the palette that appears.

6

On Your Own

Estimated time: 30 minutes

1. Select the DIAMONDB.PPT template in PowerPoint in order to modify its color scheme.

2. Change a slide background color to a bright green by using the Slide Color Scheme command.

3. Change the background shading so that it is horizontal, bright at the center, and dark at the top and bottom.

4. Change its title text color from yellow to dark purple.

5. Change the text color from white to yellow using the toolbar drop-down list.

6. Draw several circles on current slide.

7. Practice recoloring the circles and their outlines to various colors.

8. Apply the slide colors you have chosen to the template, and save it under a new name if you want to keep the new color scheme.

Adding Clip Art to Slides

Clip Art
Professionally designed images created by someone other than the programs user that can be added to slides and documents.

Effective presentations frequently rely on the use of clip art to help break up the monotony and add impact to a point. Clip art also can be used to add a bit of humor to an otherwise boring series of slides. Clip art images are created by someone other than the user of the program. They are packaged with the program or are available from third-party vendors. PowerPoint allows you to easily add and manipulate clip art in a presentation. In this lesson, you learn how to:

- Use the ClipArt Gallery
- Add clip art images to a slide
- Resize and position clip art images
- Edit clip art images
- Change the color and shading of clip art
- Convert clip art image formats
- Add other types of images to a slide

Using the ClipArt Gallery

To manage your clip art images, PowerPoint has included a new clip art manager called the ClipArt Gallery. This gallery allows you to:

- See thumbnail views of all of your clip art
- Add and delete clip art images in the Gallery

■ Categorize your clip art for easier access

■ Change names for categories and clip art images

Starting the ClipArt Gallery

There are several methods that you can use to open the ClipArt Gallery:

■ Create a slide with clip art as one object and then double-click on the clip art object.

■ Choose **C**lip Art from the **I**nsert menu.

■ Click the Insert Clip Art button on the toolbar.

The ClipArt Gallery allows you to manage the clip art in PowerPoint.

Refreshing the Thumbnail Images

When you delete, add, or modify your clip art images, you need to update the ClipArt Gallery so that the images it contains reflect what is currently available on your computer. This procedure also is used to add multiple clip art images to the Gallery at one time.

To update the thumbnail images in the ClipArt Gallery:

1. Choose the **O**ptions button on the ClipArt Gallery dialog box.

2. In the Options dialog box, choose the **R**efresh button.

You can update the images in the Gallery or add multiple clip art images via the **R**efresh Gallery button.

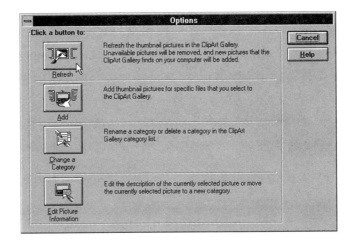

3. In the **L**ook For Pictures On box, choose the drive in which you want to search for clip art. If you press the down arrow button next to the box, you see a list of drives to choose from.

   Note: *If you choose all drives, PowerPoint searches every drive that has a letter on your system except for floppy disk drives. If you have a CD-ROM drive installed on your system, either exclude that drive from being searched or place a disk in it to be searched. Otherwise, you receive an error from Windows.*

4. When you have selected the drive(s) to search, choose OK.

At this point, the ClipArt Gallery compares the images on the drive(s) you have selected with the images it has in the ClipArt Gallery, and it does one of the following steps:

- If it locates new images, you then can add them to the Gallery; see the following steps on how to do this.

- If any images in the Gallery have changed, the ClipArt Gallery updates the thumbnail images that you see.

- If an image that is in the ClipArt Gallery can no longer be found on your computer, the ClipArt Gallery removes it from the gallery.

7

As mentioned earlier, while refreshing the ClipArt Gallery, PowerPoint may locate new images on disk; when that happens, a dialog box appears that allows you to add the images to the Gallery. At this point, you have a choice of whether or not to categorize the new images.

If you do not want to categorize your images in separate categories, press the No radio button and then the OK radio button in the Refresh dialog box. This procedure will automatically add your clip art images to a category called All Categories. If you choose to place the images in specific categories and/or give a description of each piece of clip art, follow these simple steps:

1. Click the Yes radio button and then the OK radio button in the Refresh dialog box.

You can categorize any additional clip art that the Gallery finds.

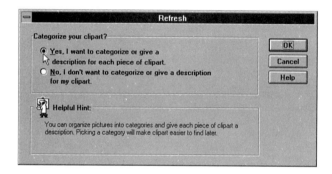

Note: *If you have a lot of images on your system, it may take the ClipArt Gallery some time to scan your drive(s) for all of them.*

2. A new Refresh dialog box appears with the current picture information. It shows the directory the image currently resides in, the file name, and a preview of the picture. It asks you to select a category from the existing ones, or type a new one. To get a list of the existing categories, press the down arrow button next to the current category. You also have the option of adding a description of your clip art.

3. Press the Add button. The ClipArt Gallery then asks you whether you want to add all the clip art from that directory into a single category. To speed up adding clip art, select Yes; everything in that directory is added to the category you named in step 2.

Adding New Clip Art Images to the Gallery

Occasionally, you may want to add images to PowerPoint's ClipArt Gallery. These may be images that you created or purchased or that came with another program. PowerPoint allows you to use these, if you want. It is very simple to add new images to the Gallery; the process is similar to the one used to refresh the Gallery.

To add specific clip art images to the Gallery:

1. Press the **O**ptions button on the **C**lipArt Gallery dialog box.

2. In the Clip Art Options dialog box, press the **A**dd button. This brings up the Add Clipart dialog box.

3. In the **D**irectories section, select the directory that contains the clip art you want to add.

4. In the Picture **N**ame box, type the name of the picture you want to add to the ClipArt Gallery or choose its name from the file list.

If you want to add one or two images, you can do that just as easily.

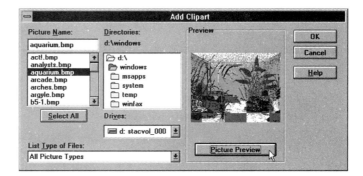

You can choose several pictures by holding down Ctrl and clicking their file names. To choose all the pictures listed in the Picture **N**ame box, choose the **S**elect All button.

5. To see a preview of a single picture before you add it to the Gallery, select the picture and then choose the **P**icture Preview button.

6. Choose the OK button.

7. In the Add Clipart dialog box, choose **A**dd.

7

8. In the ClipArt Gallery dialog box, select a category for the clip art you're adding.

9. Choose OK.

If you are adding multiple images to the Gallery, you should refer to the previous sections on refreshing the ClipArt Gallery. Those steps also are used for adding multiple images at one time.

If you want to add clip art from a floppy disk to the ClipArt Gallery, you should first copy the files onto your computer's hard drive. Otherwise, you will need to insert the disk each time you want to add one of these images to a document.

Note: *If you add a large image (such as a photo or complex image), it may take a few minutes to add it to the Gallery. Remember, the ClipArt Gallery is simply a way of viewing and choosing clip art.*

If you have problems...   If you cannot add a particular piece of clip art, the ClipArt Gallery may not support the format for the image you are trying to add; the file may have been damaged, or the file may not correspond to the extension it has been given. For example, you may have a clip art file with the extension .CGM that is not actually in a CGM format.

Changing Category Information

If you do not like the categories and names that Microsoft has given the clip art, you can change the names to suit your tastes. You can even delete an entire category if you so desire:

1. Bring up the ClipArt Gallery by either pressing the Clip Art button on the toolbar or by choosing **C**lip Art from the **I**nsert menu.

2. Press the **O**ptions button on the Gallery dialog box.

3. Press the **C**hange a Category button on the next dialog box.

   You see two radio buttons on the Change a Category dialog box.

You can rename or delete categories with the ClipArt Gallery.

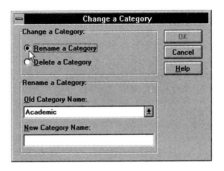

4. Select the appropriate option for your action.

5. If you chose **R**ename a Category, choose the **O**ld Category Name from the list and then type a new one.

Or, if you chose **D**elete a Category, choose the name of the category you want to delete.

6. Choose the OK button.

Caution

You can either modify the name of a category or delete a category entirely. Changing the name of a category does not affect the contents of the category. When you delete a category, the pictures from that category are added to the All Categories group; they are not removed from your computer.

Editing Image Information

PowerPoint allows you to move clip art images into different categories or change the description of pictures so that it is easier for you to find the clip art you want. You also can add new categories for your own clip art images, if you want. Changing the category name or the description of an image does not change the location or any other property of the image on your computer. (You also can change the category name by using the Changing Category Information from the Options dialog box on the Gallery dialog box; see the previous section for information on how to do this.)

To edit picture information or to change the category name or the description of your clip art images, follow these simple steps:

1. Bring up the ClipArt Gallery by either pressing the Insert Clip Art button on the toolbar or by choosing **C**lip Art from the **I**nsert menu.

2. Select the image in the ClipArt Gallery that you want to modify.

7

3. Press the **O**ptions button on the Gallery dialog box.

4. Press the **E**dit Picture Information button in the Options dialog box to display the Edit Picture Information dialog box.

You can edit picture names or change their categories.

5. Under Category, type the name of a category in the **N**ew text box. If the category you type does not exist, the ClipArt Gallery creates a new one. Alternatively, you can choose an existing name from the drop-down list by pressing the down arrow button next to the categories box.

6. Under Description, type a new description in the Ne**w** text box. This can make it easier to locate the image later, if you forget the file name of the image or the category it is in.

7. Press the OK button.

The clip art image is now displayed in the category you chose. To see the image in its new category, scroll through Choose a **C**ategory To View Below box located in the opening ClipArt Gallery images dialog box.

Note: *To add a new category to the ClipArt Gallery, you need to place a piece of clip art in that category. You can assign the new category name to a piece of clip art that is already in the Gallery or add a new piece of clip art and type in the new category.*

Adding Clip Art Images to a Slide

Adding clip art images to a slide presentation is a very easy process. As mentioned before, PowerPoint 4.0 has a new ClipArt Gallery that allows you to quickly find images from the standard clip art that ships with it. Another nice feature of the new ClipArt Gallery is that it keeps the images in a compressed format to minimize the disk space it takes up.

If you are going to add a new slide, the first couple of steps are different than if you are going to modify an existing slide to accept clip art.

Adding an Image to a New Slide

To add a clip art image to a new slide, follow these steps:

1. From the **I**nsert menu, choose New **S**lide; or press Ctrl+M. Or, with the mouse, click the New Slide button on the status line.

2. Choose one of the layouts that includes clip art as a section by either double-clicking on the layout or by clicking once on the layout and then pressing the OK button. The slide appears on-screen.

   Note: *While there are some layouts that include a place for clip art, you are not limited to placing clip art there. By choosing the **I**nsert **C**lipArt menu choice, you can add clip art to any slide.*

3. Add title and bullet text as needed.

4. Double-click on the section with the clip art. The ClipArt Gallery appears shortly.

   Note: *If this is the first time that you are using the ClipArt Gallery, it may take a few minutes for PowerPoint 4.0 to uncompress all of the clip art images.*

7

The ClipArt Gallery
makes it easy to
select the image
you are looking for.

5. The Gallery starts with All Categories. If you know that the image
   is in a certain category, select that category from the **C**ategory
   drop-down list at the top of the dialog box. The images from that
   category are displayed.

6. Scroll through the images until you find the one you need. Highlight it by single clicking on it, and then press the OK button. The
   image is added to the slide. It may look a little strange since it is
   being fit into a small area. Later in this chapter, we talk about how
   to modify the image to achieve the look you want.

The clip art may appear strange until you resize it to better fit the slide.

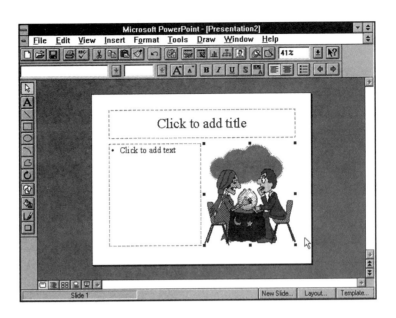

Note: *You may find it easier to size and arrange the title and bullet lists before adding the clip art. Then modify the clip art frame to the size and position that you want. This saves you time after the image is added.*

If you have problems...

If you get a message telling you that you are low on memory when you try to open the ClipArt Gallery, there are several items to check:

- Close any other applications that are running in Windows. This includes screen savers, games, and so on. This may free up enough memory to allow you to open the Gallery.

- Close any wallpaper that you might be displaying. Sure, those 256 color photos make a nice background, but they also eat up a lot of memory.

- Close Windows and then remove any DOS TSR (Terminate-and-Stay-Resident) programs you might have loaded. This can include Sidekick, PC Tools, and so on.

- Increase the size of your Windows swap file. This is done from the Windows Control Panel.

- Use a third-party memory manager like QEMM or Netroom. DOS 6.x users should try Memmaker, a memory management utility that comes with DOS.

7

Adding a Clip Art Image to an Existing Slide

PowerPoint not only allows you to add clip art images to a new slide at the time you create your presentation, it also gives you the flexibility to add them to an existing slide any time you so desire.

To add a clip art image to an existing slide, follow these steps:

1. Open your existing presentation and select the slide you wish to add a clip art image to.

2. From the **I**nsert menu, choose **C**lip Art.

3. The Gallery starts with All Categories. If you know that the image is in a certain category, select that category from the **C**ategory drop-down list at the top of the dialog box. The images from that category are displayed.

4. Scroll through the images until you find the one you need. Highlight it by single clicking on it and then press the OK button. The image is added to the slide. It may look a little strange since it is being fit into a small area. Later, we talk about how to modify the image to achieve the look you want.

Manipulating Clip Art Images

Once you have the clip art image(s) in your slide, you may want to make some changes to them. PowerPoint gives you the flexibility to resize, crop, and position the images to better fit with the other things in your slide. You also can recolor your images using one of the many colors available to you through PowerPoint, or by creating your own color. Furthermore, you can edit and convert your clip art. These topics as well as adding other types of images to your slide are all discussed in greater detail in the following sections.

Resizing Clip Art Images in Slides

After you have the clip art image in the slide, more likely than not, the image is very strange looking. It may be compressed horizontally, vertically, or both. Resizing the image helps you create the look of perfection that you want to achieve.

To resize an image, follow these steps:

1. Select the image to be resized by clicking on it with the mouse.

2. Click a *handle* on the frame and drag it to change the size and shape of the image.

Resizing a clip art image is as easy as clicking on the frame handles and dragging to the size and shape you want.

Handles
The little squares that appear on the outside of a frame when an object is selected.

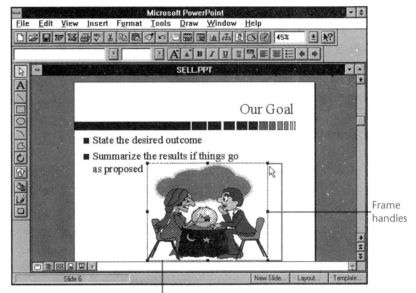

Frame handles

Placeholder frame

3. When you have sized the image to your satisfaction, click the mouse anywhere away from the image. This fixes the image to that size.

Positioning Clip Art Images

Positioning an image after you have it sized is the next step. By following the steps detailed below, you will be able to position any piece of clip art you care to add to a slide:

1. Click on the clip art image you wish to move.

2. While holding down the left mouse button, drag the image to the final location.

3. Release the mouse button to place the image.

4. Click outside the slide area to deselect the image.

To move more than one object at a time:

1. Select the arrow tool on the Drawing toolbar.

2. Starting at one corner, click and drag the dashed box around all the objects you want to move.

3. When all of the objects are selected (denoted by having handles around them), click and drag them to their new locations.

Note: *The instructions for moving an image also work if you are moving an inserted picture or any text that is on a slide. By moving objects to the front or back, you can change the look of a slide with multiple overlapping objects.*

If you have problems...

If you are having trouble clicking and dragging the box to select multiple objects, you can select them by pressing the SHIFT key while clicking on each object.

If you hold down the Ctrl key while dragging a clip art image or any object, you make a copy of it.

You can create copies of pictures by holding Ctrl and dragging the image.

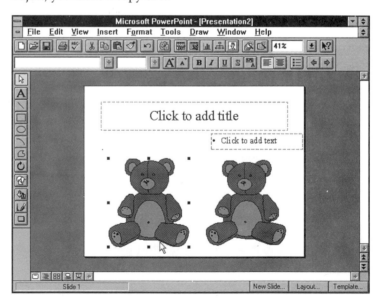

Nudge

The act of moving an object one pixel (about the size a period.) at a time.

Note: *PowerPoint 4 includes a feature called* Nudge *that allows you to move an object one pixel at a time. This can be used for precise placement of objects.*

To nudge an object into position, follow these steps:

1. Select the object to be moved.

2. Use the arrow keys to move an object one pixel at a time.

3. When you have positioned the image where you want it, click outside the image to deselect it.

Managing Clip Art Images

PowerPoint gives you two ways to manage art images. The first one allows you to edit the clip art image information. In the section "Using the ClipArt Gallery," we looked at how we can do this from the ClipArt Gallery; here, we discuss how we can do this editing from inside a slide. The second way allows you to ungroup the clip art image into groups of PowerPoint objects that you can edit individually.

Regardless of the type of managing you wish to do, start by doing one of the following:

■ If you want to manage a clip art image that you have previously added to a slide, open the presentation or the slide and select the image by clicking on it.

■ If you create a new slide, add a clip art image to it and then when you want to manage it, the image is already selected.

To edit the clip art image information from inside a slide once the clip art image is selected, follow these steps:

1. From the **E**dit menu, choose Microsoft ClipArt Gallery **O**bject. A drop-down menu appears.

2. Select **E**dit. The Edit Picture Information dialog box appears.

3. If prompted to add clip art to the gallery, choose **N**o.

4. In the ClipArt Gallery, Choose **O**ptions.

5. In the Options dialog box, choose **E**dit Picture Information.

7

6. Under Category, type the name of a category in the **N**ew text box. If the category you type does not exist, the ClipArt Gallery creates a new one. Alternatively, you can choose an existing name from the drop-down list by pressing the down arrow button next to the categories box.

7. Under Description, type a new description in the Ne**w** text box. This can make it easier to locate the image later if you forget the file name of the image or the category it is in.

8. Press the OK button. The clip art image is now displayed in the category you chose. To see the image in its new category, scroll through Choose a **C**ategory To View Below box located in the opening ClipArt Gallery images screen.

Note: *To add a new category to the ClipArt Gallery, you need to place a piece of clip art in that category. You can assign the new category name to a piece of clip art that is already in the Gallery or add a new piece of clip art and type in the new category.*

To do the second type of editing, namely, to ungroup a clip art image into groups of PowerPoint objects that you can edit individually, you must first select the clip art image on your slide

Once the clip art image is selected, choose **U**ngroup from the **D**raw menu. Now you can work with the groups and objects that make up the image. When you are finished with your changes, you may want to regroup the art so that you can move and resize it as one object. To regroup your objects, just do the opposite of the above: select all your objects and choose **R**egroup from the **D**raw menu.

Recoloring Clip Art Images

While PowerPoint comes with a wide assortment of clip art, and you can add your own images as well, not all the images are going to fit in every presentation. The time may come when you may want to change the color of a clip art image.

If you created the image, you can always use the same tool to modify it. But what if it is a standard PowerPoint clip art image, or you do not have the tools necessary to modify the images? Well, you are not out of luck. PowerPoint allows you to modify a clip art image once it is on a slide without affecting the original image it came from.

To recolor a clip art image, start by doing one of the following:

■ If you wish to recolor a clip art image that you have previously added to a slide, open the presentation or the slide and then select the image.

■ If you created a new slide, added a clip art image to it, and now want to recolor it, the image is already selected.

Once the clip art image is selected, follow these steps:

1. From the **T**ools menu, choose **R**ecolor option. Or, you can click the right mouse button within the selected image. This brings up the object shortcut menu from which you can select **R**ecolor.

You now see a dialog box showing you the **F**ills and **C**olors.

You can modify any color on your clip art with ease.

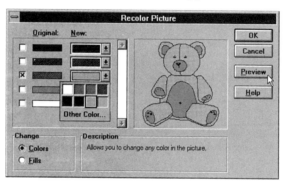

Color

In the context of clip art images, it means a solid color.

Fill

In the context of clip art images, it refers to patterned color and backgrounds, not line colors.

2. Press either the **C**olors or **F**ills radio button, depending on what you would like to change on the clip art image.

3. In the **O**riginal column, click on the color or fill box that you want changed in the picture.

4. In the **N**ew column, press the down arrow button next to the color or fill box you checked in the previous step.

5. From the drop-down list of colors that appears, select the color you want to change to. If you do not see the color you desire in the drop-down list, click on the Other Colors option.

You are then presented with the **O**ther **C**olor dialog box. (This is discussed in Lesson 6, "Working with Color on Slides.")

6. Select a color from the palette by clicking on it. If you still do not see just the right color and/or hue that you need, click on the **More Colors** command button. This displays a new dialog box where you can "mix" the colors to create your own.

Note: *If you choose a color from the Other Colors dialog box or create your own by using the **M**ore Colors dialog box, the color will be added under Other Colors. It will be displayed when you press the down arrow button for the drop-down list of New colors in step 4 above. In other words, PowerPoint remembers your special choices and displays them for you in the **R**ecolor dialog box as needed.*

7. Once you have selected a color to change to, you can press the **P**review button to see the effects of your change.

8. Press the OK button to make the change to the image on the slide.

Note: *If you attempt to recolor an image that is of photographic quality or has more than 64 colors in it, you receive the following message:*

```
This picture has more than 64 colors or fills. Recolor
Picture will list the first 64 colors and fills.
```

Cropping Clip Art Images

Frequently, you will add some clip art and realize that it is just too much. In this case, you want to crop the picture to isolate a portion of it to appear on the slide.

To crop a clip art image, start by doing one of the following:

- If you want to crop a clip art image that you have previously added to a slide, open the presentation or the slide and then select the image.

- If you create a new slide, add a clip art image to it, and then want to crop it, the image is already selected.

Once the clip art image is selected, follow these steps:

1. From the **T**ools menu, choose the Crop **P**icture command. Or, as a shortcut, you can click the right mouse button within the selected image. This brings up the object shortcut menu from which you can select Crop Picture.

2. Position the pointer over any of the handles surrounding the picture.

The pointer changes shape to a picture frame with overhanging edges.

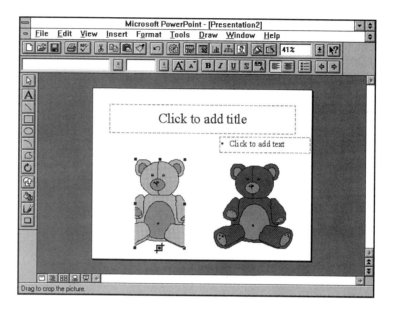

3. Click and drag the pointer to isolate the portion that you want to see.

4. Click outside the image to stop the cropping action.

Note: *You can use both cropping and resizing to isolate and zoom into an image. Simply crop the image to what you want to see. Resize the image to make it larger. Crop it again. Keep doing this until you get your desired look.*

Converting Objects

Sometimes, you may find that you want to convert an object to another object type. To do this, start by doing one of the following:

- If you want to convert an object that you have previously added to a slide, open the presentation or the slide, and select the object.

- If you create a new slide, embed an object in it, and then want to convert it, the object is already selected.

Once the object is selected, follow these steps:

1. From the **E**dit menu, choose the object to convert (this choice will vary based on the object selected). A drop-down menu appears.

2. Select **C**onvert. The Convert dialog box appears. It shows the Current Type that is the type of the selected object. Also, the available formats you can convert your image to or activate the image as are listed in the Object Type box.

3. At this point, you can either permanently or temporarily convert your clip art image. Click on Convert To button if you want to permanently convert the clip art image to an object of the type selected in the Object Type list (see next step). If you want to only temporarily convert the object to another format, while you are working with the object, click on the Activate As option button, if it is available.

4. In the Object Type list, select the format to which you want to convert or activate as the selected object. If there is more than one option in the Object Type box, press the down arrow button on the Object Type box to select the format you want to convert to.

5. The converted or activated object is displayed as an icon rather than as a picture. You can see a preview of the objects icon when Display as Icon is selected. Another feature you have when Display as Icon is selected is Change Icon button; when pressed it displays the Change Icon dialog box, which allows you to replace the icon.

6. Choose OK once you have made all your choices.

Adding Other Types of Images to a Slide

You also can add images other than ClipArt Gallery images to a slide. For example, you can add .PCX or .BMP images as either objects on the slide or as the background on the slide. To do so, follow these steps:

1. From the **I**nsert menu, choose **P**icture.

2. Use the dialog box to select an image and click OK.

3. Once the picture is on the slide, resize and position it as any other object.

Sometimes, in addition to wanting to add images other than ClipArt Gallery images, you may want to use an image as the background for your slide. To do so, first do one of the following:

■ To use an image other than ClipArt Gallery images as the background for a slide, follow the three steps above.

■ To use an image that exists in the ClipArt Gallery as the background for a slide, select a clip art image from the ClipArt Gallery (see the section "Adding a Clip Art Image" for the specific steps).

Once the picture is on the slide, follow these steps:

1. Size the image so that it fills the slide (see the section "Resizing Clip Art Images in Slides" for the specific steps on how to do this).

2. Choose the Send to Bac**k** command from the **D**raw menu. The image becomes the background.

Summary

To	Do This
Display the ClipArt Gallery	Press the **C**lip Art button on the toolbar or select Insert Clip Art from the menus.
Refresh clip art images	Select Refresh from the **C**lipArt Gallery options dialog box.
Add new clip art Images	Select **A**dd from the ClipArt Gallery options dialog box.
Change category information	Select **E**dit **C**hange a Category Information from the options dialog box.
Change image name or category	Select Edit Picture Information from the Options dialog box.
Resize clip art	Select picture and click and drag handles to size.
Reposition clip art	Select picture and click and drag to a new position.
Recolor clip art	Select recolor from the Tools menu. Select colors to change. Select new colors.
Crop clip art	Select Crop **P**icture from the Tools menu. Click and drag handles to crop.

7

On Your Own

Estimated time: 15 minutes

1. Start PowerPoint.

2. Create a new slide presentation by using the blank template.

3. Create a slide with clip art as one of the objects.

4. Open the ClipArt Gallery.

5. Change the category on the Spring Tree image from Backgrounds to Transportation.

6. Change it back to Backgrounds.

7. Add the School Supplies clip art image to the slide.

8. Resize the School Supplies clip art to make it smaller.

9. Move it around the slide.

10. Change the mug color to blue.

11. Make a copy of the image on the slide.

12. Crop one of the mugs to show just the pencils.

13. Exit PowerPoint without saving your work.

Adding Drawings to Slides

PowerPoint has a large set of tools to draw with. Some of the tools are similar to those you may have used in Draw applications; others are unique to PowerPoint.

In this lesson, you learn how to:

- Use the Drawing toolbar
- Draw lines, arcs, and freeform shapes
- Draw rectangles and circles
- Create AutoShapes
- Apply color, shadow, and pattern to objects
- Move, scale, and rotate objects
- Group and ungroup objects
- Use grids, guidelines, and rulers

Task: Using the Drawing Tools

The Drawing toolbar in PowerPoint consists of tools used to draw and apply attributes to objects. It also contains tools for manipulating and modifying objects once they have been drawn. The default location for the Drawing toolbar is vertical, along the left side of the screen. It can, however, be placed horizontally across the top or bottom of the screen, vertically along the right side of the screen, or floating at any position on-screen.

The Drawing
toolbar.

The Drawing toolbar consists of several sections, each with a group of buttons for related work. Each category is discussed in detail in this lesson. Drawing toolbar buttons consist of:

Things you *draw*:

- Lines, arcs, and freeforms

- Rectangles and ellipses

- AutoShapes

Things you can *apply* to what is drawn (called *drawing attributes*):

- Fill

- Line style

- Shadow

Draw objects can be moved and resized just like other PowerPoint objects. The Drawing toolbar also contains:

- Free Rotate tool

The Drawing+ toolbar contains additional tools for modifying draw objects. Some of these are:

- Color fills

- Shadow color

- Dashed line choices

- Arrowheads

If you aren't sure what a Drawing tool does, place the mouse cursor on the button for that tool (without clicking the button); a description pops up on-screen, just as it does for other toolbar buttons.

If you plan to embellish slides with draw shapes, you will probably want to add buttons to the standard default Drawing toolbar. Refer to Lesson 1 to learn how to customize a toolbar.

Task: Drawing Lines in PowerPoint

To draw lines in PowerPoint, just click on the Line tool button in the Drawing toolbar.

To draw a straight line:

1. With the slide you want to place the line on visible on-screen, click the Line button on the Drawing toolbar.

2. Move the pointer to the area on the slide where you want to draw the line. You don't need to be exact—you can reposition the line after it's drawn.

   The pointer changes to a crosshair.

3. Press the mouse button and drag in the direction you want the line to go.

4. Release the mouse button when you're done. A box appears at each end, showing that it's selected.

A line drawn on the slide.

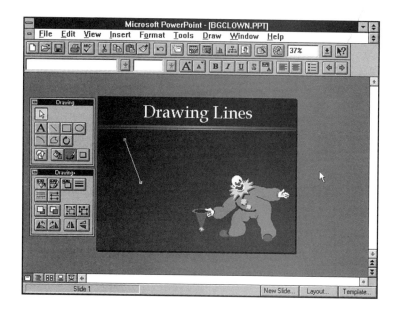

5. To deselect the line, click in any area outside of the line.

Note: *To limit a line's angle to 90°, 180°, or 45°, press Shift while you draw.*

Changing the Line Style

Any line that you draw can be lengthened or shortened by dragging on a selection handle at either end of the line. Lines can also be made wider or narrower, dotted, or dashed. You can add arrowheads if you need them, all by selecting the line and clicking the correct button on the Drawing toolbar.

To change the line style:

1. Select the line whose style you want to change by clicking anywhere on the line.

2. Click the Line Style button on the Drawing+ toolbar to change the line width. The Line Style drop-down box appears. Or, from the Format menu, choose the Colors and **L**ines command.

The Line Style drop-down list. On the slide, the default line is used on the left, and a heavier line is applied to the line on the right.

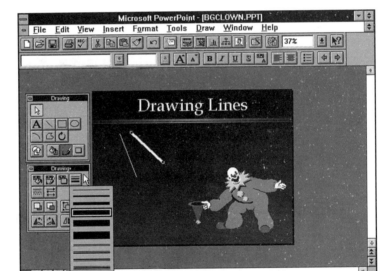

3. Select the line width you want to apply to the selected line.

To change a solid line to a dashed one:

1. Select the line you want to dash.

2. Click the Dashed Line button on the Drawing+ toolbar.

The Dashed Line
drop-down list.

3. Select the Dashed Line you want to apply.

   Note: *Whatever you choose as a line attribute remains selected as you continue to draw lines. To change the attribute, select a new one as described earlier.*

To lengthen or shorten a line:

1. Select the line you want to lengthen or shorten.

2. Place the pointer on one of the end handles.

3. Press the mouse button and drag in the direction you want to lengthen or shorten the line.

   You can also change the angle of the line by changing the angle or direction when dragging on the handle.

To add an arrowhead to a line:

1. Select the line you want to add an arrowhead to.

2. Click the Arrowheads button on the Drawing+ toolbar, and the drop-down toolbar appears, or choose the Colors and **L**ines command from the F**o**rmat menu, and its dialog box appears.

The Colors and
Lines dialog box is
shown here with
the Arrowheads
options at the
bottom right.

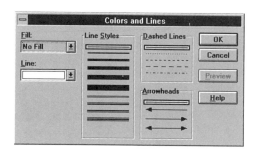

3. Click the arrowhead you want to apply to your line.

8

Using Line Colors

The original color of the line is the one assigned in the Slide **C**olor Scheme. It is easy, however, to change the line color of any line by clicking the Line Color button in the Drawing+ toolbar.

To change the color of a line:

1. Select the line whose color you want to change.

2. Click the Line Color button in the Drawing+ toolbar. Its drop-down list appears—or choose the Colors and **L**ines command from the **Fo**rmat menu, and its dialog box appears. The **L**ine color drop-down box contained in the dialog box offers the same options as the Line Color button on the toolbar.

The **L**ine Color drop-down list.

3. Click the new color you want.

   The line changes to the new color.

   The line color attribute reverts to this line color default when you draw new lines until you change the line color again. The color defaults for lines and other elements are set by the Slide **C**olor Scheme command on the **Fo**rmat menu.

   To learn how to use the Other Color selection, see Lesson 6, "Working with Color on Slides."

Task: Drawing Arcs

An arc is a segment of a circle or ellipse whose circumference is one-fourth of a completed figure. Drawing an arc and changing its attributes is similar to the process used for lines. Review the earlier sections on line styles, dashed lines, and applying line color to learn how to change the attributes of an arc.

To draw an arc:

1. Select the slide you want the arc to appear on.

2. Click the Arc Tool button on the Drawing toolbar, and move the pointer to where you want to start drawing.

   A crosshair pointer appears.

3. Drag the mouse in the direction where you want to position the arc.

   Notice that if you drag in a horizontal direction, a shallow ellipse appears. As you drag more vertically, the arc approaches more circular dimensions. As you continue to drag in a vertical direction, the arc again approaches ellipse dimensions.

Three arcs illustrate the shapes an arc can take, depending on the drag. The center arc is selected, as noted by its handles.

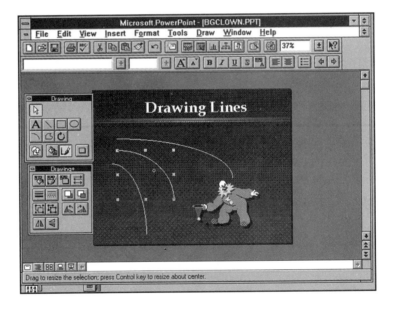

4. Release the mouse button when the arc is the shape you prefer. Eight handles appear, surrounding the arc on four sides.

   As with any object in PowerPoint, dragging a handle changes the shape of the arc.

   Note: *To constrain an arc to a perfect or* regular *quarter circle, press Shift while you draw.*

Regular shape

A shape that is perfectly symmetrical, such as a square, a circle, or an equilateral triangle.

8

To change the style and color attributes of an arc:

1. Select the arc whose line style and color you want to change.

2. Click the Line Style button on the Drawing+ toolbar and select the line you want to apply.

3. To change the arc color, click the Line Color button on the Drawing+ toolbar and select the color you want to apply.

   You can add a Fill color to an arc, so that it looks like a slice of pie. More on Fill colors comes later in this lesson.

Task: Creating Freehand Shapes

Polygon
A polygon is a closed shape consisting of a series of points connected by straight lines. Rectangles, pentagons, and triangles are typical polygons.

Freehand shapes can be either open-ended or completely closed *polygons*. They are created by dragging the mouse to make a successive series of joined lines.

To create a freehand shape:

1. Select the slide on which you want to apply a freehand shape.

2. Click the Freeform Tool button on the Drawing toolbar, and move the pointer to the slide. The mouse pointer turns into a crosshair.

3. Click and drag the mouse to start the freehand line.

4. Move the mouse in the direction of the first segment of the polygon, and click when you want to end the first line and start a second line.

5. Move the mouse in the direction of the second line and click to start a third line.

6. Double-click, and the freeform completes as an open-ended form.

   To form a closed freeform polygon, move the mouse to the beginning of the first line and double-click.

An open-ended
freehand form.

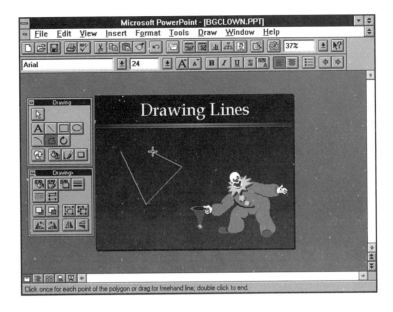

Note: *If you want to remove the last line from a figure before you have finished it, press the Backspace key. If you continue pressing, you remove lines one by one.*

The freeform closes and fills with the PowerPoint default fill color.

The shape is selected and has eight handles. To modify the freeform size and shape, drag on any of the handles.

A closed freehand
form.

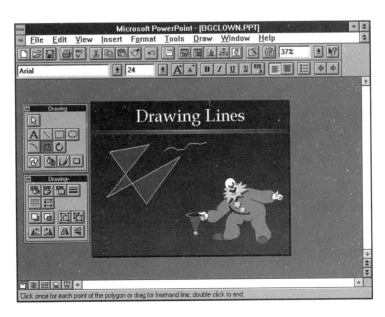

You can make as many lines as you like in any direction. If you complete the polygon by clicking on the start of the first line, the polygon fills, regardless of how bizarre the shape you may have made.

Vertex

A vertex (vertices, pl.) is the point where two lines join to form an angle in a polygon.

7. To change the shape of a polygon, double-click it. Handles appear on each vertex.

8. Drag on any vertex in any direction to change its shape.

A polygon that has been double-clicked with handles on its many vertices. Two have been dragged outward.

Changed polygon—

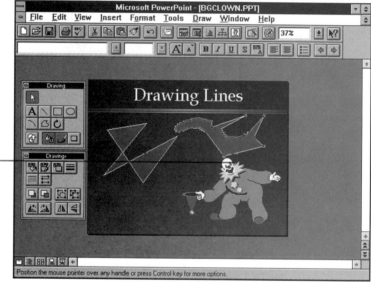

Note: *To limit a line to 90°, 180°, or 45° angles, press Shift when you draw.*

The Freeform button also allows you to draw freehand lines with a pencil icon:

1. With a selected slide on-screen, click the Freeform button on the Drawing toolbar.

2. Move the pointer over to the slide, and the crosshair pointer appears.

3. Drag the mouse while pressing the left mouse button. The crosshair turns into the pencil pointer. As you drag the mouse, a line is drawn by the pencil pointer.

4. Release the mouse button and the pencil pointer turns into the crosshair pointer. A straight line extends from the crosshair pointer to the point where you released the mouse button.

5. Click the left mouse button to draw the straight line.

You can alternate between the two ways of drawing and combine them into unique freeform shapes.

Note: *For better control while drawing, set your mouse at a very slow tracking speed in Windows.*

The figure on the right is a closed freeform that combines straight lines with freely drawn lines.

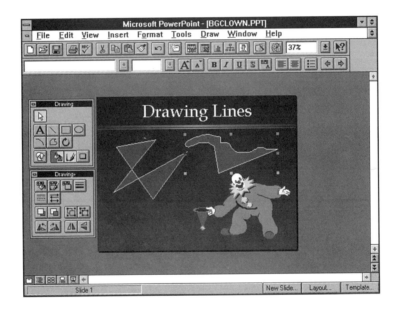

To change the fill color of a closed freehand form, refer to the section "Using Fill Colors" later in this lesson.

Task: **Drawing Shapes**

8

There are three shape buttons on the Drawing toolbar: rectangles, ovals, and AutoShapes. The AutoShape button consists of 24 different shapes that can be selected from its drop-down list.

All shapes can be resized, filled, moved, and changed to a different color.

Drawing Boxes and Circles

To draw a rectangle:

1. With a selected slide on-screen, click the Rectangle Tool button on the Drawing toolbar.

2. Move the pointer over to the slide, and drag the mouse to form a rectangle.

3. Release the mouse button, and the rectangle appears with selection handles on all four sides. The rectangle is filled with the default color from the PowerPoint slide color scheme. To change a color scheme, refer to Lesson 6, "Working with Color on Slides."

4. To make a perfect square, hold down the Ctrl key while dragging.

A rectangle and a square.

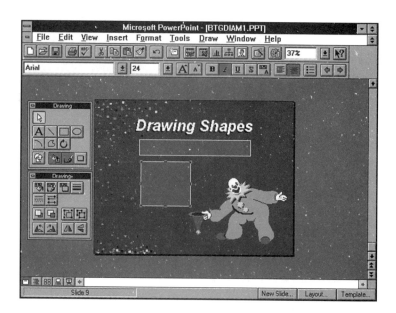

To draw an oval or ellipse:

1. With a selected slide on-screen, click the Ellipse tool on the Drawing toolbar.

2. Move the pointer over to the slide, and drag the mouse to form the ellipse.

3. Release the mouse button, and the ellipse appears with selection handles on all sides. The ellipse is filled with the default color from the PowerPoint slide color scheme. To change a color scheme, refer to Lesson 6, "Working with Color on Slides."

4. To make a perfect circle, hold down the Ctrl key while dragging.

Note: *To draw a shape from the center out, hold down the Shift+Ctrl keys while dragging.*

An ellipse and a perfect circle.

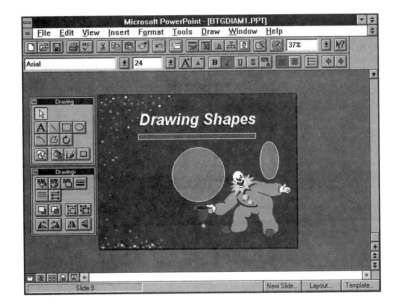

Using the AutoShapes Tool

If you click the AutoShape button on the Drawing toolbar, its drop-down toolbar gives you a choice of shapes. Any one you select is drawn automatically when you drag the mouse on your selected slide. As with other objects, AutoShapes can be resized, moved, and recolored.

To create an AutoShape:

1. With a selected slide on-screen, click the AutoShape button on the Drawing toolbar. Its drop-down toolbar appears.

8

The AutoShape toolbar from the **D**raw menu and the cascading menu of Auto Shape options from the menu bar are shown here.

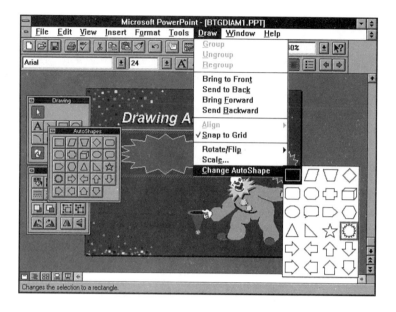

2. Select a shape and move the pointer to the slide on-screen.

3. When the crosshair pointer appears, drag to form the AutoShape.

   As with rectangles and ellipses, if you hold down the Shift key, a regular or symmetrical shape appears.

If you don't like the shape you select, you can change it easily.

To change a selected AutoShape:

1. On your slide, select the AutoShape you want to change.

2. From the **D**raw menu, choose **C**hange AutoShape, or click the AutoShape button on the Drawing toolbar.

3. Select a new AutoShape to replace your original one.

   The newly selected AutoShape appears in place of the original shape.

Text can be added to any rectangle, ellipse, or AutoShape.

To add text to a shape:

1. Move the pointer to the place you want to add the text and type in the text of your choice.

The pointer changes to an I-beam as you start entering your text.

The text that you enter becomes part of the shape you're typing into; if you add a shadow, it shadows the shape, not the text.

Text entered into two different AutoShapes. The starburst on the right has been constrained to a regular or symmetrical shape by pressing the Shift key when dragging.

2. To change the typeface and size, use the Font Style and Font Size boxes on the Formatting toolbar, or the **F**ont command on the F**o**rmat menu.

Note: *The text you enter in this manner becomes part of the shape. If you want to shadow or not shadow text independent of the shape, select the Text tool as described in Lesson 4, "Adding Text to Slides."*

8

Task: **Using Fill Colors**

You can change the color fill for any rectangle, ellipse, AutoShape shape, or any arc or freeform shape. You can also shade the background, and select color patterns to apply to any of these shapes. This PowerPoint function is applied through the Color and **L**ines command in the F**o**rmat menu, or by clicking the Fill Color button on the Drawing+ toolbar.

There are many ways to change the fill of a rectangle, ellipse, or an AutoShape. You can change the color of its fill, its shading, or patterning.

To change the fill color of a shape:

1. Select the shape you want to change.

2. Click the Fill Color button on the Drawing+ toolbar to display its color drop-down list, or choose Colors and **L**ines from the F**o**rmat menu.

3. From the Fill Color drop-down list, select the color you want to apply. To change the pattern of the fill, choose the Pattern option from the Fill drop-down list and select a pattern from the dialog box that appears.

If you want to apply a pattern, choose Pattern, and the Pattern Fill dialog box appears.

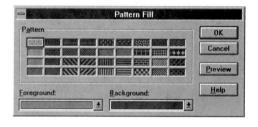

If you want your color to shade from light to dark, select Shaded, and the Shaded Fill dialog box appears.

Note: *You cannot apply both shading and patterning to one object at the same time.*

4. If you prefer a shaded background, select it.

The rectangle is filled with a pattern; the ellipse fill is shaded.

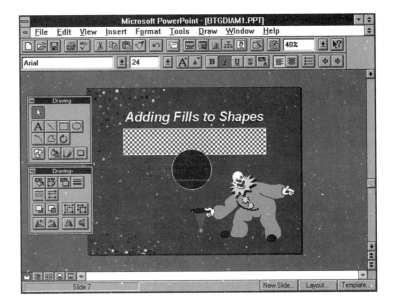

For more information on applying shaded color, refer to Lesson 6, "Working with Color on Slides."

Arcs and freeform shapes can be filled and patterned in much the same way that shapes can be.

Task: Applying Shadows

Any shape, rectangle, ellipse, AutoShape, arc, or freeform can have a drop shadow applied to it. You can specify how you want the shadow to appear—the number of points you want the shadow to have, and whether you want it to come from the right or left, top or bottom. You can also specify a shadow color. If you prefer, the shape can be embossed, rather than shadowed.

8

Specifying or Changing a Shadow Type

Shadows come in several flavors, including embossing. Colors and styles of shadows can be applied from the toolbar, or from the menu bar.

To apply a shadow to a shape:

1. Select the shape.

2. Click the Shadow Color button on the Drawing toolbar.

This is a toggle button. If you click the button while a shape with a shadow is selected, the shadow disappears. Click again, and the default shadow attributes are applied to that shape.

The Shadow Color button on the Drawing toolbar.

A drop shadow appears on the selected shape.

To change the depth and/or direction of the shape's shadow:

1. Select the shape.

2. From the Format menu, choose the **Sh**adow command.

The Shadow dialog box is displayed.

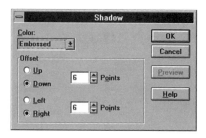

The **C**olor drop-down list allows you to select a shadow's color, delete a shadow, or select an embossed style.

The Offset box offers you a number of choices for placing the shadow. The shadow can be moved up, down, left, or right, relative to the shape.

You can also specify the distance of the drop for up/down and left/right, by typing the number of points you want to apply.

3. Select the directions for your shadow drop, and indicate the number of points for it. You can type in a number, or use the scroll arrows.

4. Click OK. The shadow attributes you select are applied to the shape.

A shadow applied to the shape on the left. Embossing has been applied to the shape on the right.

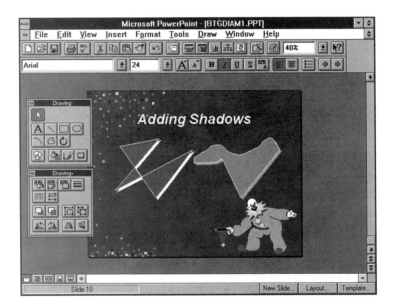

5. If you don't like the shadow effect, click the Apply Shadow Defaults button on the Drawing toolbar, and the shadow disappears.

   Note: *When applying shadow attributes to several shapes in a single slide, make sure they all face the same direction. It is visually disturbing if the shadows come from more than one "light source."*

Changing Shadow Colors

Shadow colors can be applied from either the **Sh**adow command in the F**o**rmat menu, or the Shadow Color button on the Drawing+ toolbar. The procedures are the same.

8

To change the color of a shadow:

1. Select the shape you want to work with.

 2. Click the Shadow Color button on the Drawing+ toolbar. Its drop-down list appears.

Or, from the F**o**rmat menu, choose the S**h**adow command. When its dialog box appears, click the **C**olor drop-down list for a similar selection list.

3. Click the color you want to apply.

4. Click OK.

To apply an embossed effect to an object:

1. Select the shape.

2. From the F**o**rmat menu, choose the S**h**adow command. When its dialog box appears, click the **C**olor drop-down list.

3. Select Embossed.

4. Click OK, and the embossed effect is applied to the shape.

Note: *Embossing may change the fill color of your shape. If this happens, click the Fill Color button from the Drawing+ toolbar, and select the color of your choice to reapply.*

If you have text included with your shape, it will have shadow or emboss effects applied as well.

If you don't want the embossed or shadow effect applied to text attached to your shape, use the Text tool to type in your text as an independent object.

On the left, an embossed shape with embossed text; on the right, a shape with drop shadow applied to it and to its text.

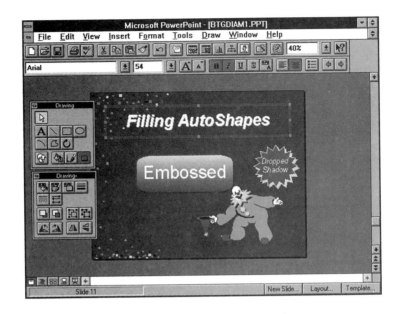

Task: Arranging Shape Objects

Shapes can be moved around on-screen, just like any other object in PowerPoint.

To arrange shapes on a slide:

1. Select the shape you want to move.

2. Press the left mouse button, and a dotted outline appears on the shape.

3. Without releasing the mouse button, drag the mouse in the direction you want the shape to move to. The selected object follows the drag movements of the mouse.

Continue dragging until you have placed the shape in its new location; then release the mouse button. Any number of objects can be moved around the screen in this manner.

8

Moving Shapes to the Front or Back

When moving shapes around the screen, you may want to move one to the front or to the back of another. As you add shapes to a slide, those shapes are layered like pieces of paper stacked on your desk. To look at a memo in the middle of the stack, you must move it to the top of the stack. On the PowerPoint screen the top of the stack of shapes is called the *front*, and the bottom is called the *back*.

To move a shape to the front or back of another:

1. Select the shape you want to move.

2. Click the Bring Forward or the Send Backward button on the Drawing+ toolbar, or choose the Bring **F**orward or Send **B**ackward command from the **D**raw menu.

   These commands bring a shape only one level forward or backward.

   If you have multiple levels of shapes, and you want to send one all the way to the back or front, you need to choose the Send to Bac**k**, or Bring to Fron**t** commands on the **D**raw menu.

If you have problems...   Sometimes it's difficult to tell where a shape is in a stack of objects. To get a shape to the layer you want, try bringing it all the way to the front by using the Bring to Front command on the Draw menu. Then use the Send Backward command to move it back one layer at a time until the object is where you want it to be.

A shape brought
only one level back.

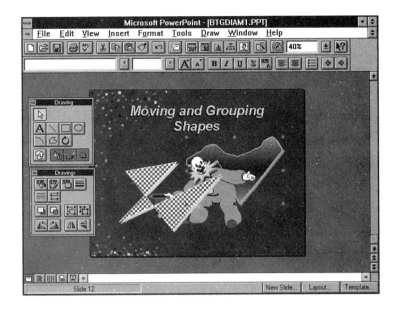

Scaling Objects

Objects can be made larger or smaller using precise percentages.

To scale a shape:

1. Select the shape to be scaled.

2. From the **D**raw menu, choose the Scal**e** command.

The Scale dialog
box appears.

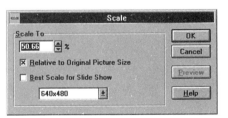

8

3. Use the scrolling arrows or type in a precise percentage for scaling the object.

   If you want PowerPoint to make the selection for you, select Best Scale for Slide Show. If you don't want to go along with the PowerPoint decision (after all, do computers always know best?), choose **U**ndo from the **E**dit menu.

   Note: *To make an object larger, the percentage needs to be a number over 100%.*

Rotating Objects

Objects can be flipped vertically or horizontally, or they can be rotated freely with the Free Rotate tool. These tools can be accessed either through the **D**raw menu or the Drawing+ toolbar.

To rotate a shape:

1. Select the shape to be scaled.

2. From the **D**raw menu, select the Rotate/Fli**p** command and then make a selection from the cascading menu that appears:

   - *Free Rotate.* Activates the Free Rotate tool to rotate an object to any angle.

   - *Rotate Left.* Rotates the selection 90° counterclockwise.

   - *Rotate Right.* Rotates the selection 90° clockwise.

   - *Flip Horizontal.* Flips the selection from left to right.

   - *Flip Vertical.* Flips the selection from top to bottom.

   The same commands can be activated through the Drawing+ toolbars.

   When Free-Rotate is selected, the pointer changes to two arrows forming a circle.

3. Place the Rotate pointer over any handle on the selected shape. The pointer changes to a square with four arrowheads.

4. Drag to rotate the shape. Release the mouse button when the rotation you desire is complete.

   To rotate in 45° increments, press the Shift key while rotating. The pointer changes to a crosshair when you press Shift.

5. To Rotate Left, Rotate Right, Flip Vertical, or Flip Horizontal, choose the appropriate command, and it is applied immediately to the selected object.

Task: Grouping and Ungrouping Shape Objects

Individual shapes can be grouped together to function as a single shape. The **G**roup command can be applied either through the **D**raw menu, or through the Drawing+ toolbar.

Grouped shape objects follow many of the same commands as single objects.

- They can be moved by dragging.

- They can be resized by dragging a handle or applying the Scale command.

- They can be recolored and shadowed by choosing the same commands.

To group several shapes:

1. While holding the shift key, select the shapes you want to group. Notice that each shape has its own handles.

Two selected shapes.

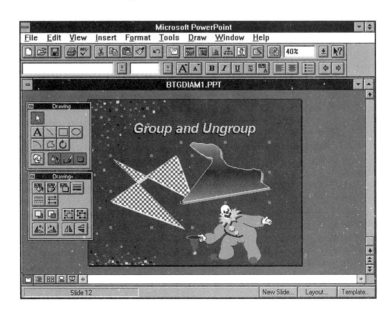

2. Click the Group button on the Drawing+ toolbar, or choose the **G**roup command from the **D**raw menu.

Notice that the handles for each individual object have disappeared. Only one set of handles is visible for the multiple shape complex.

If you have problems...   If you have difficulty determining whether an object is part of the group, try selecting and reselecting the object, while carefully watching for its handles to appear and disappear. The object is part of the group if its handles are showing.

A grouped multiple shape.

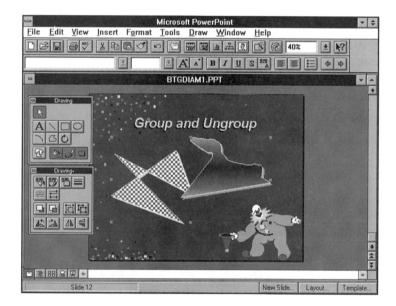

To ungroup a multiple shape:

1. Select the shape you want to ungroup.

2. Click the Ungroup button on the Drawing+ toolbar or choose the **U**ngroup command in the **D**raw menu.

Notice that handles now appear for each individual shape.

Task: Using Grids, Guides, and Rulers

PowerPoint provides a tool to help you align your work automatically—a system made up of grids, guides, and rulers.

The grid is an invisible network of vertical and horizontal lines that is part of every PowerPoint slide. There are 12 gridlines to the inch. When objects are drawn, they align automatically on the nearest grid intersection.

To use the grid command, choose **S**nap to Grid from the **D**raw menu. A check mark appears to its left, showing that it has been selected.

Snap to Grid is a toggle command. If you choose it again, the check mark disappears, and Snap to Grid is deselected.

The **G**uides command from the **V**iew menu displays guidelines that you can use to align objects precisely on a slide. A Guide consists of a vertical and a horizontal straightedge extended down and across the entire window. Each guideline can be moved freely around the window, and placed wherever you need to align objects.

To use guides:

1. From the **V**iew menu, choose **G**uides; its vertical and horizontal lines appear centered on-screen.

2. To move a guide, drag it with the pointer.

   As you move an object near a guide, either its center or its edge (whichever is closer) snaps to the guideline.

   As you drag, a numerical readout appears, giving you the distance from the center of the drawing area. If you have rulers visible, you can line up a guideline with the ruler for precise measurements.

3. The **G**uides command is a toggle. To deselect it, choose it again.

Rulers are an aid in positioning and aligning objects on a slide. PowerPoint provides both a vertical and a horizontal ruler. The 0 origin point is in the center of each ruler.

8

To have rulers appear on-screen:

1. From the **V**iew menu, choose **R**uler. A check mark appears next to the command, showing that it has been selected.

2. To deselect **R**uler, choose it again.

Note: *Pictures are images from other applications. Some (but not all) PowerPoint commands can be applied to pictures. They can be moved and resized, but usually not ungrouped or recolored. They cannot be rotated. For more information on pictures, see Lesson 7, "Adding Clip Art to Slides."*

Rulers on-screen, with guidelines.

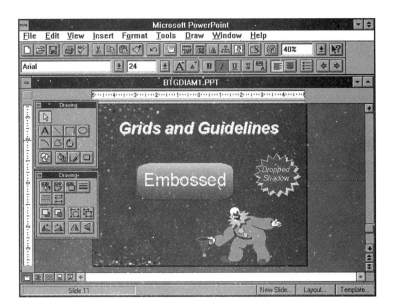

Summary

To	Do This
Draw a line	Select the Line tool. Click to place the first anchor point. Drag to create the line. Click to complete the line segment. Repeat for additional segments. Double-click to complete the object.
Change a line style	Click on the line to select it. Click on the Line Style button from the Drawing+ toolbar. Select a line style.

To	Do This
Change a line color	Click on the line to select it. Click on the Line Color button on the Drawing+ toolbar. Select a line color.
Draw an arc	Click on the Arc Tool button on the Drawing toolbar. Click to place the arc's anchor point. Drag to form the shape of the arc. Release the mouse button to complete the arc.
Draw a freehand shape	Click on the Freeform Tool button on the Drawing toolbar. Press and hold the left mouse button while dragging to form the freeform shape. Release the mouse button and double-click to complete the shape.
Add a fill to an object	Select the object. Click on the Fill Color button on the Drawing+ toolbar. Select a fill color.
Add/remove a shadow to an object	Select the object. Click the Shadow Color button on the Drawing+ toolbar.
Move an object to the front	Select the object to be moved. Choose Bring to Front from the Draw menu. To move an object to the back, select the object to be moved. Choose Send to Back from the Draw menu.
Group objects	Press and hold the Shift key. Select each object to be part of the group. Choose Group from the Draw menu. To ungroup objects, select the group to be ungrouped. Choose Ungroup from the Draw menu.
Scale an object	Select the object to be scaled. Choose Scale from the Draw menu. Type in the Scale To percentage in the dialog box. Click OK to complete the operation.
Rotate an object	Select the object to be rotated. Choose Rotate/Flip from the Draw menu. Choose Free Rotate from the submenu that appears. Place the mouse pointer on one of the handles of the object. Press the left mouse button and rotate the object. Release the mouse button to complete the rotation.
Turn on/off rulers	Choose Ruler from the View menu to toggle rulers on and off.

8

On Your Own

Estimated time: 20 minutes

1. Start PowerPoint.

2. Use the AutoContent Wizard to create the Selling a Product presentation.

3. Move to the second slide of the presentation.

4. Draw three horizontal lines across the slide.

5. Change the thickness of the second and third lines.

6. Change the lines to three different colors.

7. Draw a rectangle around the three lines.

8. Change the fill color of the rectangle to Black.

9. Change the pattern of the rectangle.

10. Move the rectangle to the back of the lines.

11. Group the lines and the rectangle together.

12. Add a shadow to the group.

13. Change the shadow type to Embossed.

14. Ungroup the object.

15. Type text into the rectangle, as part of the rectangle.

16. Resize the rectangle to fit the text and the lines.

17. Group the lines and rectangle.

18. Turn on Guides.

19. Place the grouped object exactly in the center of the slide.

20. Exit PowerPoint without saving your work.

Adding Charts to Slides

Charts are information pictures in which relationships between data elements are shown in visual format. In PowerPoint these are similar to other objects. Charts use PowerPoint's built-in color scheme. They can be moved, resized, and recolored. Charts differ from other PowerPoint objects in that they are composed of explicit, formal elements. One set of elements governs a chart's visual representation. These elements include its title and other text, the chart legend, the lines used for tick marks and axes, and the visual representation of numerical data using bars and lines or other elements. The visual aspect of charts is covered in this lesson. The other set of elements is concerned with the data, and is covered in Lesson 10, "Organizing Data and Datasheets." In this lesson you learn the following:

- How to access the Graph application from PowerPoint

- The elements on a chart

- What chart types are and how to change from one type to another

- How to apply automatic color, font, and line schemes

- How to color a chart with PowerPoint color schemes or custom colors

- How to edit, color, and format elements on a chart

- How to add text and arrows to a chart

Some elements must be included in any chart. Other elements can be left out at your discretion. Some elements must be placed exactly, and others can be relocated, depending on your design. If you have several charts in your presentation, it is important to keep your chart design consistent throughout the presentation.

Task: Accessing the Graph Application from PowerPoint

You can create charts using Graph, a supplementary application that comes with PowerPoint. You open this application by clicking on the Graph button in the standard toolbar. Charts created by PowerPoint's Graphing tool are embedded objects. They are pictures of what you created in Graph, where the actual information resides.

Note: *For more information on embedded objects in PowerPoint, see Lesson 15, "Working with Other Windows Applications."*

Graph enables you to create many different types of charts while working in the PowerPoint environment. The Graph application consists of two major windows:

■ *The Datasheet window.* This window carries default sample data. This window appears first, in the foreground, when Graph is activated. When you create a chart, replace the sample data with actual values. Close the Datasheet window when you are working with the visual aspects of the charting.

   Note: *Data from Microsoft Excel or other spreadsheet applications can be imported into Graph.*

■ *The Chart window.* This window contains the default sample chart in which data is represented visually. When you create a chart, replace the sample with the format and colors you prefer. In this lesson, you work with the Chart window and the visual elements of the Graph window.

Note: *Chart visuals can also be copied from other sources and placed into PowerPoint.*

These are the default data and chart windows that appear when you start Graph.

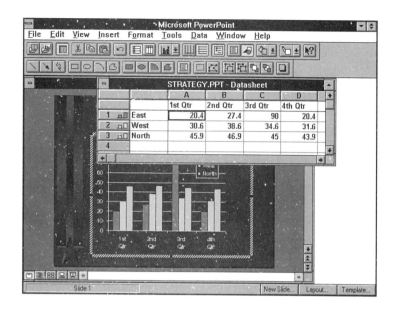

You can enter Graph either by choosing the Graph button on the toolbar or by choosing Graph from the **I**nsert menu. Follow these steps to access the Graph application:

1. Click the Insert Graph button on the toolbar, or choose Microsoft **G**raph from the **I**nsert menu. The hourglass appears while you wait for Graph to load.

    When Graph has loaded, you see a datasheet in the foreground and a chart in the background.

2. Close the Datasheet window if you are working with only visual elements.

    Note: *When you are working on a chart in PowerPoint, double-clicking the chart will move you into the Graph application.*

What Elements Are on a Chart?

A chart consists of data elements arranged visually in a restricted, formal design. A well-designed chart conveys numerical information with far more impact than a table consisting of nothing but numbers.

9

This chart shows the X- and Y-axes, the gridline, tick marks, and other elements.

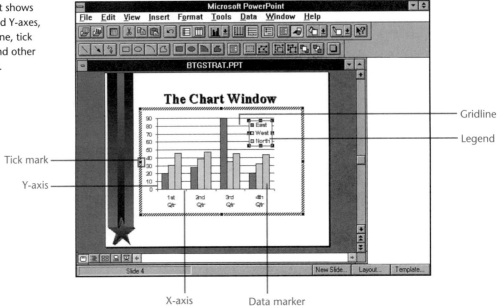

Tick mark

Y-axis

Gridline

Legend

X-axis   Data marker

Data Element
The numbers and values you want to represent visually, such as sales revenues or population percentages.

If you want to design charts that communicate more forcefully, you need to get to know their basic elements and how to use them:

- *Chart.* The complete field inside the Chart window. This includes the markers, axes, text, and all the other items that make up a chart.

- *Data marker.* The form in which data is represented in a chart. In a pie chart, the data markers are the slices; in a bar chart, the data markers are the bars; and in a line chart, the data markers are the lines.

- *Axis (axes, plural).* In a two-dimensional chart, the vertical and horizontal lines that are the reference points on which data is plotted.

- *X-axis.* The horizontal axis, which usually contains the categories for the data, such as years, countries, names.

- *Y-axis.* The vertical axis, generally containing the number references.

- *Z-axis.* In a three-dimensional chart, a third or Z-axis is included. Some 2-D charts, bar charts in particular, can be designed so that the bars have a third dimension. No data values are assigned to a third dimension in this type of three-dimensional chart.

A three-dimensional line area chart.

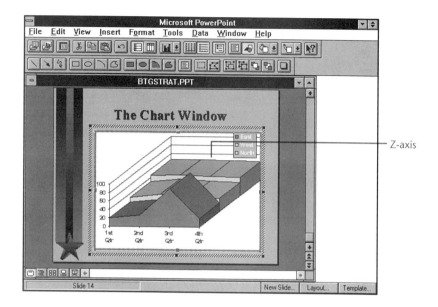

Z-axis

Note: *Data references for a three-dimensional data chart are discussed in Lesson 10, "Organizing Data and Datasheets."*

- *Tick mark.* Little lines, similar to the lines on a ruler, that mark a category or a data series on the X- and Y-axes.

- *Tick-mark labels.* Text or numbers attached to tick marks to identify them.

- *Plot area.* The portion of the chart in which the data is illustrated visually. This area includes the axes and all the data points.

- *Gridlines.* Lines that are drawn from the tick marks across the plot area. These lines are optional, and are added to make it easier to view data values.

- *Text.* Any additional text that describes the items in a chart. Text is added by typing it into an active chart. If desired, text can be attached to an item and moved with it.

- *Legend.* A key that identifies the colors or patterns associated with a data marker. The legend contains the name of the data category and a sample of the color or pattern that corresponds to it. The legend is usually in a box placed in an empty area of the chart, usually on the right.

9

Task: Working with Chart Types

The column chart that appears in the Chart window when Graph is opened is the default offering. There are, however, many other ways in which data can be shown visually. Graph enables you to choose the chart type that will best represent the information you are conveying to your audience.

The Chart Gallery includes a variety of chart types to choose from. Whichever one you choose will automatically include all the chart objects and formatting, which can then be customized to suit your preferences.

Chart Type	Definition
Area	Similar to a line chart. An area chart tends to emphasize the *amount* of change over time.
Bar	Exhibits comparisons between items at a given time. Categories are organized vertically.
Column	Similar to a bar chart, but categories are organized horizontally.
Line	Similar to an area chart. A line chart displays trends and changes in data over a given time period.
Pie	Exhibits the relationship of parts to a whole. Pie charts contain only one data series.
Scatter (XY)	Shows the degree of relationship based on numeric data between different categories. Resulting scatter clusters can also show which variables are interdependent.
Radar	Shows series relative to one another and to a central point.
3-D Area	A three-dimensional view of an area chart, separating the data series into distinct rows to reveal the differences between each series.
3-D Bar	A three-dimensional view of a bar chart that emphasizes data on two axes to allow comparison in a data series and view data by category on a third axis. If a 3-D bar chart has data for only one axis, the bars will have added thickness, but will not recede on the Z-axis.
3-D Column	Similar to a 3-D bar chart but categories are organized horizontally, across the X-axis.
3-D Line	Shows a line chart as 3-D ribbons, making them easier to view but less accurate as a data representation.

Chart Type	Definition
3-D Pie	Adds height to the pie slices so that values in the front are emphasized.
3-D Surface	Shows series as plane surfaces.

Selecting a Chart Type

PowerPoint allows you to select the particular chart which will best represent your facts and figures. Selections are made in Graph.

To change your chart type in Graph, follow these steps:

1. Activate the chart by double-clicking it.

2. From the Format menu, choose Chart Type. The Chart Type dialog box appears.

3. Under Chart Dimension, select either 2-D or 3-D formats. Associated visual choices appear.

This is the Chart Type dialog box for 2-D chart formats.

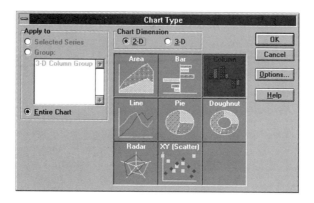

This is the Chart Type dialog box for 3-D chart formats.

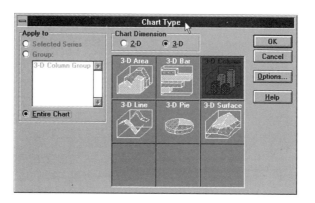

9

4. Double-click the chart type you prefer, a 2-D Pie, for example. You are returned to the Chart window, and the chart will have changed its appearance to the chart type you selected.

If you allow Pie to remain selected you can make still more changes to it.

5. From the Format menu, choose AutoFormat.

The AutoFormat dialog box is displayed.

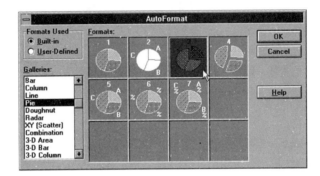

In the lower left you see a list box with a gallery of chart selections. In the center are variations for a selected chart type.

Because Pie was selected earlier, it is highlighted in the scroll box, and the Variants box (labeled Formats) contains variations of the Pie type.

Pie chart
A chart that represents data in the shape of a pie, with each data series as a separate pie wedge.

6. Change your selection to 3-D Pie in the Galleries list box.

7. Click on any of the variants in the Formats area to change your original.

If you selected a 3-D Pie with Label and Percentage attached, these will be included in your final chart.

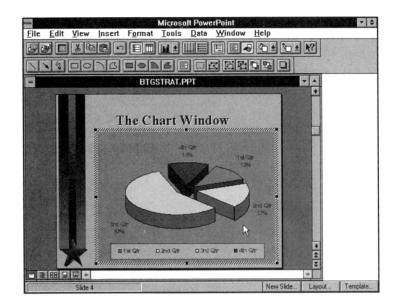

Applying Formatting Changes to a Chart

When you select a chart in the Chart window, a command designating its format appears at the bottom of the Format menu. If you select this command, you can select and apply more options affecting a chart style.

To apply changes to a specific 3-D chart, follow these steps:

1. Select a 3-D chart.

2. Pull down the Format menu.

   At the bottom of the Format menu is a command describing the chart's format.

If your chart is a 3-D Column type, the command will be named **1** 3-D Column Group.

3. Click the command at the bottom of the **Format** menu to display a Format 3-D dialog box.

At the top of the dialog box are tabs for Subtype, Options, and Axis. Click the tab for Subtype, and its options will appear at the front of the dialog box.

The Subtype tab for a 3-D column chart contains a simplified picture of your chart and four variants to choose from.

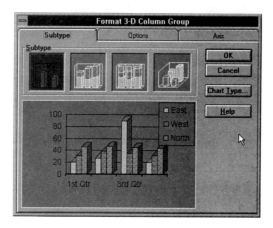

4. Click on the **S**ubtype that you prefer.

5. Click OK if no further changes are desired.

If you want to explore further, click the Options tab. This enables you to change width and spacing of your data markers with great precision.

Clicking on Axis tells you how the plot parameters have been selected.

To apply precise instructions for a 3-D chart concerning the angles at which it is viewed, choose **3**-D View from the **Format** menu. Follow these steps:

1. Select a 3-D chart.

2. Choose **3**-D View from the **Format** menu.

The Format 3-D View dialog box appears, with boxes and buttons for selecting the angle of elevation, rotation, and perspective for the data markers.

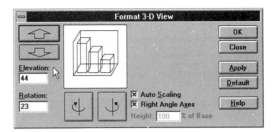

If you play around with these attributes, you can get some weird results.

To apply changes to a 2-D chart:

1. Select a 2-D chart.

2. Click the command describing its format at the bottom of the Format menu. If your chart is a 2-D Column Type, the command is named with that description, and a Format 2-D Column Group dialog box appears.

3. Click the tab for **S**ubtype.

The 2-D Column Subtype dialog box is displayed.

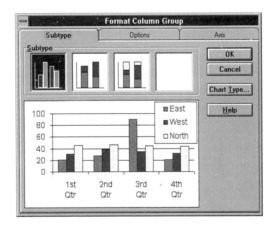

4. Click on the **S**ubtype that you prefer. Notice that two of the choices are area columns. Comparisons between data fields are not as clear in this type of chart.

5. Click OK if no further changes are desired.

   Note: *The 2-D column chart does not have a 2-D View command.*

9

Copying, Pasting, and Repositioning a Chart

You can copy charts in the same way as any other object in PowerPoint. If, however, you copy an embedded chart, the copy may not accept any of the changes that you might make to the embedded original.

To copy a chart to another slide presentation:

1. While in Slide view, select the chart you want to copy, and then choose **C**opy from the **E**dit menu.

2. Go to the presentation in which you want the chart to appear and select the slide for the copy to appear in.

3. From the **E**dit menu, choose **P**aste. The chart is copied to the new slide. Remember that if you make changes to the copy, they will not carry over to the embedded original.

4. Reposition the chart by selecting it and dragging it to a new location.

Task: Coloring a Chart

Colors in a chart are similar to colors in other visuals. There are differences, however, due to the many elements that make up a chart. Graph works with your PowerPoint color scheme to color the elements that make up a chart. Specifics for working with colors for charts are described in this lesson.

Note: *For information on using color schemes, refer to Lesson 6, "Working with Color on Slides."*

Charts can be colored in either Graph or in PowerPoint. It is better to perform some functions in Graph; others are best done in PowerPoint. It is important, at the start, to understand the different ways in which charts and chart elements can be colored in Graph.

Applying a Color Scheme to a Chart

Graph can assign color to a chart as a global or all-in-one procedure using PowerPoint color schemes. All the elements that make up the chart are assigned a color scheme at the same time. This color scheme is applied to all the elements of any other charts you make for the presentation, unless you apply a different color scheme to them.

Graph color scheme colors are assigned as follows:

- *Background.* The background behind your chart

- *Lines and Text.* The axes, grids, text, and tick marks that compose a chart

- *Fills.* These are treated as the first color in the series

- *Accents.* The colors used for the second, third, and fourth items in the series

- *Title Text.* The same as the color for the sixth item in the series

- *Shadows.* Color used to create a "shadowed" effect around the object

  Line and scatter charts use special colors assigned by Graph. These charts use thin or small data elements. In order for the dots or lines to stand out, their colors need to be bolder or darker than those assigned by a standard color scheme.

When you make changes to a color scheme in PowerPoint, the changes affect the entire chart area, for all the charts in a presentation.

Global
Applying a change to all the slides or all the charts in your PowerPoint presentation.

You can also customize colors in Graph as a *global* or all-in-one procedure. When colors are customized, though, they will no longer be part of your PowerPoint color scheme.

Note: *Graph also allows you to change colors for each element on a chart, by selecting the individual element you want to recolor.*

If you are designing a presentation that uses many charts, take the time to rearrange the colors of your color scheme in PowerPoint so that your charts are consistently represented in the most attractive color arrangement.

Changing a PowerPoint Color Scheme

To change a PowerPoint color scheme palette to accommodate better colors for charts, follow these steps:

1. Open the slide containing a chart to use for changing the PowerPoint color scheme.

9

If you are working in Graph, select a chart to work with in PowerPoint, and return to PowerPoint by clicking on the background outside the chart area.

2. Select the chart whose color scheme you want to change.

When you change the color scheme in PowerPoint to adopt better colors for a chart, all your charts will use those colors consistently, both in PowerPoint and in Graph.

3. From the Format menu, choose Slide Color Scheme.

PowerPoint's Slide Color Scheme dialog box is displayed.

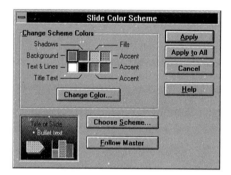

4. Select options in the dialog box:

To change the background behind your chart, select the Background color in the color scheme palette.

To change the color of the axes, grids, text, and tick marks, select Text & Lines.

To change the fill color in the series, select Fills.

To change the colors for the second, third, and fourth items in the series, select Accents.

To change the color of the titles item in the series, select Title Text.

5. When you are satisfied with your color choices, select **A**pply to apply the changes to the current slide and chart; or, select Apply **t**o All to apply the changes to the entire presentation.

If you have problems...	Some color choices do not work well together. If some of the lines or text elements of the chart disappear or become hard to read, try changing to a much darker or much lighter color.

Customizing a Color Scheme in Graph

You can also customize a color scheme in Graph. If, however, you choose a nonstandard color palette, when you return to PowerPoint those colors will not be changed to a PowerPoint color scheme. Those colors will remain the same as the colors you chose in Graph, only not in a color scheme.

The standard Graph palette includes your PowerPoint color scheme, plus additional colors for line and scatter charts. To change a color scheme in Graph, follow these steps:

1. From the **T**ools menu, choose **O**ptions.

    A dialog box with tabs at the top for Datasheet Options, Chart, and Color appears.

2. Click the Color tab to display the Slide Color Scheme dialog box for Graph.

The Graph Options dialog box is displayed.

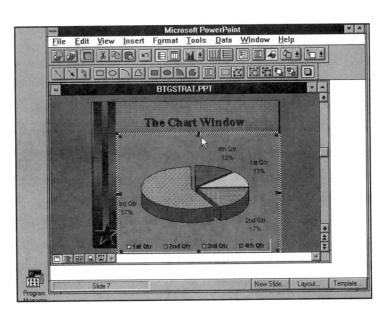

3. Select the color you want to replace, and then select **M**odify.

The Color Picker dialog box appears. Using the mouse pointer, select the new color from the color palette. Choose OK to return to the Slide Color Scheme dialog box.

If you have problems...

If you have trouble finding a color in your chart in the Slide Color Scheme dialog box, try selecting the individual element in the chart and using the color selection button on Graph's main toolbar.

---

4. Click OK. You are returned to the Chart window.

For quick color applications, select the object in your chart that you want to recolor and click on the Color button on Graph's toolbar to display the drop-down palette. Choose a new color from the palette and the object will be updated with that color.

The toolbar Color drop-down palette.

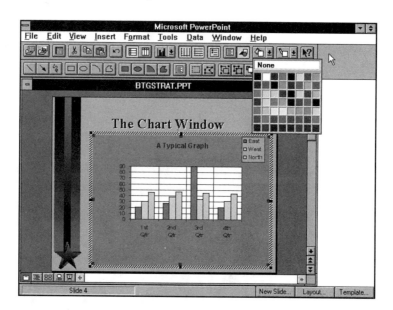

Advising PowerPoint When You Customize Colors in Graph

When you make custom color choices in Graph, they are not controlled by the Automatic color selection. Before making any custom color changes in Graph, you need to let PowerPoint know which colors are under its (PowerPoint's) control.

To ensure that the custom colors you chose in Graph will prevail as your *new* color choices when you return to PowerPoint, follow these steps:

1. In Graph, select the chart you are planning to color customize.

2. Click on the background outside the chart area to move to PowerPoint.

3. In PowerPoint, choose **R**ecolor from the **T**ools menu.

The Recolor Graph dialog box appears.

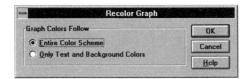

4. Choose the category of colors you want PowerPoint to control:

   Entire Color Scheme: This option cancels any custom colors you created in Graph. PowerPoint will recolor the text and background of your graph as well as the data markers such as bars and pie slices.

   Only Text and Background Colors: PowerPoint will only recolor text and background color choices created in Graph. The other custom colors remain the same as those you created in Graph.

Selecting Color for Individual Graph Elements

In Graph, you can also color individual elements by selecting them to apply colors and patterns with more precision. When an element is selected, you can change its font and location and perform other editing functions.

Automatic
When selected in a color context, applies the standard color scheme colors to the element you selected in the chart.

When you choose S**e**lected Element from the F**o**rmat menu (with a graph element selected), a multilevel dialog box appears with selection tabs at the top. To apply colors and patterns for a selected element, click the Pattern tab. If you want a color scheme that is compatible with PowerPoint's color schemes, select **A**utomatic. Each of these items is discussed in greater detail later.

9

Task: **Editing Individual Chart Elements**

So far, you have learned how to make changes on the entire chart plot. Individual items on a chart also can be changed. Some editing changes, such as changing the category names, need to be made in the Datasheet window. These changes are covered in Lesson 10, "Organizing Data and Datasheets."

Note: *Editing individual parts of a chart can only be done in the Graph application.*

Selecting Objects on Charts

Before you can reformat or edit any part of a chart, it needs to be selected, similar to editing any object in PowerPoint. There are differences, though.

In Graph, when an object is selected, its handles can be either black or light-colored, depending on the type of object it is.

If an object is marked with black handles, such as a chart legend, it can be moved and resized with the mouse, and it can be formatted.

A chart legend is selected; notice the black handles.

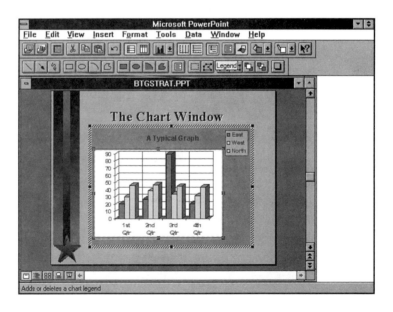

Objects marked with light-colored handles, such as data markers, cannot be moved or sized directly.

A data marker is selected, showing light-colored handles.

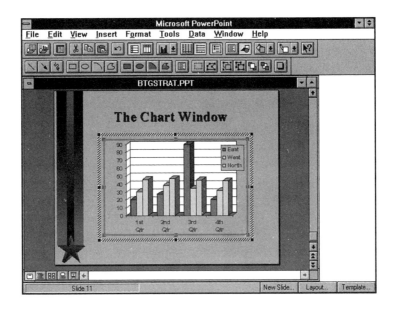

Resizing Chart Elements

To resize a chart element, drag on one of the handles of the element when you are in the Graph application. To resize a chart element, follow these steps:

1. Select a chart element and determine which handle you need to drag to resize the element.

2. Place the pointer carefully on the handle that reflects the direction of the resize. The pointer will turn into a Resize pointer.

3. Drag in the direction of the resize until the element is sized to your satisfaction.

Changing Colors and Patterns on a Chart Element

Patterns and colors are best applied by selecting the chart element you want to reformat. When you double-click the element, the appropriate set of dialog boxes appears for you to make your changes.

To recolor an element in Graph, follow these steps:

1. Select the element whose background you want to recolor or pattern.

9

The Legend is
selected in a chart.

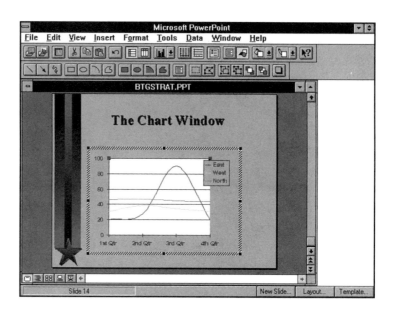

Legend
A small table in a
graph that identifies
what various data
markers represent.

2. Double-click on the element, and the element's Format (*Legend* in this example) dialog box appears. One of the tabs on the top is labeled Patterns.

3. Click Patterns.

The Patterns tab of
the Format Legend
dialog box is
displayed.

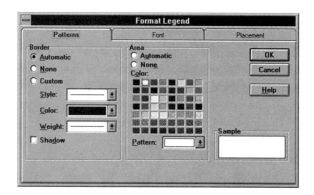

4. You can select a color or a pattern for the element you selected in step 1.

   If you want to stay in a color scheme, click **Automatic**.

5. Scroll through the **P**attern drop-down list at the bottom of the dialog box to select a pattern for the element you have chosen.

6. Click OK to apply the pattern.

Formatting and Placing the Chart Legend

The legend is the key that identifies the colors, symbols, and patterns associated with a data marker. The legend contains the name of the category, and to its right, a sample of the color, symbol, or pattern that corresponds to it.

When you first choose a chart type, Graph automatically adds a legend to the right of the plot area.

To reformat a legend in Graph, follow these steps:

1. Select the chart legend you want to reformat and double-click it.

   The Graph Legend dialog box appears, with tabs for Patterns, Font, and Placement at the top.

2. To change the location of your legend automatically, click the Placement tab.

The Placement tab options appear in the dialog box. On the left are selections for placing the legend.

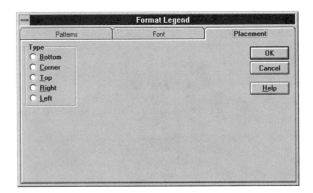

You can move the legend anywhere in the chart by selecting and dragging it with the mouse. It can be moved this way because it has black handles.

3. To change the legend type face, click the Font tab.

9

The Font tab is
displayed.

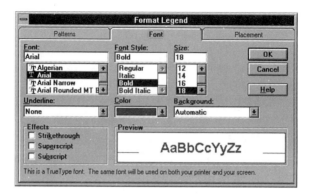

4. Select the font options you want for your legend.

Note: *For more information on selecting fonts in PowerPoint, see Lesson 4, "Adding Text to Slides."*

You also can select the font color and its background for the legend from the Font Legend dialog box.

The text printed in the legend is taken directly from the datasheet cells. To make changes to this text, you need to edit the datasheet cells containing category names.

Note: *To make changes to data categories, refer to Lesson 10, "Organizing Data and Datasheets."*

5. To change the color or pattern of the legend, click the Patterns tab and make your selections.

6. Click OK to apply all your choices.

Deleting or Adding a Legend

To delete a legend from a chart, follow these steps:

1. Select the legend.

2. Press Del, or choose Clear from the **E**dit menu, or click on the Legend button on Graph's toolbar. The Legend button will toggle the display of the selected legend.

To add a Legend Box to a chart:

1. Choose **L**egend from the **I**nsert menu.

Task: **Adding Text to Charts**

Some text is automatically added to any chart that Graph creates, such as tick-mark labels and legend text. You also can create your own additional text for subtitles, comments, source credits, and additional labeling you might need.

Here is a typical **chart** with its text elements labeled.

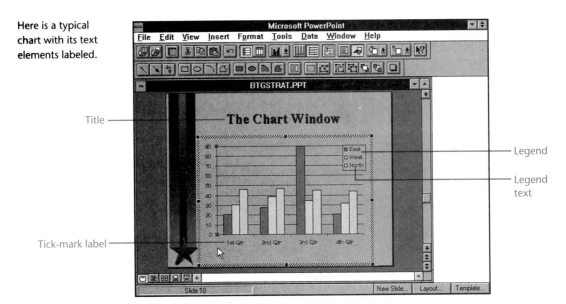

Adding Text Titles and Other Labels

You can insert text into your chart or delete it from the chart by using the Insert menu. Most text in a chart is *attached*—linked to the element that it identifies. Attached text includes titles, tick-mark labels, and axis labels. When attached text is selected, its handles are light-colored, indicating that it cannot be resized or moved with the mouse.

To add attached Title text to a label, follow these steps:

1. From the **I**nsert menu, choose **T**itles.

9

The Titles dialog
box appears.

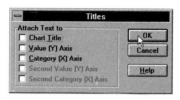

2. Select the option that pertains to the elements you want to change.

3. Click OK.

   The default selection appears, surrounded with light-colored handles. If you chose the Title command in Insert, the word *Title* appears.

4. Remove the original text and replace it with the text you want. The text appears on the screen, in position.

   Note: *If you want to change the length of a text line, press Enter for a line break.*

Adding Unattached Text

Text can be *unattached*—placed anywhere on the chart, unlinked to any other element. You place unattached text wherever it serves its purpose and is visually clear. Descriptive text, often used for emphasis, is unattached. When unattached text is selected, its handles are black, indicating that it can be moved or resized as any other graphic.

To add unattached text to a label, it is easiest to use the Text button on the toolbar:

1. Type the text directly on the chart in the location that you want.

   The text you type appears on the screen with black selection handles. You can move this text by dragging it with the mouse, and you can resize it by dragging on a handle.

2. Insert a line break by changing the size of the box, or by inserting a line break with the Enter key.

The selected text has black handles, indicating that it is unattached.

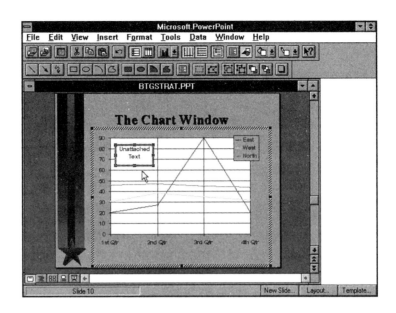

Any text can be edited to correct a typographical error or to change what you have written. To edit text on a chart, follow these steps:

1. Click to select the text you want to change.

2. Retype your entry, or use the text insertion point to delete and insert characters.

   If you decide to delete the text entirely, select it and choose Clear from the Edit menu.

3. Press Enter.

Adding Data Labels and Percentages

Data label

The text descriptions placed next to a numerical data value in a chart.

Graph will not supply *data labels* as part of the default selection. Should you want to include them, you need to make the selection manually.

To add data labels and percentages to a chart, follow these steps:

1. From the **I**nsert menu, choose **D**ata Labels.

9

The Data Label tab of the Format Data Series dialog box is displayed.

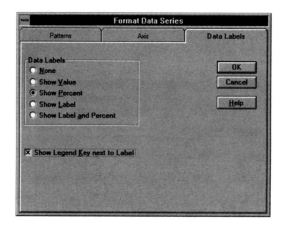

2. Select the type of label you want to display.

   To display a numeric value above each data point, click Show **V**alue.

   To display a category name above data points, click Show **L**abel. It is the same name as that appearing in the X-axis in the datasheet cells.

   To display percentages next to slices in a pie chart, click Show **P**ercent.

   If you want both a percent and a category name next to slices in a pie chart, click Show Label **a**nd Percent.

3. Click OK to apply your selections.

This pie chart, viewed in PowerPoint, has label and percentages applied.

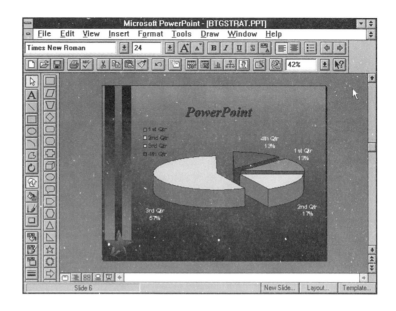

Task: Formatting Elements on a Chart

PowerPoint enables you to change several attributes of the text you place in a chart. The fonts, colors, and orientation of the text elements can all be customized to suit your presentation. The sections below give details for formatting text elements on your charts.

Formatting Text on a Chart

The Font command in the **I**nsert menu enables you to change the default formatting for any text appearing on a chart, both attached and unattached. You also can change the pattern and color of any text area and the style of the border that surrounds it.

To format text on a chart, follow these steps:

1. Select the text you want to reformat.

   To reformat tick-mark labels, select the axis.

   To reformat the text in a legend, select the legend.

2. From the **F**ormat menu, choose **F**ont; or double-click the element you selected.

9

The Font format
menu appears.

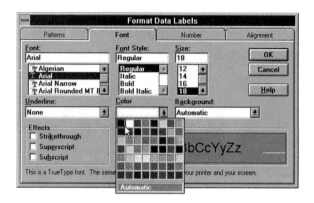

3. In the dialog box, make your formatting changes as desired in the
   Font box, the **S**ize box, and the Font Style box.

4. Select a font color from the **C**olor palette.

5. Click the Patterns tab to format the text border and area. You can
   select a shadow for your text border in this dialog box.

6. Click the Alignment tab to format the alignment and orientation
   for your selected text.

   Note: *In making color changes to text or background (under the Font
   tab), select Automatic from the drop-down palette to keep your changes
   within the PowerPoint color scheme.*

7. Click the Font tab. Under B**a**ckground, select Transparent from the
   drop-down list if you want to see the color or pattern behind the
   text area.

   If you do not want to have a pattern back of your text, but want to
   keep the color, select Opaque from the B**a**ckground drop-down list.

8. Click OK to apply your changes.

Changing the Text Orientation and Alignment

In a chart you often will want some of the text to appear in a vertical
position. You may also prefer to replace the data marker text with a
number value.

To apply changes in orientation and alignment to text, follow these steps:

1. Select the text you want to reformat.

2. From the **F**ormat menu, choose **F**ont, and then click on the Alignment tab.

The Alignment options are displayed in the Format Object dialog box.

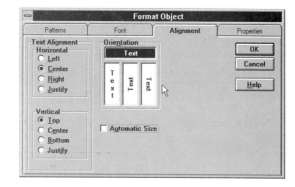

3. Select the alignment you want, from either the Vertical or Horizontal selection boxes.

4. Select the orientation you want for your text after selecting alignment. The boxes will be filled with the text you are reorienting.

5. Click OK to apply your choices.

Formatting Elements in the Plot and Axes Areas

The fastest way to get to the dialog boxes that allow you to format the gridlines, tick marks, and axes in a chart is by double-clicking the element you want to format.

It is very important to aim the hot point of your pointer precisely on the element to be formatted. If you don't hit the mark exactly, you will access the dialog box for an adjacent element.

Formatting Chart Axes and Tick Marks

To format an axis and tick marks, follow these steps:

1. Double-click the axis you want to format, or select the axis and choose the first command in the Format menu. The Format Axis dialog box appears with tabs for Patterns, Scale, Font, Number, and Alignment at the top.

9

2. Click the Patterns tab.

The Format Axis
dialog box appears.
In this dialog box,
you select the style
of the axis line, its
color, and weight.
You also can select
tick-mark types and
their placement.

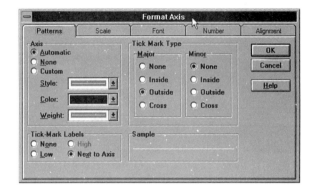

3. Select the line features you want to apply, such as style, color, and weight.

4. In the Tick Mark Labels area on the lower left, select the option you want for locating the label.

5. In the Tick-Mark Type area, select your options for **M**ajor and Mino**r** tick-mark types. For additional information, review the selections for gridlines later in this lesson.

6. Click the Scale tab to display Axis Scale options.

In a standard scale the numbers generally range from a minimum of 0 to a maximum of 100. If you are using this scale, you might want major values to be placed in units of 10, and minor units at 2. If you use minor tick marks, they can generally be placed closer together than minor gridlines, and will not clutter your chart plot.

7. Click the Font tab to display the Font options. Make your font formatting changes, including a color selection for the typeface in this dialog box.

For more details on selecting fonts in general, see Lesson 4, "Adding Text to Slides."

8. Click the Number tab.

The Number tab box from the Format Axis dialog box enables you to choose number styles.

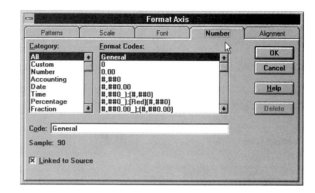

The default **C**ategory selection is for All numerical values. The default selection for Format Codes is General. Unless you have a need to make a change, the default should suffice.

9. Click the Alignment tab to display those options in the dialog box.

Choose **A**utomatic for the Graph default, or select the box whose orientation you want to apply.

Formatting Lines for Axes and Gridmarks

To make a line change to an element, follow these steps:

1. Double-click the element you want to make a line change to, and its dialog box appears with tabs for Patterns, Scale, Font, Number, and Alignment at the top.

2. Click Patterns. This tab of the dialog box enables you to select the style of the line, its color, and weight.

3. Select **A**utomatic if you want the Graph default to be applied to the element.

If you select a style, color, or weight option, the Custom option button will be selected automatically.

9

4. If you select **S**tyle, a choice of line patterns appears. Select the one you want to use.

When you make a choice, notice that it appears in the Sample box to the right.

The style options for gridlines are displayed here.

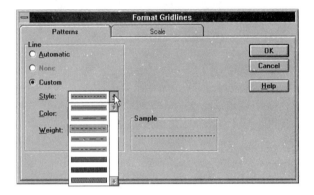

5. When **C**olor is selected, a color drop-down list appears. Click to select the color you want to apply.

The Line color options for gridlines are shown here.

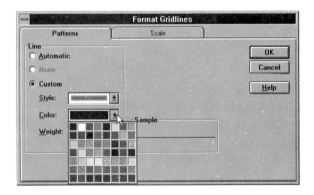

6. When **W**eight is selected, a menu showing line thicknesses appears. Click to select the line weight you want.

Here, the Line
weight options
for gridlines are
displayed.

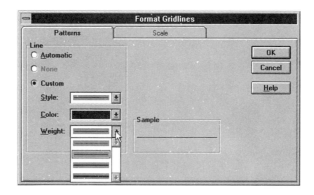

7. When you are satisfied with your selections, click OK.

Formatting Line Chart Data Elements

To format a line data element in a line chart, follow these steps:

1. Select the line you want to format and double-click it.

The Data Marker format dialog box appears.

2. Select the line style, color, weight, and any other features you want to format.

3. Click OK.

Formatting Gridlines

The Plot area contains the *gridlines*, extensions of the tick marks that denote the numerical values and categories of your data. If there are too many gridlines in the plot area, you will find it difficult to separate the data markers from the forest of lines in the background. In addition, you may find it next to impossible to aim your pointer with precision when selecting the element you want to format.

To select the gridlines you want to appear on your chart, follow these steps:

1. From the **I**nsert menu, choose **G**ridlines.

2. Select the gridlines you want to appear for each axis.

Major gridlines delineate the larger numerical values, such as 10s in a scale from 1 to 100.

9

Minor gridlines delineate the in-between values.

The numerical values you select for your gridlines are accessed by double-clicking on a gridline.

To format gridlines in a chart, follow these steps:

1. Select the gridlines you want to format, either X or Y, and double-click one. The Gridline dialog box appears with tabs for Patterns and Scale on the top.

2. Click the Scale tab.

This is the Format Gridlines dialog box with Scale selected.

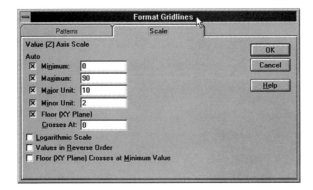

The Value Axis Scale is on the left. At the top, the title will include the axis you have chosen to format, for example Value (Y) Axis Scale.

3. Select Graph default values. The Unit breakdowns will depend on the chart type you are working with and the actual numerical values and number of categories in your chart.

After you have selected the Scale factors for your gridline, you may want to change the colors and weights:

1. Select the gridline you want to format and double-click it.

When you select a major gridline, only those will be changed. To format a minor gridline, select one.

The Gridline dialog box appears with tabs for Patterns and Scale on the top.

2. Click the Pattern tab.

The Format
Gridlines dialog box
is displayed with
Patterns selected.

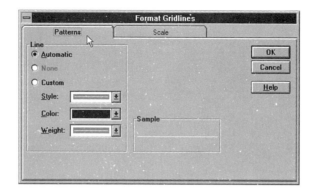

3. If you choose **A**utomatic, the Graph default is applied to the
element.

If you choose a style, color, or weight option, the Custom option
button is selected automatically.

4. Select formats from **S**tyle, **C**olor, and **W**eight.

When you make a choice, notice that it appears in the Sample box
to the right.

5. When you are satisfied with your selections, click OK.

Task: Adding Arrows to a Chart

Arrows can be added to a chart to point from a descriptive text callout to
data items you want to emphasize.

To insert an arrow into a chart, follow these steps:

1. Display the Drawing toolbar and click the Arrow button.
The pointer turns into a small crosshair.

2. Drag the crosshair pointer in the location where you want the
arrow to appear.

9

Graph inserts a
default arrow, with
handles selected.

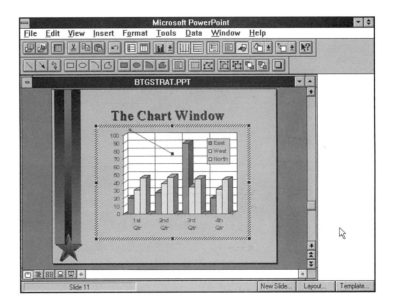

3. Double-click the arrow. The Format Object dialog box appears with tabs for Patterns and Properties at the top.

4. Click Patterns.

This Format Object
dialog box has
Patterns selected.

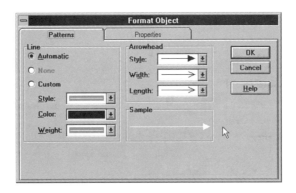

On the lower right, notice the preview of the arrow in the sample box.

5. Under Line, select **A**utomatic, or select formatting from the **S**tyle, **C**olor, and **W**eight boxes.

6. Choose the Arrowhead style you want from among the Sty**l**e, Wi**d**th, and Le**n**gth boxes.

View your selections in the Sample box as you make them.

In the Properties tab of the Format Object dialog box, you can select to size or not size the arrow with the chart.

Here is an example of a formatted arrow with unattached text.

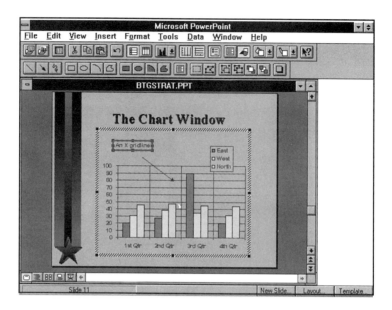

Summary

To	Do This
Add a chart to a slide	Choose Microsoft **G**raph from the **I**nsert menu. Edit the Data sheet as desired. Click outside the chart area to return to the PowerPoint presentation. The chart will be placed on the slide.
Select a graph type	In the Graph application, choose **C**hart Type from the **F**ormat menu. Select a chart type. Click OK to create the chart.
Copy a graph from one slide to another	In PowerPoint, change to Slide view and select the chart to copy. Choose **C**opy from the **E**dit menu. Move to the destination slide. Choose **P**aste from the **E**dit menu.

(continues)

9

To	Do This
Apply a color scheme to a graph	In the Graph application, select **O**ptions from the **T**ools menu. Double-click on the color you want to change. Pick a new color from the Color Picker dialog box. Select OK to return to the Options dialog box. Select OK to apply the new color to the graph.
Apply a color to an individual graph element	Select the graph element. Click the Color button on Graph's toolbar. Choose a new color from the color palette.
Resize a graph element	In the Graph application, select the graph element. Drag the element's handles to resize as needed.
Place a graph legend	In the Graph application, choose **L**egend from the **I**nsert menu.
Add a text title to a graph	In Graph, choose **T**itles from the **I**nsert menu. Check Chart **T**itle in the Titles dialog box. Click OK to insert the default title in the chart.
Add an arrow to a graph	In Graph, click the Arrow button on the Drawing toolbar. Click and hold the mouse button to anchor the end of the arrow. Drag the arrow tool in the direction and length of the arrow. Release the mouse button.

On Your Own

Estimated time: 20 minutes

1. Start PowerPoint.

2. Use the AutoContent Wizard to create the Reporting Progress presentation template.

3. Move to the third slide of the presentation.

4. Access the Graph application from the PowerPoint toolbar.

5. Close the default datasheet that appears in the Chart application.

6. Change the chart type to 3-D area.

7. Change the subtype of the chart.

8. Exit the Chart application and return to PowerPoint.

9. Resize the chart to fit under the slide bullet points.

10. Return to the Chart application by double-clicking on the chart.

11. Relocate the Chart Legend to the lower right corner of the chart.

12. Add a Text Title to the chart. It should say `Our Increasing Sales.`

13. Add an arrow to the chart pointing to the 3rd Qtr peak.

14. Add a text label next to the arrow saying `We are here.`

15. Return to the PowerPoint presentation.

16. Close PowerPoint, but do not save your work.

9

Lesson 10

Organizing Data and Datasheets

This lesson teaches you the following:

- ■ The elements in the Datasheet window
- ■ About row and column cells and their headings
- ■ Understanding data series and how they are named
- ■ Understanding what graph categories are and how best to define them
- ■ How to label a tick mark

Graphs are concerned with the *illustration* of data. Graphs show relationships based on data expressed in clear-cut, standard elements. The elements based on numbers are covered in this lesson. The elements covering the illustration of graphs are discussed in Lesson 9, "Adding Charts to Slides."

In the Datasheet window, data items must be defined and placed exactly, similar to the way you do it in a spreadsheet. If you already know how to use Excel for Windows, or another spreadsheet application, you're 75 percent there.

You can create graphs for PowerPoint using Graph, a supplementary application that comes with PowerPoint. If you haven't already reviewed Lesson 9, you should do so before continuing with this lesson. In that lesson, you learn how to access the Graph application and display the Datasheet window.

Graph creates embedded objects to be displayed in PowerPoint. You can toggle back and forth between the two applications, working in Graph to organize and format the information and adding finishing touches in PowerPoint.

Note: *For more information on embedded objects in PowerPoint, see Lesson 15, "Working with Other Windows Applications."*

As you learned in Lesson 9, Graph consists of two major windows: the Datasheet window and the Chart window.

The Datasheet and Chart windows.

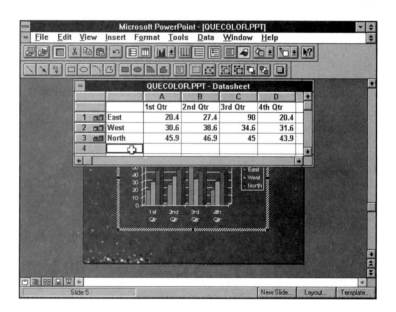

Note: *You can import data from Microsoft Excel or other spreadsheet applications into Graph.*

Reminder: You can enter Graph by double-clicking the Graph button on the toolbar or by choosing Graph from the **I**nsert menu.

Note: *Double-clicking a selected graph in PowerPoint will move you into Graph.*

Exploring the Datasheet Window

A graph consists of data elements placed into a visual arrangement.

The elements on this datasheet are labeled.

Cells

The datasheet elements are described in the text that follows:

- *Row and column control boxes.* The row of boxes above the headings (labeled A, B, C, and so forth) and the column of boxes to the left of the column headings (labeled 1, 2, 3, and so forth). When you click on a control box, the row or column is highlighted.

- *Row and column headings.* On the datasheet, cells in which the heading labels are entered. Row headings appear in the top horizontal layer of cells. These headings also appear as tick-mark labels in the chart. Column headings appear in the far left column of cells and appear as data series names in the chart.

- *Cells.* The boxes on a datasheet in which the data is entered. The active, or selected, cell has a heavy black box.

- *Data point.* A single item in a series of related data items.

- *Data series.* A row or column of data point cells. Numbers in a data series will plot a single line in a line graph, a single bar in a bar graph, and a single slice in a pie. A data series represents a category of data.

A data series row highlighted in the datasheet window.

■ *Series name.* The names that identify each column or row category. These are the names that appear in the legend. To keep all the boxes straight, notice that the series name header boxes include an identifying icon; the row or column containing the tick-mark labels header does not.

The series name column.

QUECOLOR.PPT - Datasheet	A	B	C	D	E
	1st Qtr	2nd Qtr	3rd Qtr	4th Qtr	
1 East	20.4	27.4	90	20.4	
2 West	30.6	38.6	34.6	31.6	
3 North	45.9	46.9	45	43.9	
4 South	60	70	25	95	

■ *Tick-mark labels.* Identifying text or numbers attached to divisions in a graph axis. When a data series is in a column format, these are the labels that are attached to the horizontal or X-axis.

The tick-mark or category labels row.

BGCONFET.PPT - Datasheet	A	B	C	D	
	1st Qtr	2nd Qtr	3rd Qtr	4th Qtr	
1 East	20.4	27.4	90	20.4	
2 West	30.6	38.6	34.6	31.6	
3 North	45.9	46.9	45	43.9	
4					

The text and numbers that you type into the datasheet show up immediately in the visual graph.

In this column graph, you can see the relationship between the datasheet and graph.

BGCONFET.PPT - Datasheet	A	B	C	D	
	1st Qtr	2nd Qtr	3rd Qtr	4th Qtr	
1 East	20.4	27.4	90	20.4	
2 West	30.6	38.6	34.6	31.6	
3 North	45.9	46.9	45	43.9	
4					

Note: *Graph enables you to select the particular graph that will best represent your facts and figures. See Lesson 9, "Adding Charts to Slides," for more information on graph types.*

You can type your own data into the default datasheet that appears on the screen, or you can import the data from another presentation or spreadsheet program. This lesson explores both of these options.

Task: Entering and Editing Cell Data

To enter data into a cell, follow these steps:

1. Select the cell you want to type in.

A black border surrounds the cell to show that it has been selected.

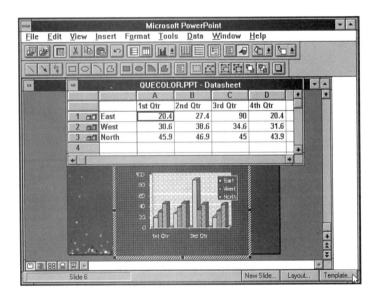

Note: *You can't enter numbers, labels, or categories into row 1, column 1 on a datasheet.*

2. Start typing the data for the cell. As you begin to type a blinking insertion point appears. Complete your entry.

A selected cell, ready for typing.

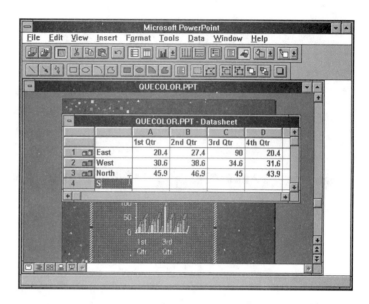

3. When you have finished typing, press Enter, or press the arrow key in the direction you want to move to.

The new data appears in the active cell, and the active cell is moved to the one you selected with the arrow key.

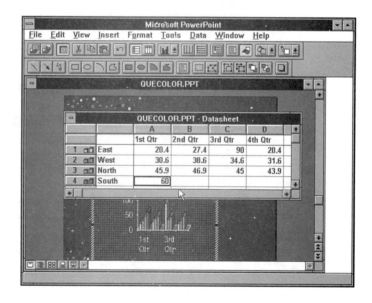

10

To edit a cell entry, follow these steps:

1. Select the cell you want to change. Selected cells appear with black borders.

2. Double-click the cell. A blinking insertion point appears in the cell.

3. To make your changes, position the insertion point or drag to select the characters you want to change.

4. Type the replacement data, and it will appear in the cell.

5. Press Enter. The active cell moves one cell down, and the new text appears in the cell you just edited.

Task: Selecting Cells, Columns, and Rows

When you are working in a datasheet, you can use either the mouse or the keyboard to move from cell to cell.

Range
A group of cells arranged in a sequence. The sequence of cells can be either vertical or horizontal, or in a group that combines both rows and columns. Cells that are not part of the sequence cannot be included in a range.

You type data entries into a single selected cell. You also can select a *range* or group of cells or the entire datasheet, depending on the tasks you need to carry out.

To select a range of cells in a column or a row, follow these steps:

1. Click in the first cell of the row group you want to select.

2. Press the Shift key and hold it while dragging toward the last cell in the group.

   All the cells in the row range will be selected.

   To select a column range, drag down from the first to last cell.

   To select a row quickly, click in the column selection box at the left. To select more than one row, drag down the column selection boxes.

   You select a column(s) by dragging through the row selection box at the top.

Two rows are selected in this datasheet.

		A	B	C	D	
		1st Qtr	2nd Qtr	3rd Qtr	4th Qtr	
1	East	20.4	27.4	90	20.4	
2	West	30.6	38.6	34.6	31.6	
3	North	45.9	46.9	45	43.9	
4						

BGCONFET.PPT - Datasheet

A column is selected in this datasheet.

		A	B	C	D	
		1st Qtr	2nd Qtr	3rd Qtr	4th Qtr	
1	East	20.4	27.4	90	20.4	
2	West	30.6	38.6	34.6	31.6	
3	North	45.9	46.9	45	43.9	
4						

BGCONFET.PPT - Datasheet

To select a range of cells that includes both rows and columns, follow these steps:

1. Select the first cell of the group you want to select.

2. Press the Shift key and hold it while dragging diagonally to the last cell in the group.

All the cells in the row or column range are selected.

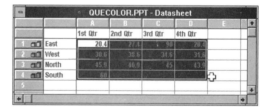

Task: Moving Around by Using the Keyboard

You can move around a datasheet using the arrow keys on your keyboard. Follow these steps:

1. To move one cell down from a previously selected cell, press the down-arrow key.

2. To move in any other direction, press the arrow key that points in the direction you want to go.

3. If you hold down the arrow key, the cursor continues moving through cells in the direction of the arrow you are pressing.

| **If you have problems...** | If you get lost in the datasheet while moving around, use the mouse to drag up and to the left until you reach the first cell of the sheet. |

Task: Adjusting Column Widths

Columns can be made wider or narrower for your convenience in viewing the data. If your columns are narrow and some of the data appears to be cut off, don't worry; you haven't lost it.

To make a column wider (or narrower), follow these steps:

1. Select the column you want to widen by clicking its heading.

2. Place the pointer on a vertical border to the right of the column heading you want to change.

The pointer changes to a column drag pointer.

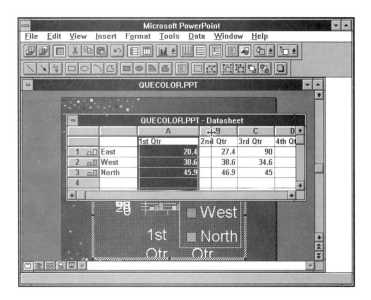

3. Drag toward the right to widen the column, and drag to the left to make it narrower.

The widened
column.

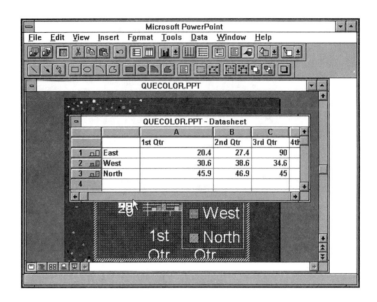

Task: Moving, Copying, and Clearing Data

In Graph, you move cell contents around using the standard **C**ut and **P**aste commands in the **E**dit menu. You can move or copy cells from one datasheet to another. Or, you can use these commands to move data within a single datasheet.

To move data, follow these steps:

1. Select the cell(s) you want to move.

2. From the **E**dit menu, choose **C**ut.

3. Next, select the first cell in the upper left of the area into which you want the data moved. Or, select the entire paste area.

4. From the **E**dit menu, choose **P**aste.

   The cells you selected and cut are moved to the new location.

To copy data, follow these steps:

1. Select the cell(s) you want to copy.

2. From the **E**dit menu, choose **C**opy.

3. Next, select the first cell in the upper left of the area into which you want the data copied. Or, select the entire paste area.

4. From the **E**dit menu, choose **P**aste.

You also can clear the information in a cell or group of cells in a datasheet. When a cell is cleared, the information is not stored on the Clipboard.

To clear a cell of its content or format, follow these steps:

1. Select the cell(s) you want to clear.

2. From the **E**dit menu, choose **C**lear.

3. Click the **C**ontents option from the submenu to clear only the data.

Click the **F**ormat option to clear only the number format.

To remove data and number formats, click **A**ll.

4. Click OK.

Use the **U**ndo command in the **E**dit menu if you want to reverse the change.

Task: Inserting and Deleting Rows and Columns

You may find that you need to insert another row or column to make room for new data.

To insert a row or column, follow these steps:

1. Select the row or column to the right of the location for the new column.

If you want to insert more than one row or column, drag to choose the number of rows or columns you want to insert.

2. From the **I**nsert menu, choose **C**ells. A new row appears above the row you selected; the new column appears to the left of your selection.

3. Click OK.

If you selected a single cell or range rather than an entire row or column, the Insert dialog box appears. Click the Insert Entire Row option button or the Insert Entire Column option button, depending on your need.

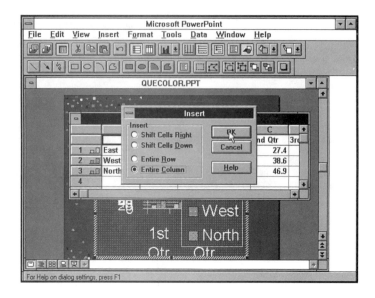

To delete a row or column, follow these steps:

1. Click on the row or column head you want delete.

If you want to delete more than one row or column, drag to choose them.

2. From the **E**dit menu, choose **D**elete. The row or column will be deleted.

If you selected only a single cell or range rather than an entire row or column, the Delete dialog box appears. Click the Delete Entire Row option button or the Delete Entire Column option button, depending on your need.

3. Click OK.

Task: Entering Data in the Correct Format

Data for graphing is frequently entered in rows. This is the format used by the sample datasheet that goes along with the sample column graph. If you follow this arrangement, type the data series names into the first column on the left. These are the names that appear in the legend. You enter the tick mark labels (category names) into the first row across the top.

Before you start typing the numbers, make sure that you have identified the name of the data series (the information that will appear in the legend) and the tick-mark labels for each group of data points (the information that usually appears under the horizontal or X-axis).

Entering Data Series in Rows

To enter data series in a row format, follow these steps:

1. Pull down the **D**ata menu and check to be sure that Series in Rows is checked so that you can replace data in the same format as the sample datasheet.

2. Enter the data series names down the first column and the category names across the first row.

3. Enter the data for each series across each row.

Entering Data Series in Columns

If you need to enter your data series in columns, you need to reverse the row format. Your data series names (the ones that appear in the legend) need to be entered across the first row, and the category names down the first column.

To enter data in columns, follow these steps:

1. From the **D**ata menu, choose Series in Columns.

2. Enter the data series names across the first row, and the category names down the first column.

3. Enter the data for each series down each column.

The data series
are entered in a
column datasheet.

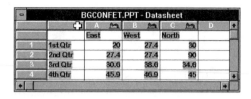

Entering Data for Scatter Graphs

A scatter graph is composed of numeric information on both axes. Most other graphs plot categories along the horizontal or X-axis, and the number values on the vertical or Y-axis. Data points on a scatter graph (also called an XY graph) are plotted on both the X- and the Y-axes as pairs of values. One data series determines the location on the X-axis, the other on the Y-axis. You choose the way you plot these values on the dialog box that appears when you have chosen XY (scatter) from the gallery.

Note: *For more information on selecting a graph type, refer to Lesson 9, "Adding Charts to Slides."*

To plot an XY (scatter) graph, follow these steps:

1. Switch to the Chart window.

2. From the Format menu, choose AutoFormat, and then select XY (scatter) from the scroll box on the lower left.

3. Select the format you want and click OK.

4. Switch to the Datasheet window.

5. Select a cell in the data series to be plotted on the X-axis (horizontal).

6. From the **D**ata menu, choose **P**lot on X-axis.

   An x will appear in the row or column heading (depending on the arrangement of your data). The data in the other data series will be plotted in relation to the values of the X plot.

An XY or scatter
graph. Notice the X
above the header
box on the far left.

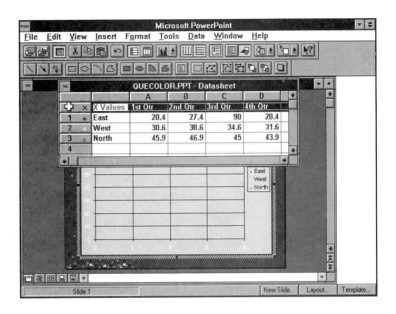

Task: Excluding and Including Graph Data

You may not want all the information you have on your datasheet to
appear in the graph. You can select rows and columns of data and exclude them using Graph's **E**xclude Row/Col. command. When you view
the graph plot, the excluded data will not appear as part of the plot.

To exclude a row or a column, follow these steps:

1. Select the rows or columns you want to exclude.

2. From the **D**ata menu, choose **Exclude Row/Col**.

3. Click OK.

   The columns or rows you excluded are dimmed on the datasheet.

A row is selected to "exclude" in a datasheet.

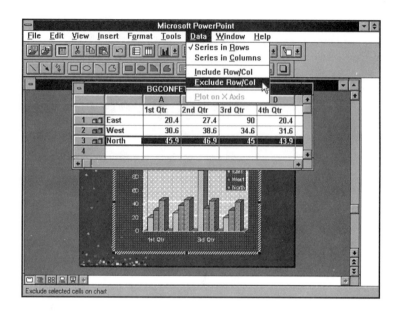

The resulting graph has only two bars.

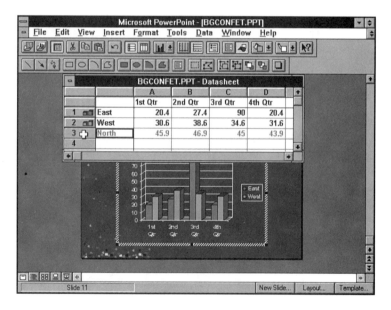

To reverse the action and include an excluded row or column, follow these steps:

1. Select the rows or columns you want to include.

2. From the **D**ata menu, choose **I**nclude Row/Col.

10

3. Click OK.

The columns or rows you included reappear on the datasheet.

Task: **Formatting a Datasheet**

If you don't like the look of your datasheet or you want to emphasize certain cell information, Graph enables you to make changes. You can change the datasheet font, color, and size. You can also change the way the numbers are formatted.

Modifying Number Formats

When formatting your datasheet, you may need to change the way currency is formatted, or the way you want a date to appear.

To change the number format in Graph, follow these steps:

1. Select the cell(s) you want to format to a particular style. A currency data series is formatted differently from one that lists dates of events.

2. From the Format menu, choose **N**umber.

The Number Format dialog box appears with all the available options.

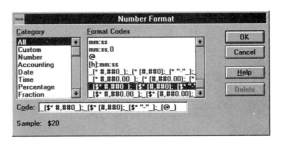

3. Select the appropriate format. You can verify your choice by looking at the sample in the lower left of the dialog box.

4. Click OK.

To reformat tick-mark number labels to include a percent or dollar sign, follow these steps:

1. If you are changing tick marks for the value axis in a column graph, click the cell in row 2, column 2.

2. From the Format menu, choose **Number**. The Number Format dialog box appears.

3. Select a format that includes the symbol you want.

4. Click OK.

Changing Fonts

When you change the font in a datasheet, the change affects all the cells in the datasheet view. It does not affect the font formatting you do in the Chart window. Select a font that will make it easier for you to work with when graphing.

To change the appearance of the data cells in a datasheet, follow these steps:

1. From the Format menu, choose **Font**.

2. Select the font name, size, style, and color you want.

3. Click OK.

Here, the font has been changed. This is a global change that affects the entire datasheet.

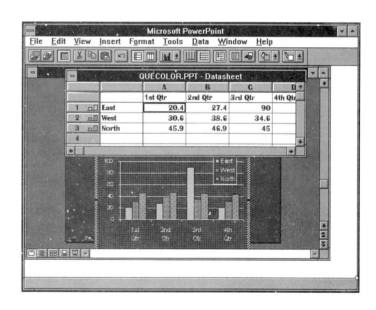

Task: Copying and Importing Data

In PowerPoint, you can open any Microsoft Excel chart, and the chart is converted to Graph format automatically. To open an Excel chart, follow these steps:

1. From the Graph **E**dit menu, choose Import Chart.

2. When the dialog box appears, select the file containing the graph you want.

3. Click OK.

   All the data and the formatting will be transferred from Excel to your datasheet and chart windows.

You can also copy data from another document and enter it directly into Graph, as follows:

1. Open the application and go to the document you want to copy.

2. Select the data you want to use.

3. From the **E**dit menu, choose **C**opy.

4. Switch to the Datasheet window in Graph.

5. Select the first cell in which to start the data entry.

6. From the Graph **E**dit menu, choose **P**aste.

Data can be imported from another document as a tab-separated ASCII (text-only) file, or in special formats used by Microsoft Excel. Check your Excel documentation for information on formats for importing and exporting between applications.

To import data as a ASCII file with tabs or other field separators, you need to first save the file in that format from your application. The file can then be imported directly into Graph.

Note: *If descriptive labels do not import to the correct cells, use Cut and Paste to move them.*

Summary

To	Do This
Enter data in a cell	Click in the cell to select it. Type the data. Move the insertion point and edit the data as needed.
Select an entire row or column	Click on the row or column selection box. The entire row or column will be highlighted.
Adjust column width	Place the mouse pointer on the dividing line to the right of the column to be adjusted. Drag the dividing line right or left to adjust.
Exclude a row or column from a chart	Double-click the row or column selection box.
Modify cell number format	Click in the cell to be modified. Choose **N**umber from the F**o**rmat menu. Select a new number format from the Number Format dialog box. Click OK to accept the changes.

On Your Own

Estimated time: 15 minutes

1. Start PowerPoint.

2. Use the AutoContent Wizard to create the Recommending a Strategy presentation template.

3. Change to the Slide view of the presentation.

4. Display the fourth slide of the presentation.

5. Access the Chart application.

6. Insert a row of cells between the North and West rows of the default datasheet.

7. Type **South** in the first cell of the new row.

10

8. Enter the numbers **34.5**, **23.1**, **45.9**, and **67.1** into the cells of the new row. Use the keyboard to move between cells.

9. Close the datasheet and resize the chart to fill the bottom half of the slide.

10. Open the datasheet.

11. Exclude the chart data for the 4th Qtr column.

12. Change the font of the data in the datasheet.

13. Change the format of the numbers in the datasheet so the numbers are whole integers, with no decimal places.

14. Close the datasheet and return to the PowerPoint presentation.

15. Close PowerPoint, but do not save your work.

Creating Handouts, Outlines, and Notes

In this lesson, you learn about the following:

- Handouts and ways to create them

- Speaker notes and ways to create them

- Outlines and ways to create them

- Ways to use the Pick a Look Wizard to help create coordinated items

In addition to helping you produce a full-featured slide presentation, PowerPoint provides you with coordinated handouts for your audience, speaker notes for the presenter, and a text copy of your outline.

Task: Using the Pick a Look Wizard To Prepare Materials

The Pick a Look Wizard can help you set up all the parts of your presentation quickly. This is a great way to get started. To use the Pick a Look Wizard to prepare supplementary materials, follow these steps:

1. From the Format menu, choose Pick a Look **W**izard.

2. Go through the dialog boxes and make the selections on each for your presentation.

Steps 4 through 9 in the Pick a Look Wizard pertain to options you can select for notes, handouts, and outline master pages.

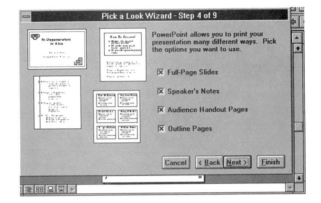

Notes options.

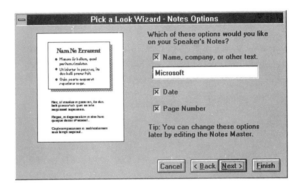

Handout options.

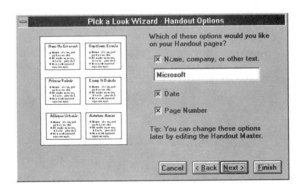

Outline options.

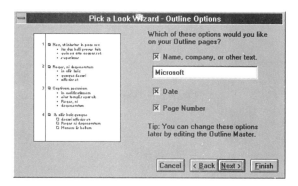

11

3. Click **F**inish when you are done. All the selections you specified are applied to your presentation.

You can make revisions and changes later, as you see fit.

Task: Creating Handouts

Handouts, printed copies of your slide presentation, can be distributed to your audience, who can then follow along more easily during the presentation. In addition, your handouts also serve as reminders that members of the audience can file and refer to later.

You can print two, three, or six slides to a page. Handouts containing two slides per page give you images with the most detail. Handouts with three slides per page give you space for audience notes and comments. The handouts with six slides per page provide less detail, but you don't need as many pages per handout set.

You can add text, your company logo, and other graphics, such as borders or clip art, to areas outside the slide image sections.

To create a handout, follow these steps:

1. Open the presentation that the handout will accompany.

2. From the **V**iew menu, choose **M**aster, and then choose Han**d**out Master.

Handout Master is
selected from a
cascading menu.

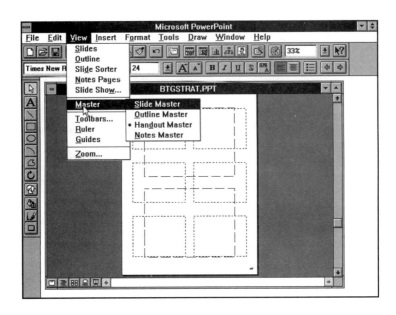

Notice that placeholder spaces (dotted outlines) are reserved for the
slide images. Slides are placed in the boxes, depending on the number of images you print. If you choose to print three slides per page,
the three boxes on the left are used by slides; the spaces on the
right remain empty.

3. Use the Rectangle tool on the Drawing toolbar to add borders to
the slide boxes, if you want. Remember that Fill must be toggled
off. You can also add text and graphic elements anywhere on the
page outside the slide placeholder areas.

Placeholder
A text or graphic
marker formatted
in a date or
time format,
for example.

Pages may already have page number and date *placeholders* on
them. You can delete the placeholders if you don't want them to
appear.

This Handout
Master is formatted
for three slides to a
page.

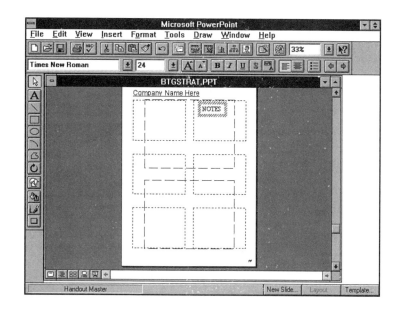

4. Print out a one-page test sample to verify that all the elements you want will appear. For more information on printing handouts, see Lesson 13, "Printing Your Presentation."

5. Save the file.

Task: Creating Notes Pages

In Notes view, each page corresponds to a presentation slide. Pages contain a miniature copy of a slide and a large space for a speaker's notes, which the presenter can use as a guide. Notes view is also a convenient vehicle for critiquing your presentation as you review and polish it.

You can print out each slide in a presentation as a notes page. A small version of the slide displays at the top of the page. The slide image placeholder can be moved or resized in the Notes Master.

Below the slide image area is a space for typing any speaker notes you might need when giving a presentation. You can print selected pages of speaker notes, or you can print an entire presentation.

You can also use notes pages for audience handouts.

Creating a Notes Page

To create a notes page, follow these steps:

1. From the **View** menu, choose **Notes** Pages.

A notes page associated with the slide you are working on appears.

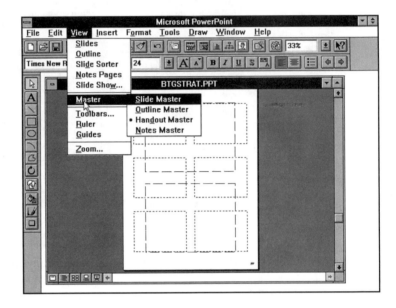

At the top of the page, a miniature image of the current slide displays. This image can be moved to another location, or resized.

You can type in your notes in the placeholder below the image. The placeholder, too, can be resized and moved for your convenience.

2. Click inside the notes placeholder box and start typing your notes.

If you have problems...	If the text you type is too small to see, change the view of page to 75% or 100% using the Zoom Control button on the toolbar.

Enhancing Notes Pages

If you use the Notes Master, you can add text, borders or boxes, page numbers, and any other material to appear on all the notes pages in your presentation.

To make changes that apply to all the notes pages in your presentation, follow these steps:

1. From the **V**iew menu, choose **M**aster, and then choose **N**otes Master.

The Notes Master page displays.

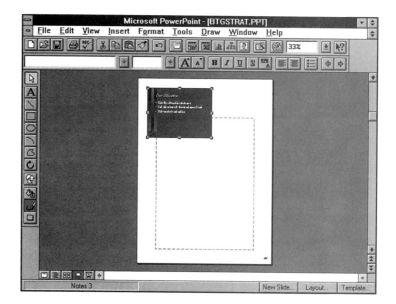

2. Move or resize either the slide picture or the note placeholder.

3. To add text notes to appear on every page, place the notes outside the slide and notes placeholder. Select the Text tool in the Drawing toolbar, and click wherever you want to add additional text.

4. From the **I**nsert menu, choose **D**ate, **T**ime, or Page N**u**mber place-holders if you want any of those items to appear on the Notes Master.

5. Print a one-page test sample to verify that all the elements you want will appear. For more information on printing handouts, see Lesson 13, "Printing Your Presentation."

6. Save your work.

Task: Creating Outlines

Outline view is a text-based visual of all the titles and body text in your presentation. This view can help you organize and reorganize your thoughts as you progress in developing your presentation.

Each title appears on the left side of the screen. To the left of the slide title is a slide icon and the slide number in the presentation. Additional slide text is indented under the title. If you have any graphic objects on a slide, they appear only as a notation on the slide icon.

Outline view helps you develop your text. Outline view is also the fastest way to reorganize your slideshow, especially as you develop content.

If you have problems...

If you have difficulty visualizing your presentation as you outline, don't hesitate to switch to the Sorter view to get the big picture.

This is how Outline view appears on-screen. A slide is selected.

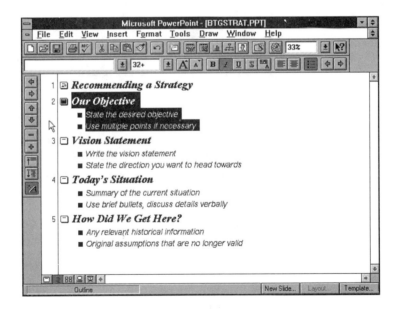

Working with an Outline Template

PowerPoint provides several outline templates that give you a head start on creating the outline for your presentation. Templates such as Recommending a Strategy or Reporting Progress might have an outline that closely fits the presentation you plan.

To work with an outline template, follow these steps:

1. Use PowerPoint's AutoContent Wizard to select a template similar to the content you want to develop.

2. Select Outline view by clicking the Outline button at the bottom of the screen, or by choosing **O**utline from the **V**iew menu.

3. Replace the title and text content with your own titles and text.

4. Edit text and make style modifications, just as you would in a Slide view.

   For more information on using outlines, refer to Lesson 12, "Viewing and Organizing a Presentation."

   Note: *Work in Outline view when you are first getting your thoughts down. Use Slide Sorter view for reorganizing the presentation in visual mode.*

To format an outline in the Outline Master, follow these steps:

1. From the **V**iew menu, choose **M**aster, and then choose **O**utline Master.

The Outline Master
appears on-screen.

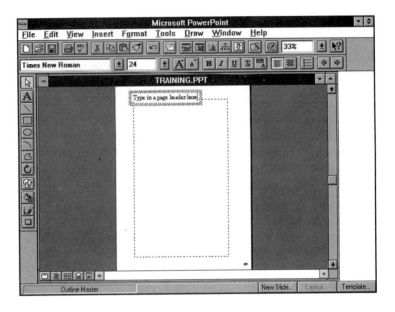

2. Use the Text tool to add headers and footers. Use the drawing tools for borders and other graphic embellishments.

3. Return to Outline view to make font changes to the actual outline text as it appears on-screen. Make sure that you are pleased with what appears on the screen because that is what prints.

4. Save your file.

   For detailed information on working with the Outline view, refer to Lesson 12, "Viewing and Organizing Your Presentation."

5. From the File menu, choose Print to print a hard copy of your outline.

   Your outline prints as it appears on-screen. (See Lesson 13, "Printing Your Presentation," for more information about printing outlines.)

Exporting and Importing an Outline File

If you want to have a copy of your presentation as a formatted text outline different from the one attached to your slide presentation, you can export the PowerPoint file to Word by clicking the Report It button on the toolbar.

You can export outline files saved as RTF files to Microsoft Word or other word processors. RTF outline files can also be imported into PowerPoint to be made into a presentation. For more information on working with Outline files, see Lesson 12, "Viewing and Organizing a Presentation."

To export an outline with the Report It button, follow these steps:

1. Have your presentation open.

2. Click the Report It button on the toolbar.

3. Your file appears as an embedded file in Microsoft Word.

   The file is converted to an RTF format. In this format, all the text levels appear in the Style Guide as Heading Levels and the formatting of the outline remains intact.

   You can apply all Word's formatting commands to your outline. Refer to your Word manual if you need more information.

This outline text in Word has been selected for a global font change.

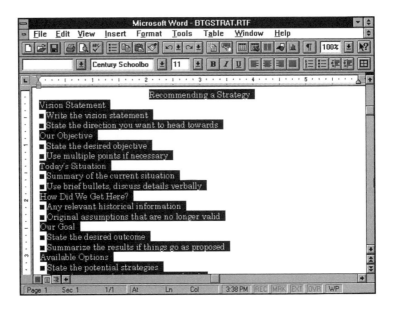

Here is the outline text in Word. A Heading 1 text style is selected for headings.

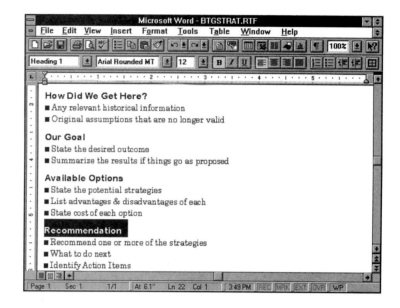

4. When you finish, click the Present It button.

   The outline you edited appears in PowerPoint.

To export an outline using Save As, follow these steps:

1. In PowerPoint, from the **File** menu, choose Save **As**.

The Save As dialog box appears.

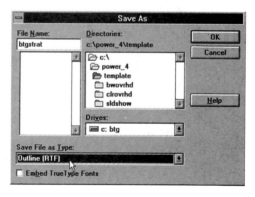

2. In the Save As dialog box, type the name you want to save your file under.

3. Select Outline (RTF) from the Save File as **T**ype drop-down list at the bottom of the dialog box.

4. Click OK. The file is saved for export to a word processor.

5. You can now open the file and edit it in a word processing program.

To import an outline file into a PowerPoint presentation:

1. From the **I**nsert menu, choose Slides from Out**l**ine.

The Insert Outline
dialog box appears.

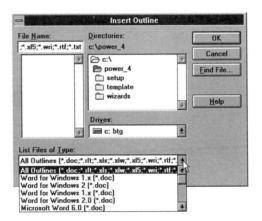

2. From the List Files of **T**ype drop-down list at the bottom of the dialog box, select All Outlines, or the appropriate application.

3. Select the drive and file folder you want to import from.

4. Double-click the file you want to import.

When you import from an RTF file, only text with outline heading styles applied is imported.

Summary

To	Do This
To create handout pages	On the **V**iew menu, choose the Handout Master option from the Master submenu. Type text notes and draw graphic elements that are to appear on each handout page.
To create Notes pages	Choose the Notes **P**ages option on the **V**iew menu. Type text notes and add graphic elements as desired.
To create a presentation outline	Choose **O**utline from the View menu. Type slide titles and use the Demote and Promote buttons to adjust outline levels.

On Your Own

Estimated time: 25 minutes

1. Start PowerPoint.

2. Use the Pick a Look Wizard to create a presentation that includes full-page slides, audience handouts, speaker's notes, and outlines.

3. Add six slides to the presentation using the New Slide button.

4. Modify the Handouts Master by adding the text **Overseas Sales** to the top of the handout master page.

5. Add a clip art image to the Handout Master.

6. Print a sample of the Handout Master with three slides per page.

7. Change to the Notes Master page.

8. Use the Insert option to place the date at the bottom left side of the Notes Master.

9. Change to the Outline Master.

10. Draw a rectangular box around the text area of the Outline Master.

11. Change to the Outline view and type **Opening** as the first slide title.

12. Change to the Slide view and print the Outline view of the current slide.

13. Exit PowerPoint and do not save your presentation.

11

Part IV
Putting It All Together

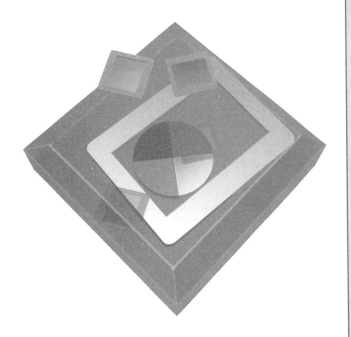

Viewing and Organizing Your Presentation

PowerPoint has the tools you need to help you organize and view your presentation as you are putting it together. In this chapter, you learn about the following:

■ Ways you can view your material in PowerPoint

■ Advantages of each viewing method

■ How to use Outline view to develop and organize content

■ How to use Slide Sorter view to organize and view your material

PowerPoint has the tools you need to help you organize and view your presentation as you put it together. From the moment you start putting your ideas down, PowerPoint can help. Ask yourself, "Who is my presentation for?" When you define your audience, ask "What do I want the presentation to accomplish?"

Get your content down quickly. At this point, don't be concerned with the niceties of color and design. If you use PowerPoint's Outline view as an outliner tool, you can move your topics around as you develop your key ideas. To make it easier, you can select a presentation similar to the topic you are developing, and use the accompanying Outline view to get started.

After you develop the basic content, you will have a better idea of how you want the presentation to look. At this point, you can run through the AutoContent Wizard, which can help you find a presentation suitable both to the content and the audience. For more about Auto-Content Wizard, see Lesson 11, "Creating Handouts, Outlines, and Notes."

After you select a starting point using the AutoContent Wizard, inspect your outline in the Slide Sorter view. Each slide shows up as a miniature, containing the text you developed in the Outline view. Slides can also be moved around in the Slide Sorter view until you finally get the sequence with the most impact.

Task: Creating a Slideshow in Outline View

To get started, take a look at the slideshow presentations that come with PowerPoint. When you create a new presentation, PowerPoint's New Presentation dialog box gives you several options for your presentation's structure. The AutoContent Wizard is the most useful option for getting a head start on your presentation's outline.

Choose a presentation that has a structure similar to the one you're preparing. Then move to Outline view to edit the outline for your presentation's content.

If none of the existing AutoContent presentations are close enough to your presentation, you can start from scratch by choosing the Blank Presentation option from the New Presentation dialog box.

This is an Outline view from a PowerPoint AutoContent slide show.

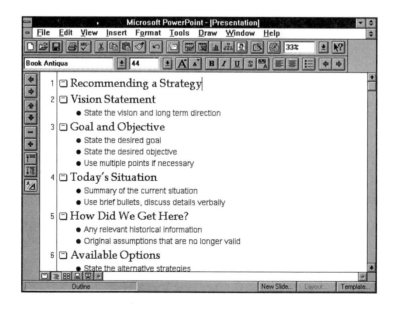

Outline view is a text-based visual of all the titles and body text in your presentation. This view can help you organize and reorganize your thoughts as you progress in developing your presentation.

Type your content as you would for any outline, and then apply templates to see how the presentation looks as a slideshow. PowerPoint creates slides to match.

In Outline view, you can move slides around ultrafast, changing their sequence. You can also move the bulleted points up and down in a slide, or move them to other slides. Paragraphs, too, can be moved up or down a level. You can also apply formatting changes as you work in Outline view.

12

To type an outline for a new presentation, follow these steps:

1. Open a new blank presentation and click the Outline View button on the bottom left of the screen.

   You are in Outline view. There is no text yet because this presentation is new. The number 1 and the slide icon appear in the left margin.

2. Type a title and press Enter.

   A second slide icon appears with an I-beam insertion point, ready for more title text.

3. To change to the second or bullet level, click the Demote button on the toolbar.

   You can continue entering more bullets by pressing the Enter key after each entry.

   To go one level up, drag the bullet to the left; it turns into a slide icon.

4. Click the Slide View button. You find a title and text for each slide that you completed in Outline view.

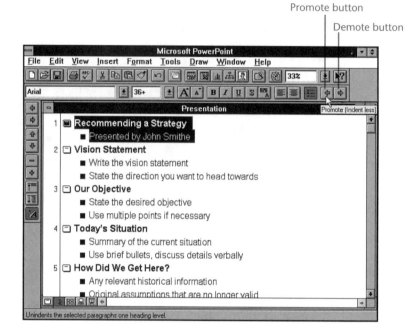

The Promote and
Demote buttons on
the toolbar.

Using the Outline Tools

The Outline View toolbar gives you several tools to manipulate the elements of your outline. Each toolbar button is described below.

- Promote button: Promotes or moves left the selected outline element to greater importance in the outline structure. You can also think of this as indenting the outline element less.

- Demote button: Demotes or moves right the outline element to lesser importance in the outline. Another way to think of this is as indenting the outline element more.

- Move Up: Moves the selected outline element vertically up in the outline.

- Move Down: Moves the selected outline element vertically down in the outline.

■ Collapse Selection: Reduces the selected outline section to the slide title only. All bullet points and subullet points for the selected slide are hidden. Use Expand Selection button to redisplay a collapsed slide's bullet points.

■ Expand Selection: Shows all bullet points (outline levels) for the selected slide. Use Collapse Selection to hide the slide's bullet points.

■ Show Titles: Displays the entire presentation's outline as Slide titles only. No bullet points are displayed.

■ Show All: Displays all bullet points and slide titles for the entire outline.

■ Show Formatting: Toggles text formatting such as bold, italic, and font selections on and off. If formatting is not shown (formatting toggled off), all outline text is displayed as a single font.

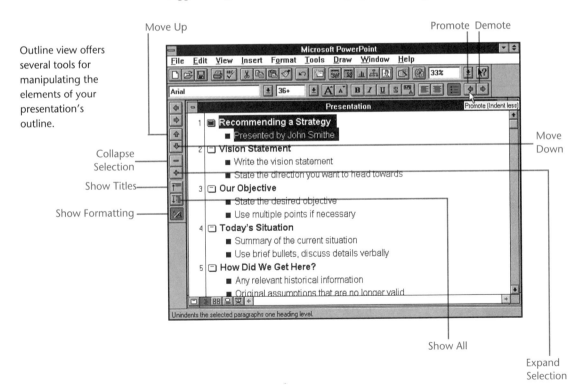

Outline view offers several tools for manipulating the elements of your presentation's outline.

If you have problems...

If you are unsure which slides you have added a bullet point to, click the Show All button on the Outline view toolbar. All levels of your presentation's outline will be displayed.

Selecting a Slide or Slide Text in Outline View

To select a slide in Outline view, click on the screen symbol to the left of the slide title. The drag icon appears.

The entire slide text is highlighted in Outline view.

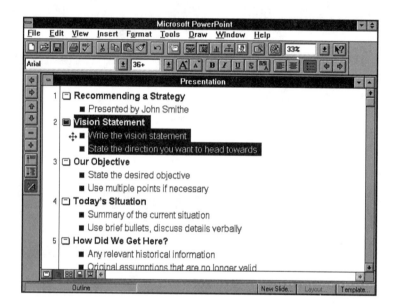

You can now move or delete the slide.

Bulleted text

These are the main points you want to make in your presentation. Each bullet item created in outline view appears on the slide when you perform a slide show.

To select *bulleted text* in Outline view, click to the left of the bullet you want to select. You can now move or delete the bulleted text.

To select text for editing purposes, highlight the text with the I-beam insertion point.

To select the entire outline, press Ctrl+M.

Adding and Deleting Slides in Outline View

As you build the content of your presentation, you add more slides.

To create a slide in Outline view and add text to it, follow these steps:

1. Place the insertion point in the slide area above where you want the new slide to appear.

2. From the **I**nsert menu, choose New **S**lide; or press Ctrl+M.

> **Note:** *You also can add a new slide by placing the insertion point at the end of the title line and pressing Enter. A slide symbol appears on the next line.*

The new slide appears in the outline with an insertion point to its right, ready for you to start typing.

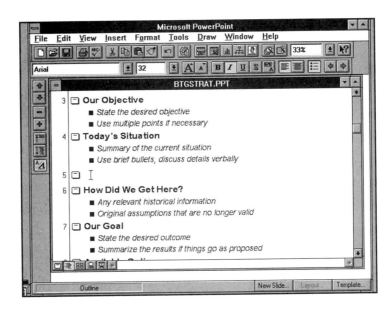

3. Start typing your text.

4. To add to a bulleted text list, place the insertion point at the end of the line of the last bullet item entered and press Enter.

A bullet appears on the next line with an insertion point to its right, ready for you to type the text.

To add a bulleted text list to a new slide that has no existing bullet points, type the text to be bulleted as a new slide positioned just below the slide the bullet text is to appear on. Then use the Demote button to demote the text you just typed to a bullet point for the slide above.

To delete a slide in Outline view, follow these steps:

1. Select the slide you want to delete.

2. Press the Backspace key. The slide is deleted.

Rearranging Slides in Outline View

In Outline view, you can rearrange the order in which slides appear.

To move a slide in an outline, follow these steps:

1. Select the slide you want to move by clicking the screen symbol to the left of the slide title while pressing the mouse button. The drag icon appears, and the entire slide text is highlighted.

Reorder
Changing the sequence that slides are presented in your presentation.

2. Drag the selected slide up or down to the desired new position.

To reorder text in an outline, follow these steps:

The drag icon appears, and the text item is highlighted.

1. Select the text to be reordered in the outline.

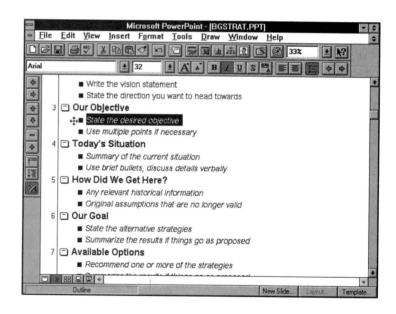

2. To move text down a level in the outline, drag the selected text to the right.

Text moves down a level, and its associated symbol appears to the left of the text line.

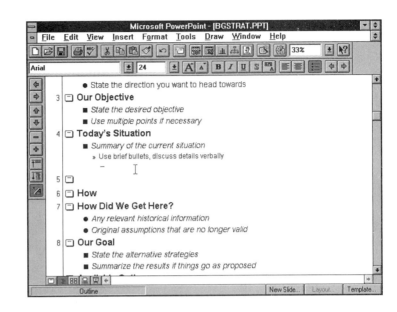

3. To move text up a level in the outline, drag to the left.

   The text moves up a level, and its associated symbol appears to the left.

   Note: *Text can also be reordered by clicking the Promote or Demote buttons on the toolbar.*

Formatting Text in Outline View

To format text in an outline, follow these steps:

1. Select the text to format.

2. Click the formatting buttons on the toolbar for Bold and Italic. Select the typeface and size in the scrolling boxes on the toolbar. To change the alignment of the text, you must change to Slide or Slide Sorter view and use the alignment buttons on the toolbar or the **A**lignment option on the F**o**rmat menu.

Formatting has been applied to the text in this outline.

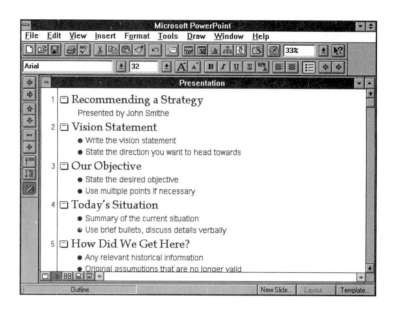

3. Print the outline to view the formatting changes.

This is the printed outline.

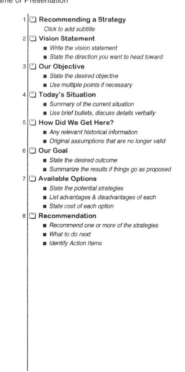

For information on printing an outline, refer to Lesson 13, "Printing Your Presentation."

Note: *Outline files saved as RTF files can be exported to Microsoft Word or other word processors. RTF Outline files can also be imported into PowerPoint to be made into a presentation. For more information on importing and exporting Outline files, see Lesson 11, "Creating Handouts, Outlines, and Notes."*

Task: Organizing Slides in the Slide Sorter View

12

The Slide Sorter allows you to move slides around as if they are real slides on a viewer box. This view shows you all the slides in your presentation as miniatures. You can change their size—making the miniature appear bigger for more detail, or smaller to allow more images to show on-screen at one time.

Slides can be dragged around for repositioning. You can also cut slides or make duplicate copies to use in other presentations.

The Slide Sorter view is also used to add transitions and timing for electronic slideshows.

Working in Slide Sorter View

Transitions
Effects, such as dissolves, applied as you move to the next slide in a sequence.

To work in the Slide Sorter view, follow these steps:

1. To look at a presentation in the Slide Sorter view, click the Slide Sorter button at the bottom left of the screen; or, from the **V**iew menu, choose Sli**d**e Sorter.

In Slide Sorter view, each slide in your presentation appears in miniature, in a numbered sequence.

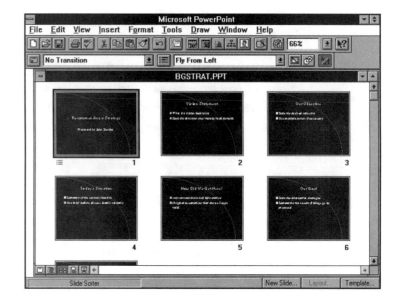

Builds

Adding a bulleted line of text one at a time to a sequence of slides. Previously added bullet items remain on-screen until the entire sequence of bulleted items is built.

If electronic transitions or *builds* are attached to a slide, icons for these appear at the bottom left of the slide. Numbers appear at the bottom right.

2. To make the images smaller so that more of your presentation fits on-screen, scroll to a smaller size using the Zoom box on the toolbar.

   To see more detail in individual slides, select a larger number in the Zoom box.

3. To select a slide, click it. A thick black border appears around the slide, showing that it has been selected.

   Selected slides can be moved, deleted, or copied.

4. To show a slide full-sized, double-click it.

Rearranging Slides in Slide Sorter View

To move a slide in Slide Sorter view, follow these steps:

1. Select the slide you want to move.

2. Press the mouse button and then drag the slide to its new location.

The move icon and an insert bar appear between two slides as you drag the icon.

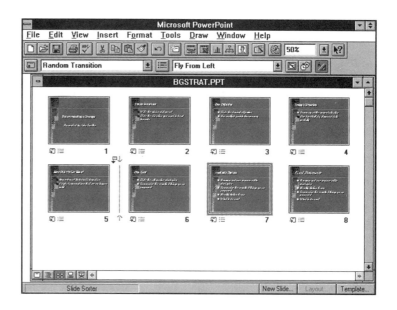

If you have problems...

If you have trouble keeping track of moved slides in Slide Sorter view, switch back to Outline view to confirm the placement of the slide you've moved.

---

3. Release the mouse, and the selected slide appears, still selected, in its new location.

   Slide numbering adjusts to the new scheme.

To copy or duplicate a slide in the Slide Sorter view, follow these steps:

1. Select the slide you want to copy.

2. From the **E**dit menu, choose **C**opy. The slide is copied to the clipboard. It can then be pasted into the same or another presentation.

   To duplicate a slide, choose **D**uplicate from the **E**dit menu. A duplicate appears to the right of the selected slide.

Note: *Copy and Duplicate are similar operations. They both enable you to create an exact replica of a slide. Copy, however, leaves a copy of the slide on the clipboard. You can then paste additional copies of the slide wherever you want. Duplicate does not use the clipboard and inserts only one slide in the presentation.*

To cut a slide in the Slide Sorter view, follow these steps:

1. Select the slide you want to cut.

2. From the **Edit** menu, choose **Cut**. The slide is cut from the presentation.

   If you want to move a slide in your presentation, use the **Cut** command to remove the slide from one location and use Paste to insert the slide in a new location in the presentation.

Note: *If you unintentionally cut a slide from your presentation, use the **Undo** command on the **Edit** menu to cancel the operation.*

Note: *To learn all about using special effects and builds and viewing your presentation as an electronic display, refer to Lesson 14, "Displaying Your Presentation."*

Summary

To	Do This
Add a slide in Outline view	Position the insertion point to the right of the line of text above. Press Enter. Use the Promote button to advance the new outline level until the slide icon appears to the left.
Delete a slide in Outline view	Click on the slide icon to select it. Press the Backspace or Delete key or choose **C**lear from the **E**dit menu.
Edit text in Outline view	Place the insertion point in the text. Edit text or drag to select sections of text.
Rearrange slides in Outline view	Select the slide to be moved by clicking on its slide icon. Click the Move Up or Move Down button on the Outline view toolbar, or press the up arrow or down arrow on the keyboard.
Collapse a slide's bullet points	Select the slide by clicking on its slide icon, or place the insertion point anywhere in the slide's text. Click the Collapse button on the Outline view toolbar.

To	Do This
Expand a slide's bullet points	Select the slide by clicking on its slide icon, or place the insertion point anywhere in the slide's text. Click the Expand button on the Outline view toolbar.
Show all outline levels	Click the Show All button on the Outline view toolbar.
Toggle formatting on and off	Click the Formatting On/Off button on the Outline view toolbar.
Rearrange slides in Slide Sorter view	In Slide Sorter view, select and drag the slide to a new position. Follow the vertical slide position line that appears for placement of the slide.

12

On Your Own

Estimated time: 20 minutes

1. Start PowerPoint.

2. Use the AutoContent Wizard to create the Training presentation base presentation.

3. Use the Pick a Look Wizard to choose a new look for the presentation.

4. Change to the Outline view of the presentation.

5. Delete the third slide of the presentation, Agenda.

6. Add three new bullet points to the second slide: **Sales, Marketing, Logistics.**

7. Demote each of the new bullet points.

8. Move the three new bullet points under the bullet "List the Topics to be Covered."

9. Change the font of each slide title.

10. Switch to the Slide Sorter view.

11. Move slide 4 so that it follows slide 7.

12. Change back to Outline view to observe the change.

13. Move slide 7 so it follows slide 3.

14. Change to Slide Sorter view to observe the rearranged slides.

15. Save the presentation with the new file name MYTRNG.

16. Exit PowerPoint.

Printing Your Presentation

If you already know how to print documents in Windows, you'll find that printing in PowerPoint is not any different. In PowerPoint, though, you can print your entire presentation—handouts for your audience, notes for the presenter or speaker, a copy of your text outline, and the slides themselves.

You can print copies of your slides as overhead transparencies, or you can create files to convert your computer slideshow into 2 1/4-inch slides for presentation with a slide projector. The process is basically the same, no matter what you are converting to print.

This lesson teaches you how to:

- Change your printer selection
- Set up slides for printing
- Print slides, handouts, notes, and outlines

Task: Changing Your Printer Selection

If you plan to print from a color printer rather than the black-and-white one you usually use, you need to select it from the list of printers installed in Windows setup.

To change a printer selection, follow these steps:

1. From the **File** menu, choose **P**rint.

2. Click the Printer button on the right.

The Print Setup
dialog box is
displayed.

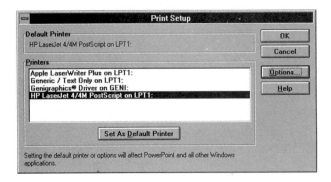

3. From the **P**rinters list, select the printer you want to change to.

4. Click OK.

Task: Setting Up Slides for Printing

Before printing your slides, make sure the appropriate slide setup is
selected. The Slide Setup command assigns the correct size to any slide
format you select. It is best to do this when you begin work on a new
presentation.

To apply Slide Setup to your slides, follow these steps:

1. From the **F**ile menu, choose Slide Set**u**p.

The Slide Setup
dialog box is
displayed.

2. From the **S**lides Sized for drop-down menu, choose the option that best suits your needs.

   Note: *If you change the option at a later time, you may need to adjust some of the text and art on your slides.*

   ■ *On-screen Show.* Settings are for 10-inch width by 7.5-inch height. The orientation will be landscape, for a standard horizontal slide presentation. (3:4 aspect ratio)

   ■ *Letter (8 1/2-by-11-inch) Paper.* Settings are for 10-inch width by 7.5-inch height. The orientation will be landscape (horizontal). This size will fill a standard letter-size page or overhead slide. (3:4 aspect ratio)

   ■ *A4 Paper (210 x 297 mm).* Settings are for 26-cm (10.83 inch) width and 18-cm (7.5 inch) height. (Between 2:3 and 3:4 aspect ratio)

   ■ *35mm Slides.* Settings are for 11.25-inch width and 7.5-inch height. (2:3 aspect ratio)

   ■ *Custom.* This option enables you to pick other dimensions by scrolling through the Width and Height boxes.

3. If you plan to start your slide-numbering sequence with a number higher than 1, indicate the starting number in the **N**umber Slides From box at the bottom left of the dialog box.

   Note: *Slide numbers appear on slide printouts only if they are inserted on the master by using the Text button to type the page number place holder characters* **##**, *or the Page Number command from the* **I***nsert menu.*

4. Select the orientation for your presentation from the Orientation Slides box area of the dialog box.

   Landscape printouts are horizontal and are the usual format for slides. **P**ortrait printouts are vertical and are generally used for notes, handouts, and outlines.

13

5. Select the orientation for notes, handouts, and outlines separately in the Notes, Handouts, Outline area of the dialog box. Portrait is the preferred selection. If, however, you prefer a landscape style for your handouts, select it.

6. Choose OK to accept your slide setup.

Task: **Printing a Presentation**

When you print your presentation, choose **P**rint from the **F**ile menu, regardless of what you plan to print—slides, notes, outlines, or handouts.

You can then select your options from the Print dialog box.

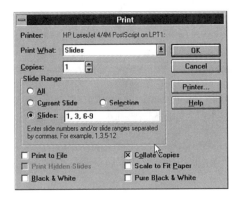

The Print **W**hat drop-down menu at the top of the Print dialog box enables you to select from a list of choices:

- ■ *Slides*. Prints your slide presentation, one image per page, on paper or as overhead transparencies.

  Note: *If your presentation contains builds, additional options appear.*

- ■ *Note Pages*. Prints the note pages for the speaker or presenter. You can print pages by selected page numbers.

- ■ *Handouts (2 slides per page)*. Prints audience handout pages with two slides per page. This option leaves room for notes and graphics.

- *Handouts (3 slides per page)*. Prints audience handout pages with three slides per page.

- *Handouts (6 slides per page)*. Prints audience handout pages with six slides per page. This option leaves little room for notes and graphics and individual slide text is difficult to read.

- *Outline View*. Prints your outline as it appears on-screen.

The Slide Range area of the dialog box enables you to select which pages of the presentation you want to print:

- **A**ll selects the complete presentation.

- **Cu**rrent Slide selects only the slide on-screen as the one to be printed.

- Sel**e**ction Prints the currently selected slide.

- If you want several slides from the presentation, type the numbers you need in the **S**lides box. You can request a range by typing the first and last numbers separated by a hyphen, and you can request individual slides out of sequence by typing them separated by commas. For example: **1, 3, 7, 9-15** prints slide numbers 1, 3, 7, and 9 through 15.

At the bottom of the Print dialog box are assorted print options:

Print to File
Selecting a print option to direct the print output to a file rather than a printer. The resulting file stored on disk can then later be copied to a printer to get a hard copy.

- *Print to **F**ile*. Prints the slides to a PostScript file; you need a PostScript driver to use this option. You use this option to send files to a service bureau for 35mm slides. You also can use Print to **F**ile to print your file on a printer other than the one you are connected to, even if PowerPoint is not installed.

- *Print Hi**d**den Slides*. Prints slides you have "hidden" in your presentation.

- *C**o**llate Copies*. Collates the copies when you print more than one copy of your presentation.

13

■ *Scale to Fit **P**aper*. Resizes your presentation automatically so that it fits the paper in your printer.

■ ***B**lack & White*. Prints quick black-and-white draft copies.

■ *Pure **B**lack & White*. Used for readable speaker's notes and handouts. This option turns all color fills to white and adds borders to them. All text and lines in the presentation turn to black. Pictures will print in a grayscale.

Printing Slides

To print slides, follow these steps:

1. Make sure that you have selected the appropriate format in the Slide Setup dialog box, as described earlier.

2. From the **F**ile menu, choose **P**rint to display the Print dialog box.

3. Choose the slide option that covers your needs.

4. Designate the number of copies you want in the **C**opies box.

5. Designate the specific slides you want printed in the Slide Range area.

6. Select a print option from the bottom of the dialog box:

PostScript

A special page description language built into some printers that tells the printer how to draw the page on the paper.

Select Print to **F**ile if you plan to send your presentation to a service bureau for 35mm slides. This option prints the slides to a *PostScript* file; you need a PostScript driver to use this option.

Note: *If you are printing to file to make 35mm slides, make sure that you have selected 35mm Slides in the Slide Setup dialog box.*

Select **B**lack & White for a quick draft copy of your presentation.

Select Pure B**l**ack & White for draft copies of your presentation if you are printing on a color printer.

7. Click OK.

Using a Service Bureau To Create Slides

If you need to present your slideshow in a 35mm slide format, it can be done easily by many service bureaus. The process is a simple one. Before you send a file to your service bureau, check with them to get the specific requirements. The bureau probably will want to know what type faces you used and what program you used to prepare the presentation to be converted.

Service Bureau
A specialized printing service that can create slides from your PowerPoint presentation files. Additional service bureau offerings typically include color copies, overhead transparencies, and color separations for four-color printing processes.

To prepare slides for a *service bureau*, follow these steps:

1. Open your presentation.

2. From the **V**iew menu, choose **S**lides.

3. Verify that you have set up your slide show in a 35mm slide format. If you have used an 8.5-by-11 view, your image will not fit properly on the slide.

4. From the **F**ile menu, choose **P**rint to display the Print dialog box.

5. Select Slides from the Print **W**hat list (depending on what is in your presentation).

    Note: *If your presentation contains builds and you are printing to file for 35mm slides, verify that Slide has been selected.*

6. Select page numbers in the Slide Range area for the 35mm slides you want to have made.

7. Select Print to **F**ile. You must have a Genigraphics printer driver installed in Windows for this option to be available.

    Note: *Consult your Windows user's manual for instruction for installing additional printer drivers.*

13

8. Click OK.

9. Enter the Output file name and click OK.

Take or upload your disk to the service bureau. They will make mounted slides on 35mm film copies from your PostScript file. Many service bureaus also are equipped to receive files via modem. Modem options and file transfer settings are accessed from the Graphics Link program in the PowerPoint program group. This program may be used to transfer slide files, via modem, directly to the service bureau..

If you have problems...	To save time and avoid possible problems printing your slide at the service bureau, contact the service bureau before printing your presentation to a file. Tell them exactly what kind of Genigraphics printer driver you have installed in Windows and its version number. Make sure they are familiar with the driver and that they confirm they can print files created with the driver. Check your Windows documentation to find the version number of your Windows PostScript driver.

Printing Handouts

The Handouts option prints your presentation in a format that your audience can refer to during the presentation. Handouts are not only useful during a presentation, they also serve as handy reminders that can be filed and referred to at a later time. You can print two, three, or six slides to a page:

- ■ *Handouts (2 slides per page).* Select this option for the greatest amount of detail in your images.

- ■ *Handouts (3 slides per page).* Use this option when you want room for notes on one side of the page.

- ■ *Handouts (6 slides per page).* Less detail will appear in your images, but fewer pages will be needed for your handout.

On the Handout Master, placeholder space for the slide image is reserved.

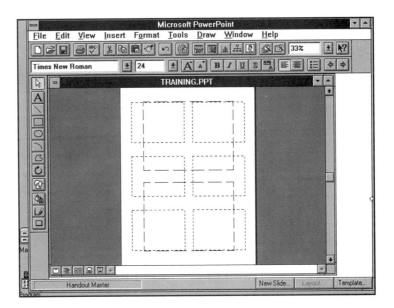

You can add text, your company logo, and other graphics such as borders or clip art to areas outside the slide image sections.

NOTES

This is an example of a three-to-a-page handout, as printed from PowerPoint.

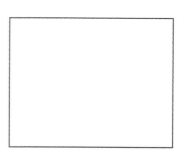

To print handouts, follow these steps:

1. Make sure that you have selected the appropriate format in the Slide Setup dialog box, as described earlier in the lesson.

2. From the **F**ile menu, choose **P**rint to display the Print dialog box.

3. Select the handouts format you want to use from the Print **W**hat drop-down menu.

Here, the option for three slides per page is selected for handouts.

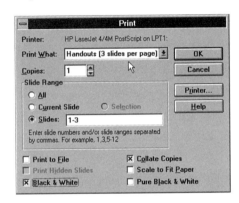

4. Select the number of copies you need.

5. Type the numbers for the pages you want to print.

   Note: *To verify that the format is correct, print a single test page before printing your entire handout set.*

6. Select C**o**llate Copies if you are printing more than one copy.

7. Select **B**lack & White if you are printing a quick draft copy.

8. Click OK.

Printing Speaker's Notes

Each slide in a presentation can be printed out as a notes page. On a notes page, a small version of the slide is pictured at the top of the page. The slide image placeholder can be moved or resized in the Notes Master.

Below the slide image area in the Notes Master is a space for typing any speaker's notes you might need when giving a presentation.

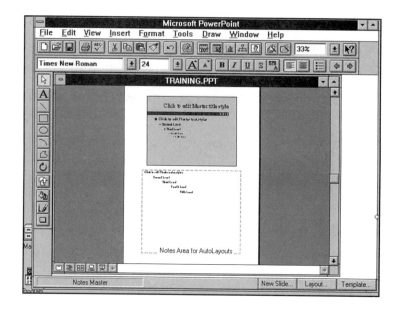

Speaker's notes can be printed by selected pages, or for an entire presentation. Notes pages can also be used for audience handouts.

To print notes pages, follow these steps:

1. Make sure that you have selected the appropriate format in the Slide Setup dialog box, as described earlier.

2. From the **F**ile menu, choose **P**rint to display the Print dialog box.

3. Select Notes Pages from the Print **W**hat drop-down menu.

4. Select the number of copies you need.

5. Type the numbers for the pages you want to print.

   Note: *To verify that the format is correct, print a single test page before printing your entire notes pages set.*

6. Make sure that you have Print Hidden Files selected, if there are any hidden files in your presentation.

7. Select C**o**llate Copies if you are printing more than one copy.

8. Select **B**lack & White if you are printing a quick draft copy.

9. Click OK.

Printing Outlines

The Outline View prints your outline as it appears on-screen. If you want to have a copy of your presentation as a formatted text outline that is different from the one attached to your slide presentation, you need to make a separate file copy of it for formatting purposes. (See Lesson 11, "Creating Handouts, Outlines, and Notes," for more information.)

This is an example of a presentation outline as it appears on-screen.

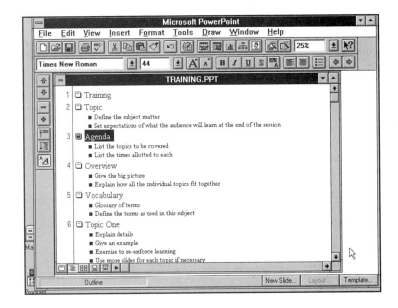

A master page is used to format your outline. To it you can add page numbers, headers and footers, borders—anything that you want to appear on all your outline pages.

To format an outline for printing, follow these steps:

1. Make sure that your slide presentation has been saved as a separate outline RTF file. Choose Outline (RTF) in the Save File as **T**ype box in the Save As dialog box. Choose a file name for your outline and click OK to save the outline.

2. From the **V**iew menu, choose **O**utline Master from the **M**aster submenu to display the Outline Master on-screen.

3. Use the Text tool on the standard toolbar to add headers and footers. Use the drawing tools on the Drawing toolbar for borders and other graphics accessories.

This is an example of header text on an Outline Master.

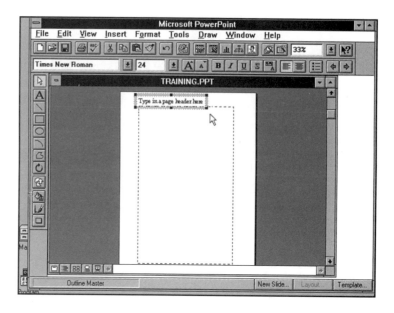

Here, a border is placed on an Outline Master.

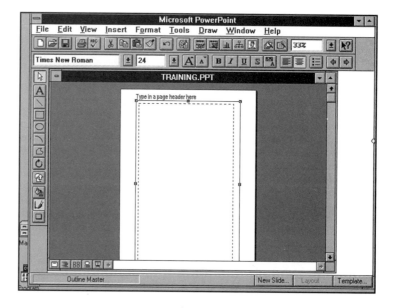

4. Return to the Outline view to make font changes to the actual outline text as it appears on the screen. Make sure that you are happy with what appears on-screen because that is what will be printed.

5. From the **F**ile menu, choose **P**rint. Then select Outline View from the Print **W**hat drop-down menu.

6. Select the number of copies you want.

7. Select **A**ll in the Slide Range area.

   Note: *To verify that the format is correct, print a single test page before printing your outline.*

8. Click OK to print.

Summary

To	Do This
Print a slide presentation	Choose **P**rint for the **F**ile menu. Select Slides from the Print What pop-up list. Choose All for the Slide Range option. Click OK to begin printing.
Print handout pages	Choose **P**rint from the **F**ile menu. Select Handouts from the Print What pop-up list. Click OK to begin printing.
Print notes pages	Choose **P**rint from the **F**ile menu. Select Notes Pages from the Print What pop-up list. Click OK to begin printing.
Print outline	Choose **P**rint from the **F**ile menu. Choose Outline view from the Print What pop-up list. Click OK to begin printing.
Print a presentation to a file	Choose **P**rint from the **F**ile menu. Select Slides from the Print What pop-up list. Click on Print to File at the bottom of the Print dialog box. Click OK to begin printing. Type the name of the file in the dialog box that appears. Click OK to complete the operation.

13

On Your Own

Estimated time: 15 minutes

1. Start PowerPoint.

2. Open the presentation created in Lesson 12: MYTRNG.PPT.

3. Change the Slide Setup to print on 8-1/2-by-11 inch paper with the note, handouts, and outline pages printed in landscape orientation.

4. Print the first three slides of the presentation.

5. Print the handout pages for the first three slides with three slides per page.

6. Change to the Slide Sorter view and select the first slide of the presentation.

7. Print the notes pages for the current slide.

8. Exit PowerPoint without saving your changes.

Lesson 14

Displaying Your Presentation

With PowerPoint's slideshow facility, you can present a show right on your computer. Moreover, when you give an electronic slide show, you can provide dissolves and other transitions between slides. You can build slides bullet by bullet. You can set the time each slide remains on-screen, and rehearse the show to ensure that it works as you need it to. Everything except the popcorn is provided.

In addition to the built-in slideshow features, PowerPoint also includes the PowerPoint Viewer. This application allows others to view your presentation slideshow even if they don't own a copy of PowerPoint.

In this chapter, you learn how to do the following:

- Display a presentation as a slideshow
- Rehearse an electronic slideshow
- Use transitions
- Build slides
- Use hidden slides
- Play movies and other OLE objects in a presentation
- Use the PowerPoint Viewer

When you finish organizing your presentation, run it as an on-screen slideshow so that you can see it as your audience will. When you run your presentation as a slideshow, your computer becomes the *slide projector*. In the electronic slideshow, all the menus and toolbars disappear. Slides take up the entire screen.

You can add special effects for each slide, and rehearse their appearance before you give your show. You can also use the on-screen show to rehearse your spoken narrative and adjust the automatic slide timings so that they fit to your talk.

Task: Setting Up a Slideshow

Before you start adding effects and setting the timings, run the show manually. To advance from slide to slide, just click the mouse.

To run a presentation as a slideshow, follow these steps:

1. Open the presentation.

2. From the **V**iew menu, choose Slide Sho**w**.

The Slide Show
dialog box is
displayed.

3. Select the slides you want to see. **A**ll is selected as the default.

If you want to see only a range of slides, type the numbers of the slides in the **F**rom and **T**o boxes.

4. Select **M**anual Advance. This option lets you click the mouse button when you want to advance to the next slide.

5. Click **S**how. Sit back, relax, and take notes.

This is a slide as it appears in the slideshow.

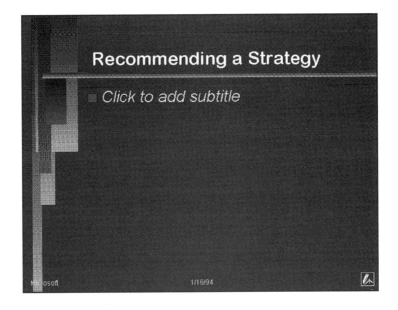

Task: **Adding Special Effects**

When you finish fine-tuning your presentation in the Slide and Slide Sorter views (as described in Lesson 12, "Viewing and Organizing Your Presentation"), you are ready to add the finishing touches—using PowerPoint's jazzy special effects. You also will want to rehearse the show to see how long your talk takes, slide by slide.

The Slide Sorter view is also your special effects workshop. When a slide is selected in this view, two toolbar boxes just above the view fill in with selections. On the left is a scrolling selection box for transitions—a visual transition from one slide to the next. You can also select the speed of the effect, and how to advance to the next slide.

14

Here you can see the Transition Effects box in the toolbar.

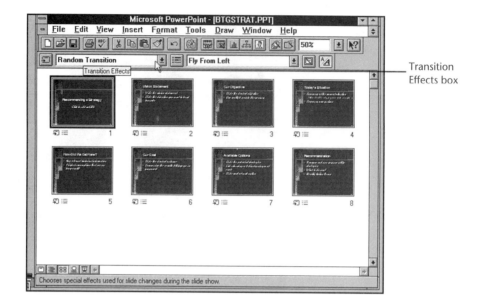

Transition Effects box

On the right is a toolbar box for builds—a visual effect for adding bulleted text one by one to *build* on-screen. That's why it is called a build.

Here is the Build Effects box in the toolbar.

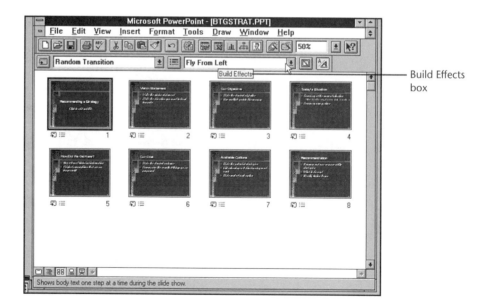

Build Effects box

Other toolbar aids allow you to *hide* slides—for example, those that you may not want to show as part of the standard presentation, but that you want to have ready for details, just in case they are necessary. Hiding slides is discussed later in this lesson.

Using Transitions

Transitions are electronic effects you can apply to a slide when it appears on-screen. Try to stick to no more than three effects styles per show, and use the fancier ones, like checkerboard or blinds, only for emphasis. You can apply transitions by using either the Transition dialog box or the Transition box of the toolbar.

To apply a transition to a slide using the Transition dialog box, follow these steps:

1. Open the presentation to the slide you want to work with.

2. From the **T**ools menu, choose **T**ransition.

The Transition dialog box is displayed.

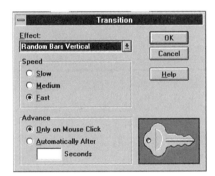

14

3. From the **E**ffect drop-down list, select the transition you want to apply to your slide.

   The transition you selected is applied to the images in the preview box.

Transitions

Special effects available while performing an on-screen presentation that add motion to the transition from one slide to the next.

4. You can control the speed of the *transition* by clicking one of the speed option buttons—**S**low, **M**edium, or **F**ast.

You can view the speed by looking at the images in the preview box.

If you are showing a series of quick, staccato slides, your transitions should be Fast. On the other hand, when you are pausing for effect, slow down the transition to match the pacing of your content.

5. Click OK after you select the best transition speed for this particular slide.

The Transition icon appears at the bottom left of the slide to show that it has been applied.

To apply a transition to a selected slide in Slide Sorter view using the toolbar, follow these steps:

1. Open the presentation in Slide Sorter view.

2. Select the slide to which you want to apply the transition.

3. Click the Transition Effects toolbar drop-down list, and select the transition you want to apply. There are numerous transitions. Experiment to find ones you like.

The Transition toolbar drop-down list is shown here.

Transition icon button

Transition icon

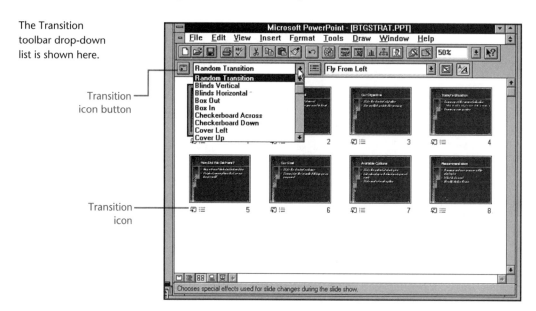

You see a quick dissolve, indicating that a transition has been applied to the slide.

4. To select the speed for the transition, click the Transition icon button to the left of the Transition Effects drop-down list in the toolbar. The Transition dialog box displays.

5. Select the speed to apply to the transition by clicking either the **S**low, **M**edium, or **F**ast button.

The effect is applied to the view image in the preview box.

6. Click OK after you select the best transition speed for this particular slide.

The transition icon appears below the bottom left of the slide to show that it has been applied.

Setting Slide Timings

Slide timing

In an Automatic presentation, the time delay between the display of slides.

Slide timings are the time delay between the display of slides during an Automatic slideshow. If you plan carefully, you can set the timing of each slide to allow you exactly enough time to talk through a slide's content.

You can set individual timings for your slides manually by typing the number of seconds in the Transition dialog box. Follow these steps:

1. Open the presentation and select the slide to be timed.

2. From the **T**ools menu, choose **T**ransition to display the Transition dialog box.

3. Under Advance, select **A**utomatically After.

4. Type the number of seconds you want the slide to display on-screen.

5. Choose OK.

You can also select slide timings in Slide Sorter view. Follow these steps:

1. Open the presentation in the Slide Sorter view.

2. Select the slide you want to time.

14

3. Click the Transition icon button at the far left of the Slide Sorter toolbar. The Transition dialog box will appear.

4. Under Advance, select **A**utomatically After.

5. Type the number of seconds you want the slide to display on-screen in the Seconds box.

6. Click OK.

Building Slides

Build

During a slide show presentation, revealing a slide's bullet points one at a time, while maintaining the slide background.

A build slide is one in which bullet points are exposed to the viewer, one at a time. Previously disclosed slides still remain on-screen—so in effect, you are *building* the point, one slide at a time.

You can dim bullet items already on-screen when new points are added, or you can keep them in full view. You can choose how you want the bullet items to appear—flying in from the top or bottom, right or left. As with transitions, keep the number of effects you use to a minimum— three at the most. For a smooth presentation, don't keep switching from one direction to another, unless you are making a definite point.

Note: *For coordinated visual impact, match a change in transition to a change in build direction.*

To create a build slide in Slide Sorter view, follow these steps:

1. In Slide Sorter view, select a slide with more than one bulleted item.

2. Click the Build Effects box in the Slide Sorter toolbar.

The Build Effects
drop-down list
appears on the
Slide Sorter
toolbar.

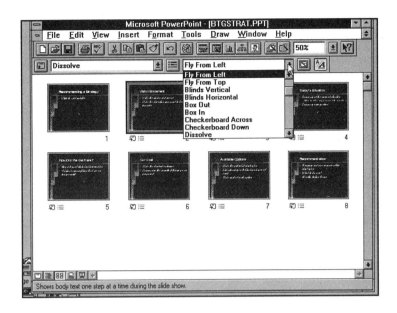

3. Select the way you want the bullets to be placed on the slide.

To create a build slide in Slide view, follow these steps:

1. In Slide view, select a slide with more than one bulleted item.

2. From the **T**ools menu, choose **B**uild.

The Build dialog
box appears.

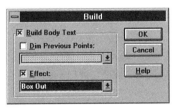

3. If you want the bulleted text to display in a straightforward build,
   building one bullet at a time until the list is complete, choose **B**uild
   Body Text.

4. If you want to dim a point as the next point appears, select **D**im
   Previous Points.

5. Click on the color box below **D**im Previous Points to select the color for the dimmed out text.

The drop-down color list for dimmed colors is shown here.

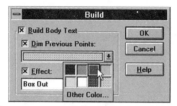

6. Click to select a color.

7. Select a build effect from the **E**ffect drop-down list.

   Try the possibilities, and select those that work the best with your presentation.

The **E**ffect drop-down list in the Build dialog box is shown here.

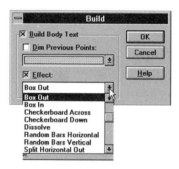

8. Click OK.

Task: Rehearsing a Slideshow

When you finish the organization of your presentation, run it as an on-screen slide show so that you can see it as your audience will. Use the on-screen view to rehearse your spoken narrative and make final changes.

Timing for slides can also be adjusted as you run a slide show. When Rehearse New Timings is selected, PowerPoint allows you to manually advance slides, and keeps track of how long each slide in your presentation displays. PowerPoint then sets the slide timing to that time.

To set the timings for your presentation, follow these steps:

1. Open your presentation and choose Slide Sho**w** from the **V**iew menu. The Slide Show dialog box appears.

   Three choices for advancing slides appear:

   - ■ *Manual Advance.* Advances at your mouse click.

   - ■ *Use Slide Timings.* Automatically advances at previously inserted timings.

   - ■ *Rehearse New Timings.* Advances each slide or bullet at your mouse click. A clock at the bottom left of the screen displays the time for each slide, and the time is recorded and attached to the slide. You can then run the show automatically with the Use Slide Timings option.

2. From the Advance box, choose **R**ehearse New Timings.

3. Click **S**how. Your slideshow appears on-screen.

14

At the lower left, a clock indicates the amount of time that the slide has been on-screen.

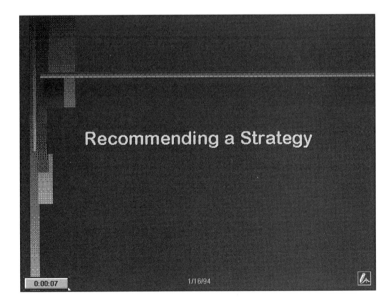

4. Click clock button in the lower left when you want to proceed to the next slide.

5. Repeat for the entire timing rehearsal.

Task: Using Hidden Slides

Hidden slides are slides you may or may not want to show, depending on questions and the need for additional information from your audience. Hidden slides can be made in Slide, Outline, or Slide Sorter views. Slide Sorter view enables you to select several slides at one time.

To create a hidden slide, follow these steps:

1. Select the slide or slides you want to hide in Slide Sorter or Outline view. Or display an individual slide in Slide view.

2. To hide the slide(s), click the Hide Slide button on the Slide Sorter toolbar if you are working in that view.

   Or, if you're working in Slide view, choose **H**ide Slide from the **T**ools menu.

   You know that a slide is hidden in Slide Sorter view when the slide number at the bottom right is enclosed in a square with a line through it.

3. To show a hidden slide, click the icon in the lower right corner of the slide before the hidden one.

The icon for a hidden slide appears in the slide preceding the hidden slide.

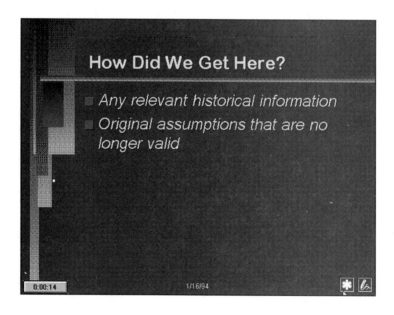

You can also show a hidden slide during a slideshow by typing **H**, or by typing the slide number of the hidden slide and pressing Enter.

Task: Running a Slideshow

When you run an electronic slideshow, use a computer with a screen large enough for your audience to see clearly. Use multiple computers or a computer projector if the room is a large one. The room can be lit with low-key lighting—bright enough for taking notes, but not to the point of distraction.

Spend time during fine-tuning to rehearse, so that you feel comfortable presenting the slideshow.

You can use the mouse arrow as a pointer as you speak. And you can annotate slides during the presentation to emphasize a point.

Don't spend too much time on any one slide. If you find that the timing starts to run over 10 seconds, you probably need to add another slide with the additional information.

Finally, add a black slide at the end of your presentation for the show finish.

To run a presentation as a slideshow, follow these steps:

1. Open the presentation.

2. From the **V**iew menu, choose Slide Sho**w** to display the Slide Show dialog box.

3. Select the **U**se Slide Timings button if you want the show to run automatically.

   Or, to run the show continually in a loop, select Run **C**ontinuously Until 'Esc.' The show continues running until you press Esc.

4. Click **S**how.

14

During the slideshow, some keyboard commands can be helpful:

- To advance a slide, you can use the right arrow or the down arrow (or a mouse click).

- To go back one slide, use the left arrow, the up arrow, or the Backspace key.

- To go to a slide, type its number and press Enter.

- To end the slide show, press Esc.

To see more quick keyboard commands to use during a slideshow, search for Slide Show in PowerPoint's Help menu.

The Slide Show Help dialog box appears with a list.

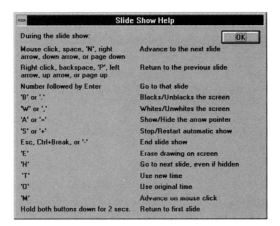

Annotating a Slide During a Slideshow

Temporary notes, arrows, and underlines can be added freehand during a presentation.

To annotate slides during your presentation, follow these steps:

1. Start the slideshow.

2. Click the pencil icon; this is the Freehand Annotation tool.

3. Press the mouse button as you write or draw.

Drawing on-screen with the Freehand Annotation tool.

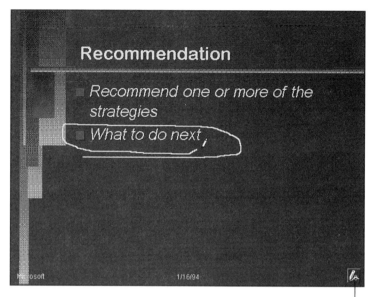

Freehand Annotation tool ──────

4. Click the tool again to turn off Annotation.

Playing Movies and Sounds in Your Slideshow

OLE

Object Linking and Embedding, portions of data or graphics from one application, such as a Excel graph, actively linked (pasted) in another application, such as PowerPoint.

Movies, sounds, and *OLE* objects can be embedded in your presentation. Use the Play Settings command in the Tools menu to direct how the embedded object should be played during your presentation. To learn more about working with embedded objects, refer to Lesson 15, "Working with Other Windows Applications." To learn more about Media Player for movies, consult Help or your Windows documentation.

To insert an object onto a slide in your presentation, follow these steps:

1. Display the slide on which you want to incorporate a movie, sound, or other object.

2. From the **I**nsert menu, choose **O**bject.

The Insert Object
dialog box appears.

3. Select the Object Type from the scrolling list box.

   If Media Clip is selected from the Object Type drop-down list, its dialog box appears. If Sound is selected, the Sound dialog box appears. Record the sound or media clip you want to insert and skip to Step 5.

   Note: *Consult your Windows manual for detail steps on recording sounds and media clips.*

The Sound
Recorder dialog
box is shown here.

4. Click Create from **F**ile if the object has been created already. A File name list box appears.

   Type the file name and path name of the file you want to insert, or click the Browse button to search your disk drive for the file.

   Note: *It's better to create and complete objects independent from your presentation and insert them when your slide show is near completion.*

5. Once you've chosen a file, click the **D**isplay as Icon check box to have the object's icon visible on the slide.

Note: *Your computer must be equipped to play sound and movies in order to select a file that runs.*

6. Click OK to complete the insertion of the object on the current slide.

You can now tell PowerPoint when and how to play the object during your presentation.

To customize the play settings of the object you inserted into your slide, follow these steps:

1. Display the slide that contains the object you want to play during your presentation.

2. Click on the object for which you want to set the play settings.

The Media Clip icon on a slide.

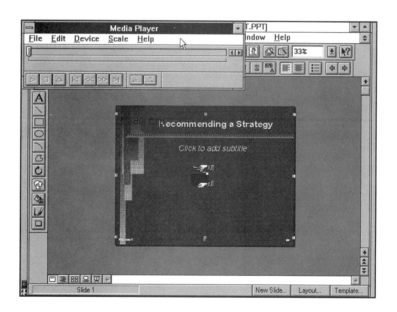

The Sound icon
on a slide.

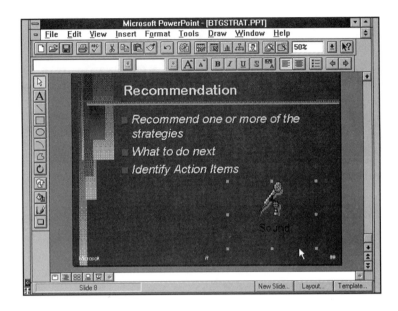

3. From the **T**ools menu, choose Pla**y** Settings.

The Play Settings
dialog box appears.
The selected object
category is
highlighted.

4. Make the selection you want:

To insert a sound, select So**u**nd.

To insert a movie, select **M**ovie.

For a slide from another presentation, and for many OLE objects, select **O**ther.

5. Select how you want the object to play from the Start Play box.

The option **W**hen Click on Object manually starts and stops displaying when you click the object.

The option When **T**ransition **S**tarts begins play at the beginning of the slide.

The option When **T**ransition **E**nds, Plus allows you to insert the number of seconds you want after the transition, before starting play.

The option Hide While **n**ot Playing hides the object except while playing.

6. Click OK.

If you have problems...   To test the Sound or Media Clip you inserted in your presentation, double-click on its icon. The sound or movie should play.

Task: Using the PowerPoint 4 Viewer

PowerPoint Viewer is a separate application that comes with PowerPoint. It enables you to run PowerPoint presentations even when you don't have PowerPoint installed on your computer, but you do need Windows 3.1 or later to run the Viewer. If you want to send your presentation to someone who doesn't have PowerPoint, you can send them the presentation file and a copy of the PowerPoint Viewer file. They can then run the presentation using the Viewer. PowerPoint Viewer will not allow them to modify or edit the presentation, though.

14

To use the PowerPoint Viewer to view a presentation, follow these steps:

1. Double-click the Viewer icon in the Program Manager, and its dialog box appears.

2. Select the presentation you want to view from the File list.

3. Click **S**how, and the presentation starts when Viewer opens.

To send a viewable presentation to someone who does not have PowerPoint, follow these steps:

1. Use Windows File Manager to copy your presentation file to a disk. It will add a file extension of PPT.

2. Copy the PowerPoint Viewer to the same disk. This file name is PPTVIEW.EXE.

3. Send the disk and instruct the receiver to use the preceding instructions for viewing the presentation.

Summary

To	Do This
Run a slide show	Choose Slide Show from the **V**iew menu. Choose **S**how to begin a manual presentation. Click the mouse button to advance the slides to the end of the presentation.
Add transition to a slide	Bring up a slide in Slide view or select a slide in Slide Sorter view. Choose **T**ransition from the **T**ools menu. Select a transition from the **E**ffect drop-down list. Click OK.
Add a build to a slide	Display the slide in Slide view or select the slide in Slide Sorter view. Choose **B**uild from the **T**ools menu. Check the **B**uild Body Text check box. Select a build effect. Click OK.
Set slide timings	Display the slide in Slide view or select the slide in Slide Sorter view. Select **T**ransition from the **T**ools menu. Select **A**utomatically After in the Advance portion of the dialog box. Type in the seconds the slide is to be displayed. Repeat for each slide.

On Your Own

Estimated time: 30 minutes

1. Start PowerPoint.

2. Use the AutoContent Wizard to create the Selling a Product base presentation.

3. Do a manual run-through of the presentation using the Slide Show option.

4. Make sure Slide 1 is displayed in Slide view.

5. Choose the Wipe Right transition for Slide 1.

6. Choose the Wipe Left transition for Slide 2.

7. Choose the Dissolve transition for Slide 3.

8. Choose the Dissolve transition for the remaining slides in the presentation.

9. Rehearse the presentation manually to observe the transitions you applied.

10. Move to Slide 3.

11. Choose a Build option for this slide. Use Build Body Text with the Box In effect.

12. Repeat the build for Slide 4.

13. Rehearse the slideshow manually to observe the builds you applied.

14. Exit PowerPoint without saving your presentation.

14

Lesson 15

Working with Other Windows Applications

One of the big selling points of Windows in general, and its applications in particular, is that it enables the user to share data between various programs. PowerPoint, being a Windows program, can share data with other Windows applications in various ways.

This lesson examines:

- The standard Windows Copy/Cut and Paste that you learned about in earlier lessons

- Dynamic Data Exchange (DDE)

- Object Linking and Embedding (OLE)

- Moving data using Drag and Drop

There are some very important differences between the four methods. In order to determine which method to use when, you must understand these differences; they are discussed at length on the following pages.

Task: Using Copy/Cut and Paste To Transfer Data between Applications

As you learned earlier in this book, you can use the Edit menu to Copy/ Cut and Paste objects within a PowerPoint presentation. What you may not know, however, is that you can also use these commands to copy/move data between different Windows programs. The Copy/Cut and Paste system is a Windows standard; every Windows application uses them in the same manner.

This section shows you how to use Copy, but you can use the same procedures for Cut operations. Just substitute Cut in place of Copy in the instructions.

To copy data to another application:

1. Select the PowerPoint object or objects that you want to copy.

2. From the **E**dit menu, choose **C**opy.

3. Switch to the program you want to copy into.

   Note: *There are three methods you can use to switch to another application:*

   - Press the Ctrl+Esc keys to display the Task List. The Task List shows all active Windows applications. Select the one you want, then press the Switch To button.

   - Press the Alt+Tab keys. Windows displays the titles of all of the applications running. Keep pressing the keys until you see the one you want.

   - If you can see any portion of the other application window, click on it to activate it.

   Note: *If the application you want is not running, you must start it.*

Press Ctrl+Esc to bring up the Task List dialog box.

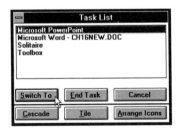

4. Pressing the Ctrl+Esc keys displays a list of active Windows applications that you can switch to.

Task: Linking Applications with Dynamic Data Exchange

Another option available to you to transfer data between PowerPoint and other Windows programs is DDE. DDE is an acronym for *Dynamic Data Exchange*. DDE works in a manner very similar to Copy and Paste.

Dynamic data exchange (DDE)

A link between two different files in either the same application or between different applications. All updates to the files are handled by the applications themselves.

Source document

The original file that is being linked into an application. This is the file in its native format.

DDE client

The program that is the repository for the copied data.

When you use DDE to share data between different Windows applications, you are, in essence, setting up a link between the two files. When you use DDE to add data to PowerPoint, the PowerPoint presentation stores only a representation of the original document and information about its location. The data does not physically reside in PowerPoint; it resides only in the original application's source file. Once you establish the link, any time you or any other user updates the information in the original (source) file, the version that is stored in your presentation is updated automatically, provided that the applications permit it. If the applications do not allow automatic updating, you can do it manually. There are a few things you should note about DDE when it comes time to show your presentation.

If you wish to show your presentation, for example, at a client site, you need to have *only* the document with you on your computer; you do not need to have with you the application that created it. If you wish to have the ability to also change your presentation at the client site, then you must have *both* the source file and the application that created it installed on your computer.

Linking PowerPoint to Another Application

Perhaps the easiest way to illustrate this concept is to set up a link between a PowerPoint slide and another program, like Microsoft Word for Windows.

To set up a DDE link:

1. Open *both* PowerPoint and Word for Windows.

   Note: *The program that you link to PowerPoint must support DDE as a client. Check your program's documentation to determine if you can use DDE as a client.*

2. In PowerPoint, select the object(s) that you want to paste to the other application—this can be a single object on a slide or an entire presentation.

15

3. From the **E**dit menu, choose **C**opy.

4. Switch to the application you want to link to.

5. From the **E**dit menu, choose the Paste **S**pecial command.

The Paste Special dialog box is displayed. Use this dialog box to create DDE links between applications.

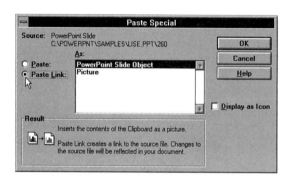

Note: *The Paste **S**pecial dialog box may look different from one application to the next. Check the documentation of the program you are pasting into; not all applications allow you to link data with other programs. If the program does not allow you to link the copied data, the Paste **L**ink radio button or its equivalent will be dimmed.*

6. Select the format you want to paste the data as, and click the Paste **L**ink option button and then the OK button. Your PowerPoint slide now appears in your Word document; it may take a few minutes for the paste to take effect.

Linking Another Application to PowerPoint

Just as you can link PowerPoint to any other Windows applications, you can link other Windows programs to PowerPoint. For example, you may want to link a Microsoft Excel spreadsheet that was created by your marketing department into a slide presentation for prospective clients. The actual object (your spreadsheet) is stored in its source document, where it was created. The PowerPoint presentation the document is linked with becomes one of several users of the data. The presentation is automatically updated whenever the original spreadsheet is updated.

Linked object
A linked object is an object created in another application that maintains a connection to its source.

Updating a Link

A linked object can be updated manually or automatically. If you choose to update the link automatically, or the applications support it, the linked object changes whenever the original object changes.

If your linked data is not being updated automatically, you need to check the source program to ensure that it supports automatic updating. You can find this information in your program's documentation.

To update a link manually:

1. From the **E**dit menu, choose Lin**k**s.

The Links dialog box appears. This dialog box gives you several options for controlling the manner in which DDE links get updated.

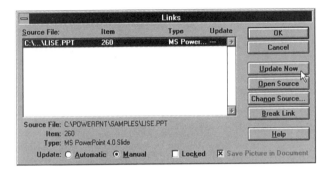

2. Click the **U**pdate Now button to update the data immediately. Most links update automatically by default.

3. Choose OK to continue.

Because the Links dialog box has a slightly different look in each application, you should check the documentation on how to use it, prior to starting your work.

15

If you delete or move the source file for a linked object, PP4 loses track of the link and cannot update it. You have to break and then reestablish the link.

Task: Embedding Data

The third and final option available to you to transfer data between programs is called embedding. Embedding takes linking one step further by actually making the foreign file an object in your presentation. This object is called an embedded object. Before you look at how to create and use embedded objects, you need to learn and understand what they are.

Understanding Object Linking and Embedding

Embedded object

An object, such as a chart, a spreadsheet, or an animation, that is created with one application but stored in another.

An embedded object is created by an application other than PowerPoint. This application is commonly called the object application. An object becomes embedded by using *Object* *Linking* and *Embedding* (OLE). Embedded Objects are the first feature of OLE; once embedded, they become a part of your PowerPoint presentation.

Another characteristic of OLE is that an embedded object can be created new, or you can embed an already existing file, like a chart, special text effects, or a sound. If the object is created from an existing file, then the object resides physically in both the application that created it and the one it is embedded in.

Object application

An object application creates an object which is to be embedded in another application.

A third feature of OLE is that an embedded object can be updated from within the host application—in this case, PowerPoint. You have the flexibility to:

- Update an embedded object only in the host application (the application it is embedded in)

- Update an embedded object manually and separately in both the object application and the host application

- Update an embedded object automatically in both applications

Each of these options is discussed in more detail later in the lesson.

Adding an Embedded Object to PowerPoint

To add an embedded object to PowerPoint, start by doing one of the following:

- If you start a new presentation or slide, open an AutoLayout that has an object placeholder on it; select and double-click the object placeholder.

- If you work with an existing slide, use the **Insert Object** choice located on the **Insert** menu.

Regardless of which of the preceding steps you do, the Insert Object dialog box is displayed. You can choose between creating a new object or using an existing one.

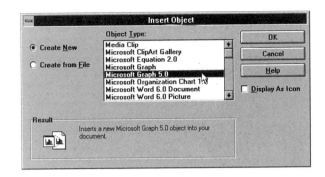

If you want to insert an existing object, follow these steps:

1. In the Insert Object dialog box, click on the Create from **F**ile option button.

2. The Insert Object dialog box changes to include a field to type in the path and file name you want to use. If you do not know the full path and/or file name, click the **B**rowse button. Peruse the various subdirectories of your disk to find the file you want.

■ As an option you can create a DDE link, instead of an embedded object, by clicking on the **L**ink check box.

You can use an existing file to create a link or an embedded object.

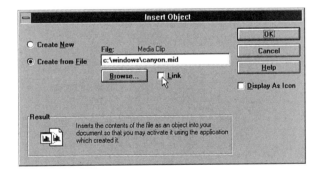

3. Choose OK to create the object in PowerPoint.

To create a new object, follow these steps:

1. In the Insert Object dialog box, click on the Create **N**ew option button.

2. From the Object **T**ype list, select the kind of object you want to create. The list includes all of those applications that can act as object applications.

3. Click the OK button.

4. Either the object application starts, or you see a window into which you can create the object. Create the object.

5. When you are finished creating the object, click outside the slide, and the object is then added to the slide.

You can create chart objects using Microsoft Graph.

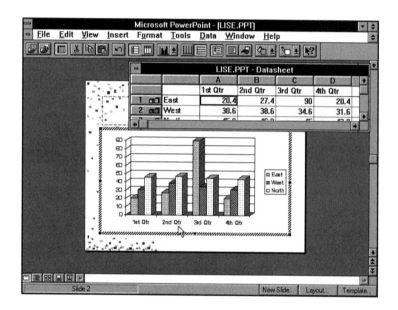

Note: *If you click the **D**isplay as Icon check box, In the insert Object dialog box or the Paste Special dialog box you see the object displayed as an icon on the slide. This can speed up displays if the object is very complex or large.*

See Lessons 10, "Organizing Data and Datasheets," and 11, "Creating Handouts, Outlines, and Notes," for discussions on how to add Microsoft Excel and Word tables to your PowerPoint presentations.

Caution

Be aware that you can embed an object only if you have that object's source application installed on your system.

Following are some of the items you can add to your PowerPoint presentations as embedded objects:

■ Text created with Microsoft WordArt

■ Equations created with Microsoft Equation Editor

- Charts created with Microsoft Graph

- Organizational charts created with Microsoft Organization Chart

- Tables and documents from Microsoft Word

- Worksheets and charts created with Microsoft Excel

- Sounds created with sound recorder

- Video clips and animation created with various programs

Once an object is embedded, you can go back and edit it very easily.

Editing Embedded Objects

Once you have created an embedded object, you may have a need to change it. Editing an embedded object is easy. OLE version 2.0 supports In-Place Editing (this is not available in earlier versions). In-Place Editing enables you to edit embedded objects without leaving PowerPoint.

Suppose that you embedded a spreadsheet, generated in Excel, into your PowerPoint slide. To use In-Place Editing to edit the spreadsheet, follow these three easy steps:

In-Place Editing

A feature supported by a few object applications that allows you to directly edit embedded objects on your PowerPoint slides, using the object application's menus and toolbars.

1. Double-click on the embedded object or its icon.

2. Edit the object (the Excel generated spreadsheet) using the In-Place editing features—the Excel menus and toolbars.

3. Click outside the object to save your changes.

15

As mentioned earlier, In-Place Editing is not available in OLE versions prior to 2.0. To edit an embedded object in earlier releases, the host application (PowerPoint in this case) starts or launches the object application (Excel in the example). The changes are made in the PowerPoint file containing the embedded object (in this case, in the PowerPoint slide containing the Excel spreadsheet) by using the object application (Excel in this example).

In-Place Editing and launching enable you to update an embedded object only in the host application. However, if you create a link between the embedded object and the source file, any changes you make to the embedded object are automatically made to the original; this works vice versa, as well. Again, establish the link by checking the **L**ink box in the Insert Object dialog box, after checking Create from **F**ile box.

So far, you saw that OLE's characteristics give you the flexibility to update an embedded object *only* in the host application, or update it automatically in *both* the object and the host applications. OLE allows you one more option: to update an embedded object manually and separately in both the object and the host applications.

Determining When To Use DDE or OLE

When deciding between using Dynamic Data Exchange (DDE) or Object Linking and Embedding (OLE), you need to consider how you are going to use the external information in your presentation. Below are a few guidelines to help you decide which type of data sharing to use.

You should consider using OLE if:

■ *You are the only creator/user of the data.* For example: You are developing a presentation in PowerPoint and want to add a new pie chart developed through Microsoft Excel. You create it using the Create New option from the Insert Object dialog box. There is only one version of this chart, and it is part of your presentation. When/if you need to edit it, you do so right in PowerPoint, without ever having to get out of PowerPoint (if you used a DDE, you would have to get into Microsoft Excel to edit the chart).

■ *Your data is static,* meaning it is not continuously updated. For example, you plan to show your presentation on other computers, like at client sites, and need to play sounds or video during your presentations. These sounds or video are already recorded and are not likely to change.

You should consider using DDE if:

■ *The data changes frequently.* If, for example, you are including in your presentation an inventory spreadsheet, you probably want to have the most current version, which would be updated automatically.

■ *The information is shared among various documents or among many users on a network.* For example, if there is a training session that is given in different rooms at the same time, you want to link to the source file. This way, the common information resides in one place, but is accessible to many users at the same time.

■ *The information comes from another user and it is updated regularly.* This would be true of an on-line profit and loss worksheet, for example.

Another major consideration in deciding which method to go with is portability. Portability means how difficult is it and what is required to show your presentation and change it while working on other computers at client sites.

If you use Object Linking and Editing:

■ To show your presentation, you need either the source file or the object application on your computer.

■ To make changes to your presentation, you need *only* the object application installed on your computer, not the source file.

If you use Dynamic Data Exchange:

■ To show your presentation, you need to have *only* the source file with you on your computer; you do not need to have the application that created it.

■ To make changes to your presentation, you must have *both* the source file and the application that created it installed on your computer. PowerPoint comes with the following programs that you can use to create objects to be linked or embedded:

   ■ Graph

   ■ Draw

   ■ WordArt

   ■ Organization Chart

15

Task: Moving Data with Drag and Drop

There is another method for moving data between applications, but it does not work with all Windows software. To work, *both* programs must support OLE version 2.0 or greater. It is called Drag and Drop. You are already familiar with the basics of it, since we learned how to drag and drop objects on a slide back in Lesson 3, "Creating Your First Presentation."

This method does *not* share data, but moves data from one application to another.

To move data using Drag and Drop:

1. Open both applications.

2. Arrange the applications so you can see both windows at the same time.

3. In PowerPoint, select the object(s) that you want to move.

4. Click on the selected objects and drag them to the second application.

You can drag and drop data between applications to move information.

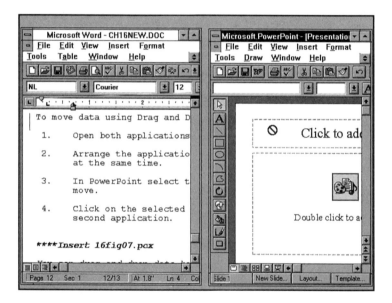

5. Release the mouse button when you have the object positioned where you want it.

Summary

To	Do This
Move or copy data between applications	Use the **E**dit **C**opy/Cu**t** and **P**aste commands to transfer data between applications.

To	Do This
Link data between applications with DDE	Copy data in the source program, and use the **E**dit Paste **S**pecial menu choice. Choose the Paste option, and then press the Paste **L**ink button.
Embed an object	Select the **I**nsert, **O**bject menu choice and then select what to embed.
Edit an Embedded object	Double-click on the embedded object. Edit it, and then click outside the slide to save the editing.
Drag and drop between applications	Select the data to move. Drag to the new application.

On Your Own

Estimated time: 15 minutes

1. Open both PowerPoint and another application like Word for Windows or Excel.

2. In PowerPoint, select a couple of slides and copy them.

3. Paste the copied data into the second application.

4. Paste the slides as a PowerPoint presentation.

5. Paste the slides as a picture.

6. Switch to PowerPoint and change the layout on the slides.

7. Switch back and verify that the update has taken place.

8. Embed a Write for Windows document in a PowerPoint slide.

9. Edit the document and add a paragraph to it.

15

Part V
Appendix

A Installing PowerPoint 4 for Windows

Installing PowerPoint 4 for Windows

To install PowerPoint 4 for Windows, your computer must comply with certain minimum system requirements. The program will run more efficiently with a faster microprocessor and more memory than the specified minimums.

PowerPoint requires that you have some knowledge of Windows in order to use the application. If you are unfamiliar with any of the steps outlined in the installation, review your *Windows User's Manual*.

System Requirements

Following are the system requirements for running PowerPoint 4 for Windows:

- MS-DOS operating system version 3.1 or later. MS-DOS 5.0 or later is recommended.

- Microsoft Windows 3.1 or later.

- A minimum of 2M of memory. 4M is recommended.

- A computer using an 80286 or higher microprocessor. An 80386 or higher microprocessor is recommended.

- Any video adapter supported by Microsoft Windows 3.1 or later. VGA, EGA, or XGA can be used. A 256-color video adapter is recommended.

■ A mouse or other pointing device.

■ Any printer supported by Microsoft Windows 3.1 can be used.

■ A film recorder compatible with Windows 3.1 is optional.

Installing PowerPoint

Before you begin to install PowerPoint, Windows needs to be installed and running. Before you start the installation, make backup copies of the application and store them in a safe place. It will take about half an hour to install the program.

Setup installs the PowerPoint application, its speller, and dictionary. In addition, several TrueType fonts will be installed, as well as templates, clip art, graphic import filters, and text converters. A separate application, the PowerPoint Viewer, also is included. PowerPoint Viewer enables you to distribute presentations so that they can be run without the need for the PowerPoint program itself.

To install PowerPoint, follow these steps:

1. If Windows is not yet running, type **win** at the C> prompt to start Windows. Then double-click the Program Manager icon if the Program Manager is not up and running.

   If Windows is open and running, close all the open applications and display the Program Manager.

2. Insert Disk 1 into drive A or drive B and close the door if you need to. Disk 1 accesses Setup.

3. From the Program Manager's **F**ile menu, choose **R**un to display the Run dialog box.

4. Depending on which drive you are using, type **a:setup** or **b:setup** in the **C**ommand Line text box; then click OK.

The Run dialog box should look similar to this.

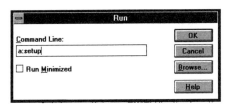

5. When the Welcome dialog box appears on your screen, click the Continue button.

6. When you are prompted, type your name and company, if appropriate, and click Continue again. The Microsoft PowerPoint Installations Options dialog box appears.

7. Click the Complete Installation or the Custom Installation button. If you are new to PowerPoint, click the Complete Installation button.

   If you decide to install PowerPoint with custom options, select the ones you want to have installed. On-screen directions will guide you. If you want to install additional files later, you can run Setup again.

8. Continue following the on-screen installation instructions given in the dialog boxes. PowerPoint will instruct you to insert and remove each of the twelve installation disks as they are needed.

9. After all the disks have been copied, a message box appears telling you that the installation is complete. PowerPoint will then display a dialog box explaining that Windows will have to be restarted to finish the installation.

10. Click OK to restart Windows.

PowerPoint can be run on a network by using the network server to store and exchange files between workstations.

A

Index

GO AHEAD. PLUG YOURSELF INTO
PRENTICE HALL COMPUTER PUBLISHING.
Introducing the PHCP Forum on CompuServe®

Yes, it's true. Now, you can have CompuServe access to the same professional, friendly folks who have made computers easier for years. On the PHCP Forum, you'll find additional information on the topics covered by every PHCP imprint—including Que, Sams Publishing, New Riders Publishing, Alpha Books, Brady Books, Hayden Books, and Adobe Press. In addition, you'll be able to receive technical support and disk updates for the software produced by Que Software and Paramount Interactive, a division of the Paramount Technology Group. It's a great way to supplement the best information in the business.

WHAT CAN YOU DO ON THE PHCP FORUM?

Play an important role in the publishing process—and make our books better while you make your work easier:

- Leave messages and ask questions about PHCP books and software—you're guaranteed a response within 24 hours
- Download helpful tips and software to help you get the most out of your computer
- Contact authors of your favorite PHCP books through electronic mail
- Present your own book ideas
- Keep up to date on all the latest books available from each of PHCP's exciting imprints

JOIN NOW AND GET A FREE COMPUSERVE STARTER KIT!

To receive your free CompuServe Introductory Membership, call toll-free, **1-800-848-8199** and ask for representative **#597**. The Starter Kit Includes:

- Personal ID number and password
- $15 credit on the system
- Subscription to CompuServe Magazine

HERE'S HOW TO PLUG INTO PHCP:

Once on the CompuServe System, type any of these phrases to access the PHCP Forum:

GO PHCP　　　　　　**GO BRADY**
GO QUEBOOKS　　　**GO HAYDEN**
GO SAMS　　　　　　**GO QUESOFT**
GO NEWRIDERS　　　**GO PARAMOUNTINTER**
GO ALPHA

Once you're on the CompuServe Information Service, be sure to take advantage of all of CompuServe's resources. CompuServe is home to more than 1,700 products and services—plus it has over 1.5 million members worldwide. You'll find valuable online reference materials, travel and investor services, electronic mail, weather updates, leisure-time games and hassle-free shopping (no jam-packed parking lots or crowded stores).

Seek out the hundreds of other forums that populate CompuServe. Covering diverse topics such as pet care, rock music, cooking, and political issues, you're sure to find others with the sames concerns as you—and expand your knowledge at the same time.

Learning is Easy with Easy Books from Que!

Que's Easy Series offers a revolutionary concept in computer training. The friendly, 4-color interior, easy format, and simple explanations guarantee success for even the most intimidated computer user!

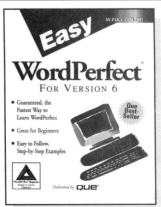

Easy WordPerfect For Version 6
Version 6 for DOS

$16.95 USA
1-56529-087-9, 256 pp., 8 x 10

Easy DOS for Version 6.2, 3rd Edition
Through Version 6

$19.95 USA
1-56529-640-0,
300 pp., 8 x 10

Easy 1-2-3, 2nd Edition
Releases 2.4

$19.95 USA
1-56529-022-4,
224 pp., 8 x 10

Easy 1-2-3 for Windows
Latest Version

$16.95 USA
0-88022-954-3,
200 pp., 8 x 10

Easy PCs, 2nd Edition
Covers IBM PCs & Compatibles

$19.95 USA
1-56529-276-6,
256 pp., 8 x 10

Easy Word for Windows for Version 6
Version 6

$19.95 USA
1-56529-444-0,
256 pp., 8 x 10

Easy Quattro Pro for Windows
Version 5.1

$19.95 USA
0-88022-993-4,
224 pp., 8 x 10

Easy Windows
Version 3.1

$19.95 USA
0-88022-985-3,
200 pp., 8 x 10

Easy WordPerfect for Windows for Version 6
Version 6

$19.95 USA
1-56529-230-8,
256 pp., 8 x 10

 To Order, Call: (800) 428-5331 OR (317) 581-3500

Find It Fast with Que's Quick References!

Que's Quick References are the compact, easy-to-use guides to essential application information. Written for all users, Quick References include vital command information under easy-to-find alphabetical listings. Quick References are a must for anyone who needs command information fast!

To Order, Call: (800) 428-5331
OR (317) 581-3500

Let Que Help You with All Your Graphics Needs!